CW01336664

MY SIX WARTIME YEARS IN THE ROYAL NAVY

Eric Denton

MINERVA PRESS
ATLANTA LONDON SYDNEY

MY SIX WARTIME YEARS IN THE ROYAL NAVY
Copyright © Eric Denton 1999

All Rights Reserved

No part of this book may be reproduced in any form,
by photocopying or by any electronic or mechanical means,
including information storage or retrieval systems,
without permission in writing from both the copyright
owner and the publisher of this book.

ISBN 0 75410 438 9

First Published 1999 by
MINERVA PRESS
315–317 Regent Street
London W1R 7YB

Printed in Great Britain for Minerva Press

MY SIX WARTIME YEARS IN
THE ROYAL NAVY

Contents

One	Introduction	7
Two	Waiting, Waiting – a Worrying Period: the Royal Navy at Last	13
Three	Scapa Flow and HMS *Greenwich*	29
Four	HMS *Havelock* – Western Approaches	38
Five	Becoming an Officer	58
Six	Coastal Forces	65
Seven	Foreign Service – the Mediterranean	86
Eight	The Home Front	96
Nine	North Africa and Algiers	101
Ten	Malta and Sicily	130
Eleven	Salerno, Sorrento and Northwards	140
Twelve	Bastia, North Corsica and Northwards in Italy	153
Thirteen	The South of France	176
Fourteen	HMS *Gregale* – Malta	183

Fifteen	England – at Last	207
Sixteen	HMS *Ferret* – Londonderry	215
Seventeen	Discharge from the Royal Navy: the Long Journey Back to Civilian Life	231
Eighteen	Victory after Six Years: Frustration and Hard Work Ahead	247
Nineteen	France, the French Language and the French Way of Life	257
Appendix I	Ports and Harbours Visited by the Author in the British Isles between 1940 and 1946	281
Appendix II	Ports and Harbours Visited by the Author in the Mediterranean between 1942 and 1945	283

Chapter One
Introduction

I was born on the 12th November, 1918, the day after Armistice Day. I waited for the end of the First World War before arriving on Earth, so that I could avoid the war. In so doing I ensured that I was the right age for the next one, not that this was part of my plan of campaign.

From an early age my parents took my brother and me to the annual service at the Cenotaph, where the impact of war was quite obvious, with plenty of severely disabled men with wives and children, and quite a number of wives and children with no husband or father. Men who had lost a leg or arm; other injuries which necessitated the use of crutches or wheel chairs.

As I became older I was conscious of 'Legion Crescent', of about ten or twelve houses occupied by disabled soldiers and their families. I do not know how they were built, but I had the impression that it was by charity.

All this was enough to persuade me that I did not wish to become a soldier, to fight in trenches, or to fire at other men with a view to killing them – in fact, to take part in war at all. My father was rejected by the Army as he was blind in his right eye from birth, or an early age, and so could not fire a rifle. He was an engineer to a firm of clothing manufacturers, with about eight factories in Kettering, my home town, and surrounding villages. His was an important contribution to the war effort, in that they were engaged in producing uniforms, an essential part of the war effort. He became a Special Constable, and amongst other duties, kept the queues under control outside shops when supplies were short. I doubt if I would be here at all if he had been in the Army.

Both my brother and I attended the local Grammar School, having won scholarships. My brother went to university, with a grant, in the days when very few families could manage to let other than the eldest son go to university.

I passed my School Certificate with honours, and a distinction in Maths, in 1933. This was in the middle of the Great Depression of the 1930s! I applied for every job that was advertised, and after five months was successful, in the meantime carrying on at school. I started work as a junior clerk in the Kettering Education Office, in February 1934, at forty-five pounds per year, plus a cycle allowance of two pounds a year. The staff comprised the education officer, school attendance officer, chief clerk, shorthand typist, and myself, which meant at least that I became involved in practically everything. I dealt with all orders from schools, checking and recording accounts, record keeping and filing, with guidance from the chief clerk.

As far as I remember, only the special school had a telephone, so if there was urgent need to get in touch with a head teacher, my bicycle and I were the link, so I soon knew all the heads, and many of the teaching staff also. Messages to the office came via the caretaker's bicycle.

The main point, however, is that I soon became involved in school attendance, and went out every morning, visiting homes, where I saw the real poverty of the depression. Many of the men working in factories were sacked, and their places taken by mothers at lower rates of pay, while their husbands would wander the streets and visit the Employment Exchange – 'The Labour'. Mothers scuttled home at dinner time, to make a quick meal out of nothing. Many houses only bought milk at Christmas, because tinned condensed milk was cheaper and needed no sugar. A major hazard of my job was avoiding cups of tea, with the lowest quality of tea and the tinned milk! I could avoid it by saying that I had just had one round the corner, but only for three or four visits. Even worse was the possibility of a slice of cake. I do not know how they did it with no sugar, fat or any goodies – it needed a cup of tea to get it down.

After I left school, I suggested an old boys' debating society and a chess society at Kettering Grammar School, and of course I was the mug who got the job of secretary of both. I also before long became secretary of a branch of the League of Nations Union, organising meetings, preaching the gospel of peace; peace not war: turn the other cheek, etc. I think I believed it at the time, but by the time Neville Chamberlain came back from Germany waving a piece of paper, saying 'it is peace in our time', I said, 'silly old fool – peace in his time perhaps, but not in mine'.

At the time I did not realise the virtues of the job I had, and the knowledge I developed of human life – in fact, I might have sat all day at one desk doing one thing, instead of which I visited all areas of society and knew most people in the town. All the doctors, nurses, police, also people at the bank where I paid in money and cashed cheques. The two earlier jobs which I did not get were in an architect's office and a chartered accountant, lines I became involved in, but not all the time. It was known that the head recommended pupils for posts in order of their exam results. The next one was the Post Office, in the sorting office, which I do not think would have been my line!

I visited the houses of the wealthy, to obtain signatures, or give them reports. I remember in particular one house of a wealthy shoe manufacturer, which scared me stiff. I went to see the widow – the maid invited me in and asked me to sit in the hall until the mistress arrived. I sat on a chair – scared to move – on one side was a Ming vase (or so I assumed) about three feet high, which my elbow was touching, on the other a mahogany table bearing expensive china items. It was a relief when I was asked to accompany the mistress into a large room, having been very careful with my elbows. I was happy to leave, getting a cheerful smile from the maid when she let me out.

Those were the days when a word in someone's ear was far more effective than the official path. If only our national leaders understood that it is possible to achieve more by kind advice and suggestion than by rigid regulation.

Two examples: I visited a house where the boy aged about ten was absent from school – the mother told me he was in bed and she did not know what was wrong. I was invited to have a look, and knew it was serious, either scarlet fever or something similar. She would not call the doctor – she owed him two shillings and ten pence already with no prospect of paying (two and a half pounds would have been a good weekly rate of pay). I told my boss, who asked me if I knew who the doctor was, and I told him. He said, 'You will see him out on his rounds later – stop him and have a word with him. Within an hour, I saw him, got off my bike, and indicated I wanted him to stop his car, which he did. I told him the boy was seriously ill and that I suspected scarlet fever. He told me he would find an excuse to call. The next day, he stopped me and thanked me! He had called in saying he was just visiting a baby in the next street, and called to ask how her baby was – then asked how the boy was. He was told he was in bed, so he went to see him, and diagnosed scarlet fever. The boy was sent straight to the isolation hospital. The doctor thanked me very much, and said he got there just in time!

Another example: when the annual fair arrived – I visited the boss, to ask for a list of children of school age, and told him which schools they were to attend. I then asked him to chase off any local children hanging around in school hours, adding, 'You know what will happen if we catch any, don't you?' He replied, 'Yes, I know – next year when I try to book the ground, it will already be booked for a cricket match.' The reader will realise that I did not threaten him. Those were the days of poverty and unemployment, but somehow people made it work. It was something that influenced me long afterwards, and when I joined the Royal Navy, I realised that on a ship in wartime, everyone depended entirely on everyone else.

My parents would always help out any neighbour who had a problem, especially in illness. I have known my mother cook a meal for another family and take it over all ready to serve. All this led me to feel that it was more important to help people than to cause them trouble, and hence I saw problems in joining the Army and being required to kill people, especially people I knew nothing about. The RAF was an option, but one could not get out of a plane in trouble and walk away. In the case of the Royal Navy, I hoped there would be the option of getting out and swimming, or grabbing a piece of wreckage.

I was in the first group for National Service, and so when I registered at Northampton, I applied to join the Royal Navy. This shook the two Royal Naval representatives, as Northamptonshire was as far from the sea as anywhere in the British Isles. I was asked if I had any relatives in the Royal Navy, to which the answer was no. I could not quote a remote relative of my mother who was seized by the press gang in the last century and never seen again!

I told them I had a neighbour who was a petty officer in the Royal Navy. I had been over the sea to Skye, but that was a short journey of well under an hour. I had spent a night on an open fishing trawler in the North Sea, and that was it!

They said they would put me forward for consideration as a writer, presumably based on my present job. I was relieved to be accepted provisionally, but did not quite know what a writer did: I was not even sure whether they existed at sea. I had a medical examination which was found satisfactory, and that was it by the 29th September, 1939, when the war had commenced.

Chapter Two

Waiting, Waiting – a Worrying Period: the Royal Navy at Last

During the next three months many of my friends had departed for the Army, and a few for the Royal Air Force, but I heard nothing. I had assumed that I should get a decision on whether I was acceptable to the Royal Navy as a writer, but I was beginning to think that the Royal Navy did not want me – a blow to my pride.

In the meantime signs of war were showing. Kettering was a centre for the receipt of children evacuated from London, an hour's train journey, and the Education Office was heavily involved. The trains had to be met, and the children to be separated according to age and sex, allocated to the appropriate schools, and the billeting officers had to distribute them to homes which had already been surveyed. They were all struggling with a bag of spare clothing. During the same period, stocks of emergency food had to be set up. The central depot was the Corn Market Hall, from which consignments went by lorry to various schools, Church Halls etc., with a central reserve at a Domestic Science Centre in School Lane in the centre of town. I had to travel with the lorry to ensure it all went to the correct depots. The driver and I would be out and about when we would hear aircraft around. Were they ours or theirs?

Having not heard either of them before we did not know whether to dive for cover or keep going. This was a problem for everyone at that time. Fortunately, they were all friendly. The people who were not going to war, were becoming engaged in air raid precautions, Dad's Army etc. It took my mind off worrying about what I should end up doing, but that would come back when I went to bed.

Despite all this my future wife and I became engaged on Christmas Day 1939, not quite knowing what our future would be. She was working at Weetabix looking after their accounts and the financial side throughout 1939. The food industry was an important factor in the country's well being. At the same time my brother, who had a degree in science, was directed into scientific work, and was a member of the team of Sir Robert Watson-Watt in radar research. Principally he was engaged on operational research, visiting various stations which were active in defence, and for this purpose he had the uniform of an officer of the RAF.

Eventually I received a notice in early June 1940 to report to HMS *Ganges* at Shotley on Monday, 17th June at 8 a.m. for training as an ordinary seaman. This again was both a relief and a shock. I was going into the Royal Navy, but not knowing what I was going into. As a prospective seaman I felt very, very ordinary.

I was to report at 8 a.m. or as soon thereafter as possible. I could not arrive at that time without spending a night in London, which would not be paid for. If I caught the first train on the Monday morning, at about 5 a.m. and dashed across London for the connection, I could arrive at Harwich at 8.15 a.m. which I thought was quite good going. When I arrived the promised transport was not there so I went to the Transport Office, which phoned for me to be collected. By the time that the truck had arrived at about 8.45 there were three of us. On arrival at the base, we were paraded before a regulating petty officer, who told us off for being late (no explanation was allowed), and we were told that the Royal Navy did not exist for our convenience, but that we existed for the convenience of the Royal Navy. If the Royal Navy said 8 a.m. that meant not 8.30, not 8.15, not one minute past eight, but 8 a.m.! The remainder of the intake were already on their way to being kitted out, and we expected special arrangements! We had to chase along and try to catch them up. What a welcome to serving our country. I was of course the exception who was not kitted out. I took size eleven shoes, and the Navy had no size eleven boots, and since they could not shrink my feet on the spot, I had to be the odd man out who wore his shoes for about a week!

I have two main memories of that first day. Firstly, the kitchen and the horror of seeing food in vast boilers about three feet across, one with soup, and one with cocoa, blocks of cocoa, dried milk and sugar, broken with a hammer, and thrown into boiling water and stirred with an object like a paddle for a canoe. Secondly, being fallen in for a lecture by the master at arms, who pointed to the iron spiked railings, and told us that they went all the way round the base; we were inside and would not go outside for three weeks. That evening when we were eventually freed for a spell, there we all were, about thirty of us, lined up inside clutching the railings, and gazing longingly at the outside world.

We did go outside under escort to be shown the air raid shelters, dug into the far side of a field opposite – rather depressing. We were told that if there was an air raid warning, and the siren sounded, we were to be out of bed and dressed, and dash across the field to the shelters. Being the East Coast just north of the Thames there was a warning just after midnight. No one told us that the siren was on the roof of our hut, made of corrugated iron, so we were out of bed like a flash, and dashing across the field clutching our trousers (bell-bottoms cannot be dealt with in a hurry by the inexperienced), shoes and boots unlaced, a right mob, when we suddenly realised that there was a rabbit in the middle of us, running along as well, because he could not get out. Hence the popular song of the day *Run Rabbit Run* or was that the origin?

After a couple of hours in misery we trudged back to our beds, hoping not to have a repeat performance that night, but the raids were all too frequent.

After a very exhausting night we were rudely awakened at 7 a.m. by the door of the hut flying back on its hinges, and a raucous voice shouting 'Wakey *wakey wakeeey*, rise and shine *rise and shine, rise and shiiine*, show a leg, *show a leg, show a leg, the sun's scorching your eyes out*' – a routine we were to get used to; anybody who was close had their bed clothes whipped off, and we all tumbled wearily out of bed, clothed in our underwear, not being entitled to pyjamas. We struggled with our blue bell-bottomed trousers, with their unusual method of fastening, the white, blouse-like top, and the blue outer top which matched the trousers, with their traditional flap, and no front opening, and the separate collar, most items held together with tapes instead of buttons. A very rude awakening!

I do not recollect clearly whether we had any duties, or whether we marched straight off to breakfast – it was quite unlike any meal at home, or indeed anywhere we had ever eaten in before. The rest of the day was a blur of parades, exercises, with a fair amount of doubling around to commands, and a small amount related to ships and the sea. We learnt a few basics like the fact that the sharp end of the ship was the *bow*, and the blunt end was the *stern*. The right had side was the Starboard side, because the early ships had a huge paddle-like appliance over the side, used to steer the ship, hence 'Steer Board', later to become 'Starboard'. Consequently, the ship could only go alongside a harbour wall on the other side, the left hand side, which became the PORT side. The toilets were at the bow of the ship known as the heads, possibly because no other useful purpose could be found for that area. As we were to find out much later on, this ensured maximum discomfort, with the ship rising up and down, and making it an uncomfortable place to go and have a slack off.

The three weeks we were to be inside the fence (the place being the annexe, with the main base of HMS *Ganges* next door) were a dull blur of routine, discomfort and unhappiness, whilst we learnt how the Navy worked and in very broad terms what went on in ships. Of course, in addition we had to do our own washing, and get our clothes dry, with no reserves to fall back on. The clothes we arrived in were posted back home. I did learn that if socks were soaked in cold water before being washed they were less likely to shrink. Needless to say we did not get a taste of rum. I suppose there was a NAAFI, but I have no recollection of it. The cheerful part was when it all ended for the day, and we were too tired except to write a brief letter home. Another cheerful part was the arrival of letters.

We were issued with a kit bag to store our clothes and belongings, and a ditty box, which was a small lockable attaché case 14" × 10" × 5", in which to store our personal and private belongings. We were taught the art of folding our bell-bottom trousers and top to pack into the bag. The two legs of the bell-bottoms were placed together, and folded concertina like in about three inch folds from bottom to crotch, and then the top rolled around them and tied with tape or cord (no such thing as string in the Navy – Nelson would not have approved of string). Looking after our clothes and belongings was no mean task.

After about three weeks, by which time we were beginning to understand something of the Royal Navy, we moved into the main base of HMS *Ganges* next door, the main feature of which was the old mast of the sailing ship Ganges, and some proper buildings which looked a bit more like the Royal Navy. We soon found out that we were to climb the mast (as high as a church steeple) to the 'half moon' about fifteen feet from the button, the round piece of wood protecting the top of the mast. We were welcome to go to the top if we wished. This last bit was not compulsory, because the Navy realised that the last bit would finish off most of the conscripts when they lost their grip.

We were assured there was no need to worry, as there was the net underneath to catch anyone who fell. Very comforting, except that it was about ten feet above the parade ground, held up by vertical steel girders cemented into the ground about every ten feet apart in a square pattern. If one landed on a girder it would either break the spine and dispose of the stomach, or alternatively treat the skull like a turnip – and we did not know how we were expected to guide ourselves in a high speed spin.

The covered drill shed of colossal size did impress me however. On the end wall, very appropriately in letters about eight inches high was the poem *If* by Rudyard Kipling which I had never come across before. I thought it particularly appropriate, ending with:

> If you can treat with triumph and disaster
> And treat those two impostors just the same;
> ...
> Yours is the earth and everything that's in it,
> And – which is more – you'll be a man, my son.

It was not quite so comforting in the middle of a hard day's slog! I have a script version of all four verses of it in colour, and framed, hanging in the kitchen!

Of course, everyone was required to take the swimming test, and pass. I was very relieved that I could swim. We had to line up and go down a water chute into the deep end and swim. Anyone who showed any knowledge of swimming was pointed at by the instructor, who shouted, 'out you – swimming test', and I was one. Anyone who could not swim and who tried to struggle to the edge was pushed off with a long pole, until the petty officer thought they could take the test, or were eventually allowed out when about to drown, to try again later.

I went to the shallow end to take the test. This entailed putting on a 'duck' uniform of white thick stiff material, bell-bottoms and top. Everyone who took the test was given two pieces to struggle into, of the wrong size. I had a colossal pair of bell-bottoms which tried to slide down and strangle my legs, and a top I could scarcely get into, which virtually prevented me getting my arms above my head, and jumped in. The person dishing out the uniforms either had a sense of humour or was malicious! I made it slowly to the deep end, to be told, 'right, away from the edge and stay afloat for ten minutes.' At least the test was helpful for surviving from a sinking ship! One could comfort oneself by thinking of the poor boy entrants to the Royal Navy who no doubt saw glamour in the uniform and the sea.

In the classroom we were introduced to matters more appropriate, like which end of a gun the shell went in, and which end it came out, and how it was elevated and aimed, (we were not told that the ship would be rolling like a 'bath bun' at the time); the theory of mine laying, and how mines were swept (a weird expression – 'sweeping at sea'), torpedoes and how they operated (and blow a ship up, if you happened to be on the receiving end) – this inevitably led to keeping a sharp look out at all times. We learned how to 'sweep' an area with binoculars, both around the horizon, as well as in the skies. I was to appreciate this later, as the reader will see, when he hears of my first action station!

And surprise, surprise, we went down to the sea in ships. Well, actually we went down by bus, and saw the sea and ships, which by now we had almost forgotten. We went down once to learn the art of rowing a boat, or 'boat pulling'. I had rowed many times on a lake, and occasionally on the river at Bedford, so I knew which end of an oar was which. We caught a few crabs, even if we could not eat them.

There were four or five oars on each side of the boat, and one man on the tiller. After a few circles, we had to achieve a straight line, or we would never have got back ashore. Then we went in a sailing boat about twelve feet long. We learnt how to put the sails up and lower them (or did we learn?), and the philosophy of tacking, sailing against the wind – and somehow we got back ashore. We were becoming fully paid members of 'Harry Tait's Navy', or on a higher scale, we could have joined the Swiss Navy (if we could find it).

We were billeted in a building which had a double row of beds, head to foot down the middle, and a row on each side, sleeping about forty or so in total, with tables at the entrance by the door for our meals, which had to be fetched in bulk from the kitchen and served out, by two mess men, a duty we all shared in turn. They had to wash up as well and dry tea towels over the heating stove. There were four class leaders, of whom I was one, each with a 'watch' of about ten men, who would take it in turns at various duties about the establishment. I do not know how we were chosen, and I do not think we were particularly anxious to take it on. One had been in the scouts and this was no doubt a factor, and I think one had been in a youth club.

There was one trainee who stood out in more ways than one. He was a Sheffield steel worker, in his early twenties, who was built of steel, and knew how tough he was. He could eat anything and everything. He put food in his mouth and swallowed and it went down his throat. I doubt if he used his teeth. He scared everyone including the leaders. His first trick was to creep down under the beds at night. Underneath the bed of a leader, he would stop on hands and knees, heave up and tip the bed on its side, with the leader sprawling, in a mass of bedding, and everyone waking up to look, while he struggled to get it upright, sort it out and get back in. Of course, no one 'knew' who had done it.

Came the night when I was the only leader who had not been dealt with. Somehow I kept awake, listening – my bed was on the left hand side of the central block and I lay on my right side with the bedclothes loose on that side. Despite the work of the day, somehow I managed to keep awake. Between half an hour and an hour after lights out, I heard a soft shuffling sound approaching from further up the row. It stopped under my bed and I waited a few seconds then swung my fist under the bed and was relieved when it violently hit something and a grunt was emitted. It felt like someone's head but I was not sure what part, although I thought it was the face. I expected my bed to turn over and trouble to follow. I was relieved when the shuffling retreated, and after a while I dropped off to sleep.

At breakfast someone said, 'We were expecting your bed to turn over last night – what happened?' I looked at the steelworker and he looked at me. I said, 'Nothing at all. I slept well all night.' I watched his face and eyes and saw a look of gratitude that I had not let him down. He showed his appreciation by then becoming one of my supporters. I saw the results within twenty-four hours when I ordered, as a class leader, someone to do something, and he was slow to respond. My protégé barked out 'You heard what the leader said – get on with it!' I cannot remember whether we had a drink together in the canteen, but I am sure we exchanged cigarettes from then on.

In the Navy, I was to find out later, friends like that were more use than the high and mighty, who were usually the slowest to react in an emergency. If he reads this, my thanks for his noted support! On parade I gained experience of being in charge of a few men – marching them off parade and taking charge of a group in performing various duties. I do not know how boy entries to the Navy had survived this place, I doubt if I would have done so as a boy.

Of course we had to climb the mast to begin with up to the first platform via the shrouds like a complex rope ladder of six or eight vertical strands on both the port and starboard sides. The complication was getting on to the platform. The shrouds went to the mast, where they all closed up leaving at most a toe hold, and further shrouds started lower down the mast, and sloped outwards towards the edge of the platform, and then up against the mast. We had to climb up, and then switch to the second shrouds which sloped outwards, so if anyone missed their foothold, they would be hanging in the air. They had somehow to recover, and if lucky a more secure friend would help. Having stood on the platform we then came down, when we started off hanging over the edge and swinging inwards to get a foothold. What a life!

Then later on we had to repeat the performance with a second set of shrouds going to a platform near the top (the half moon) of the mast – still more difficult and more dangerous. The ground looked very remote. There was then an option of going to the top via a rope ladder alongside the mast. I went some way up, but chose not to go to the top, and stand on the button. No one fell off – I think they thought treatment in the sick bay would be even worse.

We had a certain amount of shore leave in the evenings and at weekends, but there was little to do other than go to a pub and have a few drinks, and feel the outside world. I went once to the pictures in Ipswich. I was warned to be careful not to sit next to any females, as they would grab me in their arms and demand money for favours. I succeeded in keeping clear.

We went on the rifle range several times, to perfect our aim. We needed to be able to point and fire a gun in the right direction, and this was part of the tuition. I was quite good at it, and every time got some 'bulls', feeling quite proud. Someone then told me I would end up in the Royal Naval Beach Party, amongst the first to land. I do not know what happened, but after that, I would miss the target altogether. I would get the occasional bull, but never more than two. Whoever was next to me on both sides, started getting better results, one or two each, and felt quite proud! The Royal Navy, like other walks of life, is full of surprises!

We had duties on coast defences around the area, where there were some slit trenches and barbed wire. Once, we were taking huge coils of barbed wire from lorries on to the beach and laying them out as defence against invasion. They were very heavy, and were carried on balks of wood, with a sailor at each end. On one occasion getting down a sloping sea wall on to the beach, my colleague slipped and the full weight came on my left leg, which was half bent. I managed to stop the wire falling on me, but that did not help my thigh muscle. I was limping back, and saw the doc, who gave me liniment and put me on light duty. This of course happened the week before I was due for the one and only weekend leave, from Friday evening to Sunday evening, and I was booked on a coach going up north and through Kettering on the way.

The doc told me I was not allowed to leave the base, whilst on sick leave. He said he had relented before, only to have the sailor not return and send a sick note from his doctor. I told him that the bus would put me down by the bus stop, and I would arrange to be picked up at the same place. He relented as long as I gave him my personal promise to return. I did, and did return! It was a brief but happy weekend. I have a photo of my future wife lying on the lawn wearing my sailor's cap, of which the ribbon said only HMS as names of ships were not allowed in case it gave information about ships to the enemy.

We had a degree of elementary information about ships and the sea, and the way the Navy did various things. I remember we were shown how to rig sheer legs (nothing to do with the ladies, regrettably!), and other aspects of rigging on ships, including splicing, and putting an 'eye' in the end of a rope or wire. Sheer legs were two poles lashed at the top, with a rope across the bottom and which were about ten feet apart, and each had two ropes going outwards and secured to stop them pulling together. Then a weight, such as a gun barrel could be hoisted up, with a block and tackle. I felt that a crane was much more efficient, but of course there would be no cranes at sea.

Finally, we were all issued with a hammock and bedding for our departure to Portsmouth Naval base. The hammock was a rectangle of canvas, with about fifteen to eighteen eyelets on each end, and about ten cords doubled passed through a metal ring, and the two ends tucked through the loop. Then the cords were secured to the eyelets in the canvas, and one hoped to get a hammock with the bottom on longer cords, so that we did not fall out, and felt comfortable, which we did not. There was a rope from the ring at each end which hung from a support under the deckhead (or ceiling); a couple of blankets, which after use had to be rolled up in the middle of the hammock, and lashed round to make a huge sausage, to be carried on the shoulder, or by the lashing. We could have made an entertaining performance in a London theatre, especially trying to swing up above the hammock holding a bar which went across the messdeck, and then dropping into the hammock. Much more complex at sea on a ship rolling in an Atlantic Gale. Why did we apply to join the Royal Navy?

And so we left on Friday, 23rd August for RNB Portsmouth, which turned out to start with five days at an annexe at Leigh Park House, where we had tents on the lawn. Fortunately these were camp beds and not hammocks. An outstanding memory was the toilets, never to be forgotten! A canvas screen with trees behind and then a long trench about four feet wide and five feet deep, over which was a long pole thirty feet long, like a telegraph pole, secured at each end about two feet above the ground. Passing water was no problem, but the next stage was a menace. One had to lower the bell-bottoms, retreat backwards, and sit on the pole beneath which was a mess of 'you know what', giving off a renowned odour of course. This was difficult enough, but when someone else sat down, the pole bounced up and down and vibrated. One had to carry out one's duty, with the constant fear of being catapulted off to disappear below forever. The Royal Navy certainly had some original ways.

We had several days here before entering the barracks at Portsmouth, where we spent about a week. We tried the hammocks, having been told not to leave anything valuable below, and to keep our boots in the hammock in case of theft. It was bad enough being in a hammock for the night, but with all our belongings as well, what a time we had. This was relieved by Hitler, who arranged air raids, so that we dashed out to the shelters under the parade ground. If the bomb missed the building there was a fair chance of hitting the parade ground. So be it! It is all a blur, but we went off several times in the daytime to Ford Aerodrome to clear up bomb-damaged buildings, and look for bodies, not a very welcome task. Luckily, on the second day I was detailed off to the kitchens, where I was given the job of working the Dawson Deluge dish washer, which had constantly been breaking down. I had the magic touch, and kept it going, probably by not overloading it. I was detailed to the kitchen all the time. No doubt the cook spoke to the Petty Officer in charge of us. At least I had my meals in peace after the crowd had gone through, and it was preferable to looking for bodies!

When we fell in for the evening, I succeeded in placing myself where I was detailed for a watch on fire patrol, or perimeter guard, which was preferable to the shelters, and would be a watch of four hours only. On one occasion, in a heavy air raid, we went to the top floor of one of the mess blocks to see what was going on. We were then walking between the buildings, when we heard and saw a flash, and threw ourselves flat. There was an almighty blast of air – a parachute mine had hit the Petty Officers' mess, where they were mostly in the cellars, and the building was flattened. By the time we landed again the ground was already covered in broken glass, and we all cut our hands and knees. One member of our patrol, still in the building, was at the bottom of a flight of stairs, and was blown back to the top before landing on his share of broken glass.

We fell in on parade every morning and marched round in front of the Commanding Officer of the barracks to the Royal Marines Band, followed on occasions by a march round the City behind the band. One memory of the barracks parade: the band played 'Run Rabbit Run', which was accompanied by a male voice rendering of the song. We heard later that the Commanding Officer had forgotten to switch his microphone off, before he started singing to himself. A lighter moment in our training!

During our stays in Portsmouth we were allowed an occasional night ashore, when a civilised meal in normal surroundings was a priority, as well, of course, as a drop of beer. I used to get a bed for the night in Aggie Weston's Hostel on the Southsea sea front, and I always asked for a bed on the top floor. My theory was that if the place was hit, I would rather be on top of the rubble than underneath it, unless, of course, I was blown clear, either for a hard landing on the rubble or road, or a soft landing in the sea or on the sand!

About ten days before we left Portsmouth, we took a test in seamanship, in which overall I was classed as 'exceptional' with ninety-one per cent. Not bad for someone who really knew nothing about the sea, and was metaphorically out of his depth for some time yet. I came first in 'Log, Lead and Line' and 'Bends and Hitches', (not that sort, but rope work!) and in 'Compass and Wheel'. I came third in semaphore, seventh in boat work, and was not much good at dropping anchor, as I was twentieth in 'Anchor and Cables'. Perhaps I did not really want to go to sea at all! In gunnery I was highest overall with seventy-two per cent, having got seventy-two per cent also in gun drill, and oral knowledge. I suspect that the reason for my successes was that I had taken quite a few exams before, and was more skilled in the art than most of the others.

And after all this I was about to be posted to a depot ship – was I too valuable to go to sea? No, the Royal Navy did not work like that. I think it was more a lottery where we all ended up.

Our final stay in barracks was relatively short, and at the end of August, we were technically capable of active service, and received postings to various ships, which could be shore establishments, or seagoing. I think that generally they were to real ships. I and a colleague (who worked in Northamptonshire) were posted to HMS *Greenwich* at Scapa Flow, a very long way away. We joined a train which made the journey all the way to the North of Scotland, by a most circuitous route. We identified some station names as we stopped. My memories of what and how we ate are blurred, but in the end we were on the ferry to the Flow.

Chapter Three
Scapa Flow and HMS *Greenwich*

Shortly after arriving at our destination we boarded the ferry for the Orkneys, a journey of about thirty miles to a port we were to land at. We then transferred to an open boat from HMS *Greenwich*, fortunately with an engine and made the final journey to the ship. We had to pass through the boom defence at the entrance to the area and it was not a particularly attractive sight, in fact quite depressing to see these islands and hills with nothing on them, hardly any houses or buildings in view. The appearance of HMS *Greenwich* was also something we were not expecting. It was a very old merchant ship moored at both ends to buoys and obviously never moved. It seemed strange that we had joined the Navy to end up on an immobile ship, whereas we thought we would be going to sea. It seemed that maybe the Navy didn't really want us after all.

We climbed the ladder on to the deck clutching our kit bag and anything else we could carry, our sole possessions in the world at the time. The Master at Arms allocated us to either the port or starboard watch, the crew being divided into two basic watches with divisions within them. We were also allocated to our mess and shown where the mess deck was. We soon discovered that the holds of the ship now had decks put into them to make sleeping accommodation, but one hold left contained coal to run the ship's engines. The engine for propelling the ship had been removed years ago and the coal was for heating and for the electricity generation. We realised that the ship was quite incapable of going to sea and we should never get to sea on this ship.

The seamen's mess deck had a gangway running fore and aft in the centre with long tables on either side which would seat roughly fifteen people, The leading seaman sat at the end, and he was in charge, with about seven people seated on either side. The seats were a wooden bench on either side and that was where we were to have our meal.

In each mess there would be two seamen appointed every week as cooks of the mess, which did not mean they did the cooking, but they prepared all the meals for cooking. These went to the galley where the cook in charge cooked them all ready for the appropriate mealtime. The leading seaman of the mess had to decide in consultation with the cook what he put up for cooking for any particular day, as there would be a limit to the number of roasts that could be cooked or the number of pans that could go on top of the cookers, so this was all predetermined. The two cooks prepared the food, took it in the appropriate trays or dishes to the cook, and they were labelled with the number of the mess and left with him. He would have them ready at the right time. The two mess men would then go along and recover the food and would be responsible for serving it to the rest of their particular group. The food was good within the limited resources which were available to the ship in those circumstances. Of course, after the meal was over, the two cooks had the job of doing the washing up and drying all the crockery and so on, ready for the next time.

A major benefit of serving on HMS *Greenwich* was that it was very largely manned by Royal Fleet Reserve seamen who had served most of their life in the Navy and had returned to service during wartime. What they didn't know about the Navy was not worth knowing, so we could pick up a lot of very useful information from them which I don't think we would ever have got on any seagoing ship. This extended both to the way of doing things, the way of avoiding doing things, and the way of ensuring that you did what would be of personal benefit as far as possible.

After the meal we would fall in on the upper deck together with the rest of the crew to be allocated our duties for the day. We soon learnt an interesting tradition of the old seamen. After lunch the leading hand would report to the Officer of the Day, 'Thirteen mess present and correct, sir except Brown, sir, birthday, sir.' The Officer of the Day would ask where he was – 'in the oilskin locker?' And the leading hand would reply, 'Yes, sir.' This is because on a birthday every man was allowed unofficially to have a sip of the rum of every other member in that mess who drew a rum ration. This meant of course that he was quite drunk and incapable in the afternoon and could not go on duty, so he was laid down in the oilskin locker with a pillow under his head, and the interesting point was that the Officer of the Day would go down every hour or so to look at him and make sure that he was still breathing and in order.

There were more important advantages of having all these experienced seamen there. We very quickly learned how to splice ropes, wire guard rails and all the other similar requirements of a seagoing ship. There were such duties as washing down the deck in our mess apartment and all the rest of the ship, which was shared around.

However, I acquired another interesting function which was to go round on the ship's boat where there would be about four of us delivering supplies to the various seagoing ships in the area. Some of these came from our own ship, others came from various ships which were around, including a refrigerator ship which had all the meat in it. Going down into the hold of the refrigerator ship to obtain meat and other substances was a very chilling experience, especially in the middle of winter in the Orkneys, and when one came back on deck it felt like mid-summer, even on an icy cold day. But it did not feel like this for very long, and one soon felt the chill again. We would have to load what was required into a net in the icy hold, and the four corners of the net would have rings in them and these would be brought together and hooked on to the hook of the hoist which would then lift them up by power, and swing over our own little boat and lower them into there. The main problem was one had to very careful not to let a side of meat drop on your foot in the hold because when it was frozen it was like dropping a heavy iron weight and this would certainly have finished off the foot completely.

One major disadvantage of HMS *Greenwich* was that it was not a seagoing ship and therefore was not allowed duty free goods, which meant we had to pay normal price for cigarettes and any beer we could get on the ship. We were allowed to go ashore, as far as I remember, one evening a week, possibly two, to a canteen which was on the shore close to the ship, where one could have beer. However, each person going on shore was allowed only two beer tickets which would enable them to have two pints during the evening so nobody ever got drunk. I soon discovered that the two people who went on patrol to make sure that order was kept were not allowed any beer at all, but I found out that if they helped to recover the beer mugs from various people in the room when they were empty and take them back to the bar, the barman would express his appreciation. If when they put the beer mugs down they turned the handle of one of them towards the barman he filled it up, and so the patrol got their ration of beer. The only difference was that they could get more than everybody else with the result that the seamen on shore leave went back to the ship stone cold sober, whereas the duty boys went back feeling very merry indeed.

One could go for a walk ashore whilst on leave, but bearing in mind that there were tracks through the heather and nothing significant to see, a hundred yards or two would be quite enough to turn one back to civilisation. I remember on one occasion going to Kirkwall, the capital of the Orkneys, which meant a journey by boat of some time and then the walk to get into the town. I discovered that about thirty minutes there was quite enough to satisfy me because I couldn't find anything worth seeing, and I was soon ready to go back to the ship again.

My friend Jones and I after a few weeks discovered that on the notice board it was announced that a course for people wishing to study for able seaman was to be held on HMS *Maidstone*, the main seagoing headquarter ship in the harbour. Since this would involve getting away from our ship for a morning it was a very appealing idea, so we put in an application and this was granted. We started the course which was in the morning from something like 9.30 till 12.00, which meant that we would have a cup of coffee and a break on the *Maidstone*, and we would meet a few people from the *Maidstone*, and from other ships around the harbour.

The main attraction apart from possibly helping our position in the Navy, was that the *Maidstone*, unlike the *Greenwich*, was a duty free ship and this meant that we could go to the canteen at the break and buy duty free cigarettes. Since the cap ribbons worn by everybody in the Navy did not any longer show the name of their ship and merely said 'HMS' the people in the *Maidstone* canteen could not identify who came from their ship and who from other ships, and so we were served with the duty free cigarettes without any question. We would normally come back on board with about six or eight packets of cigarettes concealed in various pockets in our uniform and go into the mess and put them into the bottom of our lockers.

One day when we boarded our own ship again the sentry told me that the Master at Arms wished to see me as soon as I came on board! This created a major sense of panic because I felt sure he knew that we had been buying duty free cigarettes and was going to search me. So I quickly went down the first gangway to the lower deck which I came across, ran along it until I met somebody who I knew, and showered my packets of cigarettes on him, saying, 'Lose these where ever you can! I've got to see the Master at Arms.' Back I went and approached the office of the Master at Arms from the normal route, knocked on the door and went in when he called me. To my relief he said to me, 'I see you put in an application to draw your rum ration, Denton. Do you really drink rum or have you been told to get it by some of those senior men in your mess who want to drink it for you?' I said, 'Oh no, I'm very fond of rum and I intend to drink it myself,' to which he said, 'All right I'll approve it, but make sure you do – I don't want to see any drunkenness about.' The next day I had my rum ration and that of course cheered up my view of the whole of Scapa flow and the Navy.

One activity that took place, I think on a Saturday evening, was housey housey or bingo as it is now called. I came down off watch to hear the caller saying, 'One more ticket to go, who'll have it?' So I promptly said, 'I will' and bought the last ticket. The game proceeded and I won the top prize much to the annoyance of everyone else. Of course, I did not share their concerns.

One evening I saw somebody finishing off a ready cut wool rug and that struck me as being quite a good idea. I sent away for the materials which duly turned up and set it out in the mess and started to work on it with everybody looking on. After a while I had to go on watch for four hours, and when I came back I found, to my surprise, the rug half finished! It didn't give me anything to do but at least it occupied everyone else, and I ended up with the rug. I rolled it up and with a dirty towel wrapped it up and had to go and take it to the officer who had to approve the outgoing mail. It had to be tied up in his presence to show that I was not smuggling anything out. He was rather concerned about the towel and what was that going for? I said, 'Well, my wife will wash it – it is there to protect the rug and she will send it back to me.' He let it go. Of course, it never did come back.

There was so little to do that one had to occupy oneself with any means possible. At least I got to go round to other ships with the drifter carrying supplies and met a few other members of the crew and got a bit of variety which other people did not. Eventually, at the end of November, I was called into the Master at Arms's office to learn that he had been informed that it was all a mistake me being appointed to HMS *Greenwich* and that I was to return to Portsmouth as soon as possible, in order that I could be drafted to a seagoing ship. It appeared that I had been recommended for a commission and had to have a certain length of seagoing time before I could gain a commission, and a depot ship did not count as seagoing time. If I was to get a commission it was a bit disappointing to know that I had wasted three months, together with my friend Jones. However, I realised sometime afterwards that I had a great advantage in that I learnt all the 'tricks of the trade' of the Navy as they should be, rather than as they have to be on a seagoing ship, which is never running to any normal routine.

Within a few days we were all packed up, went across on the ferry and got on to the train for Portsmouth which was to take us pretty well the whole way there by a very circuitous route. We were not given any rations but given an allowance because there was going to be on the train the first catering unit run by the British Red Cross Society.

Unfortunately, when we went forward along the train to get our midday meal we were amazed to discover that all the carriage doors were locked so that nobody could get from one carriage to the next. Having had some experience with locks in my early days, when it was a hobby of mine to develop the art of picking locks, I found a cordial bottle which had a spring top, levered off the wired fastening, and re-bent it so that I could use it as a sort of hook to get at the inner works of the door. I soon found out how to open the door and started going forward. Eventually, I came face to face with the guard who said, 'What's all this going on? Interfering with British Rail property, that's a criminal offence for which you can be put in prison.' He then saw the crowd of angry sailors behind me, each waiting for their meal and feeling rather hungry, and promptly disappeared into his little cabin and shut the door.

We continued our journey and got into the canteen. I was the first one to place my order so I had a good choice of menu and sat down to a very attractive meal. After a long and arduous journey we eventually arrived back at Portsmouth from where we had departed in the month of August – three months earlier.

Chapter Four
HMS *Havelock* – Western Approaches

On arrival in Portsmouth my colleague and I were told that we were to join HMS *Havelock*, a destroyer working from Liverpool on the Western Approaches. We left the following morning for Liverpool and I cannot remember now whether we went by train or whether it was Naval transport. However, after a long journey across country we reached Liverpool, to be told that the ship was at sea for another two or three days, and we were taken to a church hall, I think it was, a few miles north of Liverpool in a rather desolate environment. Here we and a few other Naval personnel were sleeping on temporary camp beds and having meals prepared in the kitchen of the hall, so there was no degree of comfort at all. Going outside was not particularly attractive either, because there was virtually nothing in the neighbourhood: we could not find shops we could reach within reason, not even a pub. It was a relief, therefore, after about three days when a truck arrived to take us down to the docks to meet our ship.

We arrived on the dock side to see a destroyer moored to the quay alongside. I think it was a destroyer although it would be very difficult to say. It was quite a shock when we first saw the *Greenwich*, and it was an even bigger shock when we saw the *Havelock*, or what was left of it. It was not suffering from the acts of the enemy, but from the act of the weather. Above deck all the lifeboats had gone having been washed overboard – one had gone complete with its davits. All the guard rails on the ship had been washed away and the mast had disappeared. The bow of the ship was bent upwards by about twenty degrees or so for a short distance, and the forward gun, complete with mounting, had been twisted upwards by the force of the waves until the gun was pointing about forty-five degrees up into the air when it should have been pointing out horizontally. This clearly indicated to us the severity of the Atlantic gales which we were to suffer before long.

It was no better when we went on board and went down to the messdeck where there was water swilling around, presumably because the upper deck had been strained and water was coming through and accumulating, and the pumps would not pump it out. If we were going to sea on HMS *Havelock* we were certainly going to experience the rigours of being at sea in the Atlantic in the middle of winter.

However, the first problem was for the ship to go back into dock to be restored to its normal condition, and after a day or two we were sailing up the west coast of Scotland, around the north and down the east coast to the Tyne where we went to the shipyard of Swan Hunter at Wallsend. Needless to say we did not experience flat calm on that trip and the weather was quite rough, particularly around the north of Scotland.

Now I had gained my first experience of keeping watches at sea, four hours on and four hours off. The watch system in the Navy was four hours from midnight till four in the morning known as the middle watch, followed by the morning watch from four till eight, and the forenoon watch from eight to twelve. The afternoon watch was twelve to four, and this was followed by the dog watches. These were two hourly periods, the first one from four to six, and the second from six to eight, followed by the resumption of the four hour watches from 8 p.m. to midnight. The resumption of the watches after the two hour breaks meant that everybody changed their watch every day so that they weren't doing the same periods all of the time. The body took some time to adjust to this weird system of getting one's rest.

I am not sure what duties I had in that brief period but I vaguely remember being on duty on the forward gun when I was on deck. There were all the internal duties to carry out, and each person was in a mess of approximately fifteen people. There was a series of long tables with a bench seat on either side running from side to side of the ship, with a centre gangway.

Each mess had seven sailors sitting on either side of the table and the leading hand at the end. Each mess under the leading hand catered separately for itself, and the leading hand had to obtain the food from the store, and it had to be prepared in the mess by two men who were on duty each day to do this. An agreement had to be reached with the cook to make sure that he had the facilities for cooking whatever was required by each mess on every day. For example, if everybody wanted a roast this would not be possible due to the size of the ovens. I had my share of this duty which seemed to include principally peeling potatoes and preparing vegetables. And washing up afterwards.

Also, we had to do all our own washing and hang the washing up to dry. For this purpose the Chief Engineer allowed a certain amount to be hung in the boiler room where it would benefit from the heat. It was not quite the life we had been used to and it took quite a bit of getting used to. However, when we got into dock at Wallsend things were slightly different.

Since the ship was clearly going to be out of action for a month or so the Captain was able to grant leave to parts of the ship's company, and there was shore leave within the area. This particularly benefited me since I had an aunt who lived at Monkseaton just north of Newcastle. I could reach her by electric railway quite easily. So I could go there and have a normal meal from time to time, and also if I was allowed a night ashore I could spend the night there.

I was on duty one night, as a sentry, together with one other sentry and a leading seaman. In the middle of the night the leading seaman told me to go down to the officers' mess at the stern of the ship, and get some coffee so that we could all have a hot drink. I did this with considerable misgivings, because I didn't quite know what explanation I could give for being down there when I was supposed to be on watch on the upper deck. However, I went, got the coffee and crept silently back up the stairs hoping no officers would wish to go to the lavatory during the period I was there.

Whilst I was down there I heard a peculiar humming noise apparently coming from the deck above. I didn't know what it was, but when I went back I told the leading seaman. Alarm appeared on his face and we dashed to the stern to discover that the stern mooring had parted company and the ship was drifting away from the quay. I had to run back far along the ship, get ashore, dash along the quay holding another mooring rope by the eyes that were spliced in the end, and slip it over a bollard, while the remaining sentry secured it around a bollard in the ship. I went back to the ship and all three of us heaved away to get the ship back into position. Just as we were finishing and securing it, the Officer of the Day, who had been asleep below, heard the noise and came up to see what was going on. He was very annoyed that he had not been called out immediately, but was somewhat mollified by the fact that we had saved the situation. We had been doing those things which we ought not to have been doing. This was something which I would come across quite frequently in the Navy.

Within a few days, we crossed the river to enter what I believe was called Smith's Dock on the other side of the river. I can best identify this by saying that it was on the south side of the river and the roadway ran along on the land side of the dock. The roadway, where Catherine Cookson lived, ran up the hill almost opposite the dock gate. Needless to say I was not aware of the existence of Catherine Cookson at that time, but I must have walked past her house. Repairs to the ship started immediately we were in dry dock, although I have to say that living on a ship in dry dock is not a very happy existence, because none of the water systems are working nor are the lavatories, commonly known as 'the heads'. We had to use the facilities ashore which were specifically provided for ships going into dry dock. When I was on watch ashore I would go ashore with one or two of my ship mates to the nearest pub and would sit having a few beers. There was absolutely nothing else to do.

When I was on duty it was rather more interesting because I would probably be a sentry on the dockyard gate at which there were two sentries and the night watchman of the dock company. If anybody who was technically on duty wanted to go across the road for a drink we would permit them on the standard terms, namely that when they returned they brought a bottle of beer with them which was left in the watch house.

I soon discovered that there were approximately eighty bottles under the watchkeeper's bed in the watch house. This meant that when I was on duty I could go in and have a swig at a bottle any time I liked, and there was a tendency for the people who were on duty to be rather more inebriated, when they got back, than the people who were on watch ashore. The Navy moves in mysterious ways! We were in dock over Christmas and some of the crew had Christmas leave at home but I was not one of the lucky ones, so I spent Christmas with my aunt and uncle in Monkseaton which was quite enjoyable. I did, however, get about a week at home out of the period and that was a very pleasant experience. Regrettably, my future wife was working so I could only see her in the evenings and weekends, and I used to go the couple of miles on my bicycle to her work place at Burton Latimer. We could cycle home through the country together. We would then normally have a meal together, either at her house, or at mine, and spend the evening wandering around the town, calling in places for a drink, and occasionally going to the pictures. Memories become blurred but I can remember one time when she was lying on the lawn with my sailors cap on, posing for a photograph which I still have.

The time came when the ship was ready to return to Liverpool and resume its former duties. A list of duties were published on the notice board and, to my surprise, and horror, my duty for action stations was mast head lookout. I rather gingerly enquired from the crew what happened to the mast head lookout when the mast went, trying not to show my concern. The reply was, 'The captain called him down two minutes before the mast went' so I said, 'I hope to God his judgement is always as good.'

In due course I was to discover that mast head lookout was a marvellous post to be in when the ship was in action, or when escorting a convoy which was threatened. I had a grandstand view of everything that went on all around the horizon. On the other hand, if I did not report anything I saw before anybody else lower down reported it I was in trouble. This led me to adopt a technique of keeping an eye on the bridge lookout and the stern lookout to see in what direction they were looking through their binoculars. If they maintained their look in any direction for more than a few seconds, I promptly trained my view in that direction with my binoculars, and, of course, I got a better view than they did and so I got my report in first!

With our gunfire we attempted to stop serious incidents happening. But if a plane succeeded in getting in from the rear between the lines of the convoy and flew up between them there was no means of stopping it because any guns we fired at them would be liable to hit our own convoy, so we were prevented from using them. The plane, however, was not prevented from taking any action it wished.

I remember one occasion when there was a ship loaded with ammunition more or less on our port beam while we were in the middle of the convoy. A plane came over and a bomb was released and I saw it hit the ship. I thought, *Those poor blighters on the ship are going straight up in the air.* The ship blew up and to my surprise I saw a small boat pulling away from the ship with the captain and all the crew in it. They well knew what the risk was and had the boat ready hanging on the davits. The minute the bomb hit the ship the captain ordered 'abandon ship', and everybody got into the boat and started rowing. They were very, very close to the ship when it exploded but, fortunately, the pressure of the water on either side took the explosion upwards over their heads. Little bits of the explosion were liable to land on us, though, and other ships in the convoy, so one had to be very careful about exposing one's head in those circumstances. As masthead lookout there was no way in which I could protect my head so I would have to rely on dodging if anything came in my direction.

By now I had discovered the background story of HMS *Havelock*. Five destroyers were ordered by Brazil prior to the outbreak of war, and were completed just about on the outbreak of war, so they were never handed over to Brazil but were commandeered by the Royal Navy. Because Brazil has a very long coastline and only two suitable ports, one at either end of the country, their destroyers had to have an exceptionally high fuel capacity to enable them to do their job. This meant that whereas the ordinary destroyer would normally stay at sea in the Atlantic for approximately twelve days, the destroyers of the Atlantic Advanced Striking Force could stay at sea for approximately fourteen or fifteen days, and the record for HMS *Havelock* whilst I was on board was seventeen days! The basic organisation was that there would always be at least two of them on duty in the Atlantic, probably one with a convoy outgoing and one incoming. There might be another one as well from time to time. So if a convoy was in serious difficulty, or heavily attacked, one of the nearest would be detached to join the convoy and help them out. This meant going at virtually full speed whatever the weather, and explained why the *Havelock* was in such poor condition when I first joined her.

Needless to say, I gained experience of these high speed journeys to come to the rescue of somebody in difficulties.

Sometimes it would be a lone merchant ship which had been torpedoed or something like that, and was detached from the convoy, and needed its survivors picking up. It was very dangerous for a destroyer captain to stop his ship to pick up survivors for longer than three or four minutes. So we had a scrambling net (with a mesh design) on both sides of the ship fastened to the guard rails on either side towards the stern of the ship, and rolled up and lashed to the guard rails ready for use in emergencies.

When we got alongside any survivors in a boat or in the water the net would rapidly be rolled over, the ship would stop and we would have to get the occupants on board as quickly as possible, preferably within two or three minutes. This meant that one or two of our crew would jump over the guard rails, holding on, and rapidly drop down the net with their feet on the lower mesh. They would help a survivor up the net, most of whom would be weary and not able to get their own weight up, so they needed help. Other seamen would be leaning over the rails to grab hold of them as soon as they could reach and help them the last bit of the way up.

I remember one time when the weather was pretty rough the net went over the side. I went over as well and went down to the bottom. The person who particularly needed help was a heavily built Negro who must have weighed over two hundred pounds. I was holding on with my left hand while I got my right arm under his right shoulder to help him up whilst he had his arms on the net also. The ship rolled out of the water and we were all high and dry in the air. It was then that I realised the full weight of this man was on my left arm and I quite thought my left arm was going to be pulled out at the shoulder joint. I gave a shriek of pain and one of my mates realised what was happening and jumped on the other side of him, dropped straight down and got his arm under his left shoulder so that we shared the load. By then the ship had rolled the other way and we were on the net clear of the water. With great heaving and tugging we got him up on deck where he lay exhausted. We would like to have laid exhausted, but we had other things to do. We wanted to get the ship moving as quickly as we possibly could, because if there was a submarine lurking and it fired a torpedo we would have been hit along with everybody else on the ship.

War can have some very peculiar twists at times. On one of our earlier journeys in a convoy I saw fourteen ships sunk and we came back into Liverpool with something like eighty-four survivors on board. We had had no bread for ages and were living on dry, hard biscuits and tinned corned beef for the last four or five days. By the time we reached Liverpool we were really in a pretty depressed state. As this was the largest number of survivors ever brought in by one ship from a convoy, we found that we were to be welcomed home by the Mayor of Liverpool and the chaplain to the Royal Navy. I had the duty of sentry on the ship's gangway with my rifle and bayonet. As they approached, I went to present arms and I was so tired that my right arm missed the rifle which ended up being supported only by my left hand, with the bayonet point about two inches in front of the chaplain's stomach. Fortunately for both of us he came to a very rapid halt and I recovered my poise, rescued the rifle, presented arms and apologised. I quite expected to be placed on a charge of attempting to murder the chaplain and spending my next few days in the cells despite all the hard work that had been done during the trip. The ship's captain, who was present at the situation, must have fully realised the position, because I have no doubt he was probably just as tired as everybody else, and nothing was said.

When I went ashore my first thought was to have a meal and I went to the top floor of Lewis's department store where there was a restaurant. I sat at a table towards the middle of the restaurant looking at the menu and the waitress came up to me and said, 'What would you like to order, sir?' I said, 'What I would really appreciate most is a plate of bread and butter, because I have not tasted bread and butter for ten days due to rough weather and shortage of supplies.' She turned round and went out and came back within a matter of minutes with a plate full of bread and butter. I cannot remember what I ordered for the main meal, but I suppose it was something like egg and beans on toast or something else of that sort. Off she went. I really appreciated the service that I got after such a poor food outlook over the last week or more.

The interesting point is that whenever I went ashore after that I went to Lewis's restaurant, sat in the middle of the floor in approximately the same position and every time the same waitress would come in, but without waiting for me to place an order, she would bring me a plate of bread and butter. That is the sort of thanks from a member of the public that one appreciated so much.

It was not long before I realised that my favourite sight was the Liver Bird above the skyline of Liverpool. When I saw that, I knew that very shortly we would be inside Gladstone Dock, and when the dockgates closed that meant that we could not go to sea for twelve hours whatever happened. That was like heaven!

Of course, there were other joys from time to time. On one occasion the midshipman on the ship, who I suppose was a year or two older than me, asked me if I would like to accompany him to the theatre. A midshipman is a trainee officer joining the Navy full time. I said, 'I would, but I don't think it would be seen as very good conduct if you were to go to the theatre accompanied by a sailor, would it?' To which he replied, 'I would like you to come no matter what anyone else thinks.'

The result was we went to the theatre and I sat next to him. I cannot remember now what the show was but it was a remarkably enjoyable evening. Afterwards, when we came out he said, 'Now, I think we'd better go for a drink,' and headed for one of the best hotels. We went in, sat down and enjoyed ourselves over a pint or two of beer. I'm sure everybody will realise how much one appreciated this sort of treatment by other people.

Another episode not on quite the same level was that I wanted to post about six packets of duty free cigarettes home to my father as a special present. I knew that one was always liable to be searched at the gate to the docks by the civilian guards on duty. I also knew that smoking was prohibited in Liverpool docks because of the risk of fire. So just before I reached the open space before the dock gate, I lit up a cigarette and came round the corner puffing away at my cigarette so that the smoke showed up well. As I headed towards the gate one of the sentries shouted his head off and pointed towards me, jumping up and down in the air. He was obviously pointing in my direction so I just looked around behind me, and I could see nobody doing anything at all, so I just carried on. When I reached him he was shouting out, 'Put that cigarette out, put that cigarette out! Don't you know that there's no smoking here?' I said, 'Oh, I'm very sorry, I didn't know, it's my first visit, I had no idea,' and stamped the cigarette out. He said, 'Well, don't ever let it happen again.' So I walked past him with my load of duty free cigarettes. I appreciated very much his tolerance. I presume my father did as well. It was a risk I did not think I dare take twice.

There were other pleasures of Atlantic convoys, not necessarily when one was at sea with a convoy. On return to harbour, for example, we might occasionally go into an unusual port to escort one or two ships that wished to go there. Once we went to Londonderry to leave a couple of smaller ships which had to dock there. Once we went into the estuary leading to Belfast where ships from time to time would want to go to Larne.

On more adventurous occasions we would go up the west coast to leave ships at Greenock or anywhere around there and once, I remember, we went up to Loch Ewe, just inshore from the Isle of Skye to take several ships there which wished to continue their journey around the north of Scotland.

When we were about to leave Lock Ewe, the Captain called me over when I was on bridge lookout, and told me to give him a course to get out of the harbour. The shock was a bit sudden but I succeeded in producing one, and then told him when to alter course again to clear the estuary. On leaving we were leading a number of merchant ships which had come round the north of Scotland from the east coast and were joining another convoy lower down to continue their journey.

Climbing the mast on a ship at sea, particularly on a destroyer in rough weather in the Atlantic, was something quite different from climbing the mast at HMS *Ganges*, the shore base, on dry land. The masthead lookout post was like a rather larger version of a dustbin, about four foot six deep, and was secured on the front of the mast where a yardarm running the width of the ship was attached and used for hoisting flag signals. The mast was secured to both sides of the ship by rigging which was quite strong and of steel wire. The ladder one had to climb went from the deck about eight feet back from the mast, to the yardarm. It was wire at the sides with wooden rungs to climb up. This all sounds very simple, except that the ladder did not keep still in a gale. One would start to climb up it, get about six or eight rungs up when the ship would roll to the left and the ladder would swing round on to that side with the poor helpless climber hanging on for dear life. The ship would then roll to the right and the ladder would then swing to the right hand side of the ship, again with the poor climber hanging on for dear life. With experience, one discovered that it would be stationery in one position for a few seconds, and those were the few seconds when one would take another two or three steps up and hang on tight again. Eventually, when about totally exhausted, one had reached the yardarm. Although the feet could go on climbing to the yardarm, the arms had no such facility and had to hang on round the mast to get up to the level of the top of the lookout post and then drop down inside. They would be relieving somebody who was already there, so when the climber reached the lookout post he would probably go round the right-hand side of the mast while the person who was there already climbed out and went round to the left. The previous lookout could start going down the ladder as soon as the climber was clear of it. All very complex.

When the lookout had reached the box and had the binoculars handed over to him, he was expected to be as alert and acute as if he was still standing firmly on the deck below. Although it was a very perilous matter, after a while I realised I had a grandstand view of everything that was going on, and far superior to anybody else on the ship. The corollary was of course that I had to report everything before anybody else saw it and that did require a great deal of alertness.

The aircraft we were particularly looking out for were Foch Woolf Couriers and later Foch Woolf Condors. On more than one occasion, I would find myself looking down on the wingtops of these planes because they would endeavour to get in and fly along between two rows of ships so that nobody could fire at them as they would then be firing at the next row of ships. The plane on the other hand could fire at any ship they wished, and could drop anything they had; if they had a torpedo they would release that in-between the row of ships. Although it was quite exciting to see them from above it was not very comforting to know they might blow you out of the water.

I saw large numbers of ships sunk, and sometimes we would go to the rescue of the seamen who had abandoned ship and were in the lifeboats in the water with a lifejacket on. Although we were not particularly happy about being stationary in the Atlantic when there were enemy planes and submarines bent on destroying anything they could, it was something we had to do. The more we picked up the more uncomfortable life became below decks because they all had to stay on board until we got back to Liverpool. This meant them sleeping in the mess deck wherever they could, on top of lockers, on the deck or anywhere with the aid of a few blankets or whatever was available. They also had to share our food.

When we received our training, we never received any instruction in how to eat a meal on a ship in a howling Atlantic gale, which would be pitching and tossing, and rolling from one side to the other like a... bath bun! We discovered that it was fatal to put the plate with the food on it, down on the table – it would either land upside-down in our lap or in the lap of the sailor opposite. If the ship was rolling it would slide along the table and end up on the floor. The technique was to hold it and the fork in the left hand, holding the plate on the table, and making a few quick cuts with the knife in the right hand; then, change hands and do some quick shovelling with the fork, or the fingers. It was not unusual after the first course to dash out to the WC to be violently sea sick, before returning for the next course. One good aspect was that I discovered that the rum ration tasted just as good coming up as going down!

The ships of the Atlantic Advanced Striking Force not only had to dash around doing everything for everybody, but had not been designed for the purpose of taking on any function that came along whether they were equipped for it or not. As far as I'm aware, the five ships of the Atlantic Advanced Striking Force survived to the end of the war although how they did I really do not know.

When we returned to harbour, before we went into the Gladstone Dock, we had to go alongside a tanker somewhere in the river and refuel so that we were ready for sea again straight away. Whilst we were in the dock we had to have ammunition and supplies given to us, which all had to be taken on board and stored away in safety. A no less important requirement was to fill the ship with drinking water once again, and we had to be very careful when we were at sea about how we used it to make sure that we didn't run out. We were very rapidly being transformed from ordinary seamen into fighting men.

My friend and I had the thought in the back of our minds that as we had been earmarked for a possible commission, we might at least get a position with better accommodation and facilities than the poor ordinary seamen got on the lower deck. There were some advantages. Once, when we had escorted a convoy to the point at which we handed it over in mid Atlantic, instead of turning straight back, we went to Iceland. I cannot remember now what the reason was but we had no boats on board at all, whatever had been replaced had been washed away by then. Whilst it was very nice to see Iceland in the vicinity of Reykjavik Harbour, it was very frustrating to be able to gaze at a city apparently untouched by war, and not be able to get ashore.

I am sure we all wished the captain had rented or hired a boat from the shore to get us ashore for a brief spell of walking on dry land. We might even see an occasional young lady ashore but that was all we could see. It was a great surprise to me to discover that Iceland was green all over. When later on we passed close to Greenland it was an equal surprise to see that Greenland was icy all over. However, anything connected with normal civilisation was a great pleasure after all the hardships of being at sea in the Atlantic in winter in a gale.

We were never in Liverpool long enough to have anything like a proper look at the city. About all we could do was go ashore, have a meal without having to hold on to the plate, and have a few drinks of beer in a pub somewhere. Nevertheless, we regarded it with a great deal of affection. After a while we acquired the ability to climb the mast with a little more dignity than when we first went on board. This was partly because we learnt to assess the direction of the sea and what was likely to happen – we would keep an eye on the sea and wait for a large wave to pass and then hope that the next few would be a little less. But climbing the ladder of the mast one would swing round the mast to one side, then to the other side, and it was very hard work holding on and keeping your feet under control.

The first time I climbed the mast to take up duty it was no easy journey, and by the time I got to the top I was just about completely exhausted. I was relieved by my friend and when he reached the top I said, 'Hello Jonesy, how are you?' He looked at me as if to say, 'You know jolly well how I am,' and I quite thought he was just going to let go and crash down on to the deck or land in the icy waters if the ship happened to keel over one way or the other. However, eventually he managed to squirm round the mast and he got in and I went down. Whether he saw anything when he was up there I don't quite know but I didn't hear any complaints.

Getting into one's hammock at sea in a rolling gale was no easy matter. The hammocks were slung fore and aft, and one held on to a bar across the deck head just below the beams and swung upwards and across and dropped down into the hammock. This is a good theory except if the ship happened to go down into a trough of a wave just as you were swinging up, you would end up flat against the deck head pinned to it by the pressure of the ship going down, and when it stopped you would of course drop back again. If your timing was perfect as it dropped you could manoeuvre your body sideways to land in the hammock. If you were unlucky you would miss the hammock and go back to the deck. If you were really unlucky you would crash down on top of the table or the floor.

It was then necessary to go to sleep and it required a good bit of training to discover how that worked, especially when anybody who happened to be passing, who got caught by the sea, was liable to hit your hammock with his shoulder. It did seem at times as though ship design had been specially prepared for the maximum degree of discomfort possible. We regarded the officers as living in great comfort because they had bunks and all that sort of facility as well as respectable wash places. But, I suppose from their point of view the movement of the ship would be just about as bad as up at the front.

Firing guns for the people who were on duty as guns crew was no easier. They had to fire the gun when the gun was pointing at the target which meant keeping it in the general direction and as soon as they saw it in the sights pulling the trigger. With a rapid firing anti aircraft gun this was somewhat easier because one had to spread the fire over an area anyway to get a successful result. Rather like playing dice where the winning combination never came up.

There were many times when I had just got into my hammock and dropped off to sleep, when action stations would go. We had to jump out of our hammocks, quickly get on as much clothing as we could, and dash up to our duty post. On some of these occasions, when the situation was severe, the masthead lookout would not be relieved because that would cause an interruption. He remained, and I would take on the duty on the bridge as bridge lookout.

One day, when I was theoretically dressed but I hadn't got my woolly jumper on, action stations went and I could not see the possibility of getting back into the mess to pick up my woolly jumper, then return to the gangway and reach my destination. So I ended up standing on the bridge with my cotton top on, my under-vest and no woolly whatever. Action stations lasted for about thirty minutes by which time I was just about frozen to death. All in a day's work.

After such an event, the captain could receive an order to proceed to the assistance of another convoy fifty or eighty miles away, which was in worse trouble than our own. So off we set at high speed through the sea, whatever it was like, and in whichever direction. We had to console ourselves by thinking that the country was relying on us to get the ships carrying essential foodstuffs and supplies to England ashore without damage. This was appreciated as I was to discover later on when I was staying in a hotel with my future wife. This would be when I had leave and I discovered that every hotel in the country gave the people who were serving in the Royal Navy accommodation and food at half price as a tribute to their work in keeping their supplies going. When I knew of that I learned to take full advantage of it including staying at some hotels I could never have afforded to visit unless I only paid half price.

We received orders to leave HMS *Havelock*, to arrive at Portsmouth on the 11th April to commence our training and assessment to become commissioned as officers in the Royal Naval Volunteer Reserve. My memory is dim now, but I remember some sort of interview and assessment on board ship, so that the captain could submit his report on our period on the ship, and his recommendation (we hoped). Subsequent events seemed to indicate that this must have been in our favour!

Chapter Five

Becoming an Officer

I arrived at HMS *Victory*, the Royal Naval barracks at Portsmouth, on the 11th April where some twenty or thirty ratings were gathering to be considered for a commission. The details of what happened are a little vague because after being at sea in the Atlantic for almost four months one's mind became acclimatised to being at sea. At sea we walked on a rolling surface rather than a steady one, and when coming ashore it seemed most peculiar on a steady surface to be standing upright which gave one the impression that the ground was rolling. There were other differences, including a very important one – the food and the plates stayed in the normal position on the table whilst having a meal.

We all knew that we had to behave ourselves and keep our noses clean because it was very difficult to know what the people who were in charge of us were really looking out for. Theoretically, it was future promise rather than present behaviour, although one's present behaviour had to be static and controlled, to hold the prospect of doing the job properly in the future. We were in the barracks for approximately twelve days whilst we received various lectures on all manner of things, some of which we already knew, some of which were new to us. It was very worrying wondering whether we were going to make the grade, because the last thing anybody wanted was to go back to a ship at sea as a seaman, particularly in the Atlantic. If one had to go as an officer at least the living conditions would be more bearable. We had a certain amount of leave ashore and again had to be very careful not to show any signs of bad behaviour. Even walls have eyes.

On Wednesday, 23rd April, 1941 I appeared before the final board to decide upon whether I was suitable to go forward for a commission. Fortunately I was, so that was a great relief. Needless to say, the whole thirty or so people were not seen on the same day so one could not entirely judge from what had happened before. We then joined the 'ship' HMS *King Alfred* at Lancing College near Brighton, and in beautiful peaceful surroundings. Life here was more civilised and we had beds and bedside fittings, respectable washing facilities, and the building was very beautiful because it was designed for private fee-paying students. We had certain duties to perform, and I recall particularly when I was on fire duty, which required that if any part of the premises caught fire we were supposed to go at once and put it out. For this purpose we had a trailer pump and were taught how to operate it but nothing happened thankfully. The only snag was that we didn't have anything to pull it round the grounds, to reach the fire, so we had two long ropes attached to the front and a couple of crew had to balance the pump on its two wheels while the remainder of us pulled on the ropes to take it to the position required. Fortunately, it never happened and we never even tried it, so I don't know what would have happened if there had been a fire, and I don't think anybody else did either.

After a short period here we moved to HMS *King Alfred* at Hove which was based in the new swimming pool built at Hove. The pool was boarded over and was used for general training purposes, and we slept on bunk beds in the car park down below which was not used for parking at that time. Not exactly luxurious surroundings, and I seem to remember we had a white band round our uniform caps with the officer's uniform to indicate that we were not yet fully qualified officers. This, however, is a dim memory.

An important aspect of being an officer was the ability to give orders clearly and concisely, in a manner which ensured that they were obeyed at once, whatever the consequences. Practice consisted of a party of twenty or so going on to the cliff top at Hove where there was a large expanse of level grass, nicely trimmed. In turn, we would all be placed in command, and had to fall the rest in and march them about in a neat and orderly fashion. There is one very clear memory. One of our team fell us all in, in a double line, and commenced to march us about, in a somewhat hesitant manner. After a while the double line was marching towards the top of the cliff, anxiously awaiting the call to change direction before we all disappeared over the cliff edge. Nothing happened, until one anxious marcher called out, 'For God's sake, say something, even if it's only goodbye.' To our relief a rather weak cry of 'Halt' reached us, and was instantly obeyed, whilst we awaited the next move with some anxiety. Eventually, 'About turn' came hesitantly, and was readily obeyed, to be followed by 'Quick march'. I am not sure how it ended – he may have been trampled underfoot. He probably got high marks for his reaction to an impossible situation. Whether he became an officer I know not!

On Thursday, 3rd July, 1941 I became a sub lieutenant RNVR, HMS *King Alfred*. At this stage I moved into lodgings in a private house in Hove which was a couple of doors from the corner of the road on which there was a pub. We had to be very careful about looking properly dressed and well behaved and so on, and there were only a certain number of establishments ashore we were permitted to visit as an officer. I was very daring, however, and as I had civilian clothes with me, I used to don them in the evening and move a couple of doors up the road to have a pint or two in the pub, unofficially. After all I was only applying one of the golden rules of being an officer, which was to tell people to do as I say, not as I do! We still attended lectures and talks in the King Alfred establishment in Hove, but I cannot remember very clearly a great deal about them. We also went to Newhaven harbour to gain experience of handling and taking charge of ships. Small ships, of course, such as trawlers and drifters and we would actually go out of the harbour to be at sea and get the knack of handling ships in these conditions. These would all be single engine ships but I have a vague recollection that there were one or two ships with twin engines that we tried and these may well have been built for the Navy for various purposes.

We were all required to express a preference for what branch of the Navy we would like to serve in and what type of ship. I expressed a preference for Coastal Forces having seen a Coastal Force launch and been on one once, and I thought this would be very pleasant. I realised that if I went on a destroyer or something of that size I would be likely to see only the major ports around the British Isles, and not see quite so much of the country as I would like. If I was in Coastal Forces I would get into all sorts of smaller harbours and places where I would get a varied interest and would get a chance to see some life away from the strict rigours of the Navy.

My future wife and I had decided that we would get married as soon as I left *King Alfred* and arrangements were made for the wedding to be on Saturday, 19th July, 1941. It was a little difficult for Marjorie who had to make all the arrangements, including deciding upon the church and who was to be invited. I just had to turn up with the wedding ring which I bought in Hove having made sure what her size was. I remember getting home on the evening of the Friday night at about 8 p.m. I went to visit her to discuss the arrangements, and it transpired that there were certain things for me to do the following morning. I had to go on my bicycle a mile or two to the nursery to get all the flowers and roses for people to carry and to wear on their lapels. I met my wife on the day of the wedding before the wedding, which I believe is supposed to be unlucky, but I can assure everybody that it did not affect our luck in life later on. We realised we would not get much out of the marriage in terms of being together but, on the other hand, if we were married, my wife would receive the marriage allowance, which would be very useful to save up for getting established in the future.

The wedding went off very well indeed and everybody seemed very happy. One memory in my mind is of the photographer trying to take a photograph outside the church. The path did not go straight away from the door, it went around in a large oval meeting again away from the church. As we were having our photographs taken, he was sitting in the middle of a bush in order to get the right focus and the right number of people in, so we probably looked quite an amused crowd.

As I had not had any proper leave since joining the Navy over a year earlier, I was promised faithfully that I would have fourteen days' leave before I was posted to a ship. We had our honeymoon in Ambergate in Derbyshire as few people went to the coast for their honeymoons in those days with the war on. On the 22nd July which was a Tuesday, I received a telephone call from my father to say a telegram had arrived from the Navy requiring me to return to HMS *Victory* at Portsmouth, at once, for a course in Coastal Forces. So much for my leave, and that seemed to be an experience I suffered from frequently in the Navy.

However, at least I was apparently getting my wish to join Coastal Forces. Even in those few days, we had a very happy time at Ambergate; there was a dog at the hotel where we stayed and we used to take him for walks in the countryside. We would walk alongside the canal, although when we returned to Ambergate many years later we could not find out where the canal was, and we didn't know how we managed to find it when we were there before.

There followed for me a trip down to Portsmouth to find out where I was to go and what I had to do. I discovered that I had to go to HMS *St Christopher* at Fort William. I turned around and got on another train heading back. I stopped at Kettering to spend a night with Marjorie, and then carried on. The train passed within sight of our hotel at Ambergate and I could see the window of the room upstairs we actually occupied. It seems a great pity the Navy could not give me another two or three days and let me go direct. I could quite appreciate that I was an important person now that I had a commission, that I had to keep the whole thing secret from Adolph Hitler, because, no doubt, he was watching me to see where I was going – what! what!

At Fort William I discovered that I was billeted in the old station hotel which was commandeered by the Navy during the war. My bedroom looked out over the railway line, but fortunately there were only about two trains a day so it didn't cause any disturbance. There was no food in the hotel so every meal had to be taken in the Naval eating establishment which was a bit further down the road towards the water. From memory the food was quite good, and there were only a few of us there to receive experience in the handling of Coastal Force motor launches.

Chapter Six

Coastal Forces

The Coastal Force launches were one hundred and twelve feet long with a three pounder saluting gun mounted on the forecastle which could just about manage to lob a shell into the water two or three hundred yards from the ship. Not much comfort if one happened to be attacking an enemy ship or an enemy ship was attacking us. The ship had a machine gun mounted on either side of the bridge which was armour plated and it was some three feet or so above the deck level to improve the visibility, and there were steps down into the wheel house which was just in front of the bridge. The deck below provided the quarters for the crew, and underneath the bridge was the coxswain's cabin on the port side, and on the starboard side was the galley, which in ordinary terms we would call the kitchen. Then came the engine room with two Hall Scott Defender engines. The V type engines drove twin screws. The advantage of twin screws was that if one screw was going ahead and the other was going astern the ship could be turned around fairly quickly, without moving forwards or backwards to any great extent. One had to run the engines reasonably slowly at that stage so as not to tear the ship apart. After the engine room were the petrol tanks and these were self sealing which meant that if an incendiary bullet hit them they would be sealed immediately so there would be no air and the bullet would have no effect. It was not very convincing!

Then came the wardroom which was the officers' quarters and there was one room only which was used for eating, sleeping – everything. There were bunk beds on either side which had to be used as seats in the daytime with the blankets all being put away in lockers underneath. There was a table for meals and a couple of moveable chairs. A small wardrobe on either side and a central unit between them with drawers for clothing and so on and, luxury of luxuries, a cabinet above for keeping a few bottles of wine. All the quarters below deck which were not storerooms had portholes, opened in harbour but closed at sea, with a metal cover. Next, astern on the port side was the officers' bathroom which had the luxury of a shower with a rubber container to put underneath to catch the water and pour away afterwards (weather permitting and the ship not rolling). There was a toilet which, of course, went up and down when you were at sea. On the starboard side was a small kitchen where food could be kept hot or heated up, and little else.

Next astern, a hatch on the deck which gave access to a small stern compartment, underneath which were the propellers and a rudder mechanism. It was used for storing all sorts of equipment required on the ship. There was a mast just behind the bridge which could have a light on the top lit up if we were at sea at night in an area in which we wished to show lights. There was a yardarm for hoisting signals.

I should have said that at the bow of the ship was a small compartment gained by a hatch from the upper deck which contained the ship's cable which, when the anchor was dropped, would be drawn upwards and out over the bow of the ship by the weight of the anchor and the weight of the ship pulling on it. The cable would be secured when enough cable had been paid out. It looked very attractive as a yacht type of ship but hardly as practical as it could have been if one was to engage the enemy.

On the after deck, above the ward room, was an Oerlikan gun which was mounted in the centre of the ship with a structure around it known as a bandstand, with steps so that the gunner who operated the gun would stand with his shoulders in the shoulder rest and walk round and round, and up and down the steps to get the right angle to fire at the target.

There were seven depth charges on either side of the ship at the stern, which would have to be set for the depth at which to explode, and rolled over the side. Obviously, this required the ship to be steaming at a reasonable speed so that it got out of the way before they went off and, hopefully, blew up a submarine.

I would go every day on one of the launches in the harbour to get experience of handling the ship – how all the apparatus worked, how the guns were fired and so on. It was quite pleasant to be at sea in a reasonably sheltered area where there was no immediate enemy around, and the only threat would be from bombing by an aircraft. One soon acquired the knack of handling the ship and became, theoretically, fit to go to sea on one.

I was then ordered to join a small Coastal Force unit at Sarisbury Green, based in the community centre. I was living then in a house called 'Greenways', next door to the centre, which was very comfortable after some of the places I had previously been in. I was to stand by for the completion of ML285 or Q285, as its official designation was, and would be its first lieutenant. It had been built at a shipyard on the Hamble River, or I should say a boat building yard on the Hamble River, and was nearing completion. So the following day I went down to see it and had perhaps one of the biggest shocks of my life. The hull was coated in copper sheathing which told me instantly it was designed to go abroad.

So much for my theory that in joining Coastal Forces I should see the coastline of England. At dinner in the mess that evening I was grumbling about my ill fortune, only to find that a fellow officer who had been appointed to ML273, which clearly was not going abroad, would dearly love to go abroad, even if it was to the West coast of Africa which seemed to be suggested. The place would probably be Takoradi or Freetown.

We agreed that we would change over if we could possibly persuade anybody to allow this to happen. Perhaps the heavens were with us after all, because the following evening a senior official from the Admiralty was to join us for a day to have a look at what was going on. I was duty officer that evening so it fell upon me to receive him and entertain him in the mess whilst all the more senior people disappeared to their wives and sweethearts in other parts.

Although I was not particularly well experienced in this art at that stage, I received him when he arrived, showed him to his room and then met him in the mess where we had drinks prior to the meal, charged to my account, and sat together to have our meal, chatting about the things that were going on. Afterwards, we had a few whiskies in the mess and when things seemed to be at a suitable stage I mentioned to him that this other officer and I would rather like to change over commands as he wished to go abroad very strongly, and I had no particular wish to go abroad at this stage. He took out his cigarette packet, pushed up the cigarettes and on the back of the part holding the cigarettes, wrote down my name, the other person's name, and the numbers of the two ships. He then said, 'Yes I will see to that when I get back to the Admiralty.' There was me thinking I'd wasted all this money on drinks and entertainment and that he would never see that again because he'd never look on the back of his cigarette packet. However, to my great relief, about two days later a signal arrived switching over our appointments and we were both very, very happy!

The ship to which I was appointed was by now lying alongside in the boatyard and I would go on board everyday to keep an eye on things. The captain had not yet been appointed. At the weekend my wife managed to come down for two or three days so that we could stay in a hotel, and she could have a look over the ship, which she quite liked.

At this time the wife of a very senior officer in the area came to launch another motor launch from the shipyard, and we went to watch the ceremony. Afterwards she came on board 273 for me to show her around and tell her all about it. I was not exactly skilled in the way of this particular vessel because I hadn't yet been to sea on her, but nevertheless we did quite well.

The captain turned up and the crew were beginning to arrive. He was a highly skilled ships' officer having an Extra Masters certificate and had served as a Chief Officer on various liners. He was now appointed to Coastal Forces! Rather a change in the type of vessel he had to handle, but his knowledge of the sea and all activities was of immense value. His standards were very high. After a few days of sailing around the area and getting experience we set sail for

Portland where we were to be based for a while getting used to the ship and building up our experience.

In the early days after commissioning, we were engaged in various activities along the south coast, designed to get the officers and crew working together as a unit, as well as becoming used to the functions of the ship and its activities. Strictly speaking, it is called a launch and these vessels were built in yacht building yards to a basic design similar to that of yachts except that because they had twin engines, they had a square stern about five feet across. Overall, Coastal Force motor launches were one hundred and twelve feet long from bow to stern, and drew four foot six forward at the bow, and five foot six, approximately, at the stern.

In addition, we had an Asdic (anti submarine detection indicator) dome attached to the keel and slightly ahead of the wheel house. It was about two foot six across and elongated, and this meant that one had to allow a depth of a little over seven feet, to ensure that one was in sufficient depth of water not to damage the dome or hit a mine. They were for detecting and attacking a submarine. On a large vessel they could be manoeuvred to focus on any point in any direction from the ship. Ours were firmly fixed and transmitted a beam on both sides so if we passed a submarine or a submarine was on the beam it would give an echo and we would know that there was one there. Unfortunately, it didn't tell us on which side of the ship it was and so it was then necessary to steer the ship twenty degrees to one side or the other and continue steaming ahead. If the echo came again whilst steering to starboard that would indicate that the submarine was on the starboard side. If after a certain distance it had not been picked up again it meant it must be on the port side and then the ship was altered in its course so that it located it. Once the submarine had been located, the ship swung hard round in that direction and in due course this would locate the submarine. One could gauge the distance away that the submarine was by the time it took for the echo of the submarine to return to the ship. One then went full speed ahead and when it was estimated that the ship was over the submarine, depth charges were fired in the hope that the submarine would be blown up. Excellent in theory, but not very easy to operate in practice, particularly if the weather was rough. However, the submarine would know that it had been detected and this would possibly be enough to send it scurrying away in another direction.

The ship and crew had to get used to all this sort of activity which was rather complicated. In addition, we would go to sea and a target would be towed by another ship and we would practise gunfire. With our three pounder gun this was a bit of an academic exercise. It did mean, though, that we were beginning to get experience of the ship and develop a degree of confidence in it. In addition to our training along the south coast, we would also have formal official functions to fulfil.

Sometimes we would be escorting two or three small merchant ships along the coast from one port to another, mainly in daylight, and this gave us the opportunity to go into various ports which we would otherwise not have entered. I remember on one occasion we went up the Hamble River to let a senior Naval Officer land at Hamble Quay to perform some duty ashore in the area. At various times we went into Portsmouth and Gosport and I have a vague recollection of going somewhere in the Isle of Wight for some purpose.

From time to time two of us would be out on patrol in the channel at night about two to three miles off the coast, steering up and down a certain area. Bearing in mind that we were armed with a three pounder saluting gun and a couple of Lewis guns that fired from the bridge and would be totally ineffective against a submarine, we considered that the sole object of the exercise was that if a submarine or any enemy craft fired on us and hit us, we would blow up and the people ashore would know that somebody was coming close and would take more appropriate action. This illustrates that in the Navy we did not always feel that we were going to sea for the direct purpose that we were supposed to be, but do not tell anyone!

By now we knew that we were part of the 25th ML flotilla which, when it was complete, would be four vessels in each of two divisions. My captain was leader of one division, which was comprised of two vessels. I have never understood why we were the twenty-fifth flotilla because there were by no means anything approaching this number of flotillas of coastal launches in service. Coastal Forces comprised motor launches, motor torpedo boats, and motor gun boats, which were heavily armed and could proceed to any situation fast and had a fairly stable performance – the guns could be fired with more accuracy than those on our ship. Whether the whole lot were numbered together I do not know.

In due course we discovered that we were to proceed to the west coast to be based somewhere in the area of the Irish Sea. At that stage we did not know where but we fully appreciated that it would involve sailing around Lands End, which is not an entirely attractive proposition for a small ship, bearing in mind the gales that could be experienced there and the roughness of the seas. Eventually, two of us set off on this journey and I cannot remember if we stopped anywhere on the way round but I think we probably stopped in the vicinity of Plymouth for the night. We accepted the hardships of going round Lands End because it meant we were getting away from the dangers of the Channel to something a little calmer.

We set off on the journey round Lands End and arrived in the Bristol Channel to discover that our base was to be in Milford Haven. We berthed at Milford Haven briefly and were told where our base was to be. Surprise, surprise – everybody, I presume, will know that the good old Naval ship, the *Warrior*, is now in Portsmouth Naval Museum, as an example of the fine old ships of the Navy. I believe the peculiarity was that it was the first steam ship built for the Navy. The experts say that it had no function during the recent war, but this is where they are incorrect. It was, in fact, the base of the 25th ML flotilla and that is where we used to berth at night and when we were not on duty.

Our ship was alongside HMS *Warrior*, and to get ashore we had to go up on deck on the *Warrior*, over to the other side where she was moored and down through a long tunnel which carried an oil pipeline ashore to storage tanks. Our administrative centre was ashore in a small hut, as far as I remember, and there were two or three Wrens there, and probably a Wren Petty Officer. Going through the tunnel was one of the major hazards of service in the Royal Navy. Theoretically, it was lit by electric light and being a tunnel containing an oil pipeline it was liable to be bombed. Consequently, it was fitted with blast walls periodically to stop any blast passing through the tunnel, and these walls were built alternatively on one side and the other. This was all very fine when the lights were on, but periodically they failed. When walking through one could hear footsteps approaching from the other direction, but in a tunnel with baffle walls it was quite impossible to judge how far away the other person was. In any event, everybody would walk through the tunnel with their arms stretched out in front of them so that they didn't crash into one of the blast walls. As soon as one felt the wall one crept around it and carried on. It was not unusual suddenly to find someone's hands in your face and they would find your hands in their face. The hazards of warfare!

At this time we would, in turn, get a short period of leave at home. As the ship of the senior officer, we had a third officer on board, who was building up experience in order that he could become the first lieutenant on another launch when a vacancy occurred.

Coastal Forces was referred to by other people in the Royal Navy as 'Costly Farces'. The Admiralty headquarters responsible for Coastal Forces was situated in Hanover House in West London. Consequently, we became known as 'Costly Farces of Hangover Hall'. A somewhat uncomplimentary description but it must be said that if we were costly farces it was due to the design of the ships and of the way in which they were used, rather than the performance of the people on them. I have to blow my own trumpet at times because nobody else will! I can remember that when I was returning from leave I called in at Hanover House to pick up some documents which could not be sent by normal means because they were either secret or confidential.

We would get general duties in the area we were in, and one ship had constantly to be on standby at anchor opposite Milford Haven quay to go to sea at once in any emergency. This might be in the unlikely event of a ship being attacked or more likely that it was suffering from some sort of breakdown and was not able to proceed into port normally. The duty ship would be anchored in the centre of the river opposite Milford Haven, and in the event of a real emergency we would have to slip the anchor cable and proceed to sea picking up the anchor cable later. For this purpose a rope was attached to the cable with a buoy on the top so that we would know where it was on return. On one occasion, when we returned and the tide was running rather strongly we tried to recover the cable and the rope parted, so the whole thing went to the bottom. The only remedy, then, was to steam across the line of the cable with a drag line and hope to grapple the cable somewhere and then haul it up. This was a very hazardous exercise, particularly as the tide was always running one way or the other in that estuary. Eventually, we managed to grapple it near the anchor so that we lifted the anchor up first which otherwise was holding the cable down. But we were all pretty fed up by the time we were back to normality.

Once, when the captain was on leave, I had to take the ship to sea with the third officer to escort a small convoy of, I think, three merchant ships southwards where they would be met by another escort. We had picked them up somewhere in the region of Tenby and were steaming south across the Bristol Channel when the weather deteriorated and the wind started blowing in strongly from the Atlantic. A heavy fog descended so that I lost sight of the three ships totally. I searched around but nothing I did could locate them, so I decided to turn back and have a look and see if they had slowed down. Again no luck. I then decided to head back into the Bristol Channel and as I was passing the Island of Lundy I saw the three merchant ships lying happily at anchor in the lee of Lundy. After a few choice Naval swear words, I dropped anchor and lay there and had a good night's sleep. We resumed our journey the next day until I could hand them over to the escort they were due to meet.

From time to time we would go around the south western corner of Wales, escorting a few ships northwards or alternatively meeting some to bring them southwards towards Milford Haven. It was customary to go round the west of Skomer Island which lay off the south western corner of Wales – i.e. St Brides Head. Local legend said that if the tide was flooding northwards it would be so great that one could not override it with the engines. Conversely, if it was flowing southwards the same applied and the local fishermen, if they wished to go one way or the other, would merely get in the centre of the gap between the island and the mainland, switch off their engines, and let the tide carry them through. The theory being that the bulk of the water would keep well clear of the rocks and shallows, and the ship would go through in deep water even if it might be spinning around one way and the other as it went. We decided to try it once but never again.

I think that everybody in Coastal Forces was appalled when they heard the reports of the attack on San Nazaire harbour in northern France. This was because two Coastal Force motor launches identical to ours were involved, and one of them was severely damaged and the crew, so far as I remember, were captured and spent the rest of the war in a concentration camp somewhere. It came as quite a surprise to find that wooden ships carrying two thousand gallons of high octane petrol should be chosen to lead this sort of force.

There is a large dry dock at San Nazaire and a German warship was in dock undergoing repairs. The idea was to destroy the dock gates so that the water would rush in and the ship would be battered around in the ensuing melee and damaged on the sides of the dock. The two ships carried a few soldiers who were to be landed to place explosives in the area of the dock gates. This operation proceeded, but unfortunately one of the MLs had its bow severely damaged or blown off, presumably by shell fire from the defences. I believe that the other one survived the operation and put out to sea again, although it was not in a very healthy condition.

The worrying part of all this for us was that we learnt that we were to be the next flotilla for this sort of operation. Consumption of alcohol went up considerably, in order to try to dull our brains and allow us to get some sleep at night. Well, that was our story!

At this time a new policy was beginning to show up. Merchant ships coming over from America had a deck cargo of four or five assault landing craft. These were the type that would raid the beaches and put ashore a group of twelve to fifteen soldiers who would then proceed to do their work ashore. These small craft were metal and rectangular in shape and not particularly manoeuvrable or easy to control. I believe they had diesel engines. They would arrive in docks such as Cardiff and Swansea and we would have to go in to escort four or five of them around the coast, heading south towards the area from which any cross-channel landing might take place. On each of them there would be one person who was a motor mechanic and one a seaman, theoretically. The mechanic would have been working in a garage and would have had a short course in the care of these engines, and that was it. The other person probably had no training at all, certainly no training at sea. The vessels would be lowered over the side of the merchant ship into the sea and the two man crew would embark never having seen one before, or been to sea before. There would normally be two of our launches with them but not always, sometimes only one, and we would have something like five or six of them following astern of us. In a flat calm and with the sun shining, this probably went reasonably smoothly, and we always spent the night in a port or a harbour somewhere.

Unfortunately, when the weather began to deteriorate slightly, problems would arise. Quite frequently this would be that the crew on one of them had become so seasick that they just abandoned the controls and left the boat to its own devices. It might just happen to follow on ahead of where it was going previously and we would have to manoeuvre alongside it as it was travelling along. One of our crew would jump on board to take over the controls and try to restore the boat and its crew to normal. There could be occasions when our crew were responsible for two or three of the craft and the few remaining would still be manned by their original crew. Our man would stay on board until the crew had recovered sufficiently to take over again when the craft would be manoeuvred alongside so that he could jump back on board.

In the worst cases the first indication we would have of trouble was when one of these craft started going round in circles behind the rest and nobody was aware that there was a problem until it started to happen. This then meant stopping the whole convoy and us going back and, with a little careful manoeuvring, timing it so that we came alongside the craft sufficiently closely for a member of our crew to jump over, get on board, and bring it back to a normal direction. In these circumstances it was virtually impossible to forecast where we would arrive at night when it was time to take shelter in a harbour somewhere. All this confirmed the view that we were becoming a part of the assault forces for a landing.

One time we were heading down the north Devon coast towards Lands End when we received a radio signal in code, which we could not convert into plain language, with the use of any code we had on board. In some way we knew that it was urgent, quite apart from the fact that it had been transmitted to us at sea, which indicated a degree of urgency. We did not know what to do but continued on our course for a while contemplating what course of action we could take. We spotted a telephone box ashore where the beach looked fairly calm and reasonable and there was a short climb up a hill to reach the telephone box. We decided the only course of action was a telephone call to base to find out what was going on. The captain instructed one of the landing craft to take him and put him ashore and wait for his return. He climbed up the hill, went to the telephone box, and telephoned headquarters to discover that they had assumed that we were in a different area and sent the signal in the code for that area, which we could not understand because we had not got the appropriate code book on board.

The message was to the effect that we were to turn around and head in the other direction because the craft were now going to be heading north up the Irish Sea and would be assembling somewhere up north. The implication of all this became quite clear to us. The landing across the Channel had been abandoned, and the landing craft were now heading north to go abroad as deck cargo in order to undertake a landing probably somewhere in the Mediterranean. At that time we assumed it might be the south of France. This did not relieve us of the thought that we were going to take part in a landing but rather that we were going to take part in one a long, long way from home. We turned round and headed back towards Milford Haven once again.

Marjorie, who had a week's holiday, had come down to the area in the hope of spending some time with me at nights. It started off by my telling her to come to Cardiff which she did, and I met her in the hotel and spent the night there going back to resume the ship's voyage in the morning. The next port of call was on the north Devon coast and it might have been Watchet or Minehead; I can't remember for certain now. However, she went there but we did not. This was when we turned around and started heading north so all I could do when we docked was to telephone her at the hotel where she was and tell her to come back again and then we would meet once again in Cardiff. We then went on to Swansea but after that we had to abandon the idea and she went back home.

We spent some time ploughing up and down the west coast of England, Wales and Scotland, sometimes escorting landing craft, sometimes small groups of merchant ships. In the case of the landing craft we had to go in to harbour at night and this meant choosing any suitable harbour which was on our route. This enabled us to call in various places which we would not otherwise have visited. A popular port of call was Holyhead, on the isle of Anglesey, where we would go alongside the quay where the ferries from the Isle of Man spent the night. There was nothing much to do ashore by the time we got there and the main source of exercise would be walking up and down the quay.

Frequently, we would have a very interesting evening meal because, to use the Naval terminology, a member of the crew saw something on the quay and picked it up to see what it was and it would come away in his hand. By some strange coincidence it would always be something edible which fitted in nicely with our evening meal. As officers on board we accepted that the cook was very good at his job and did not question where he got his supplies. That was his responsibility.

On another occasion we went into Douglas on the Isle of Man, as far as I remember escorting a single merchant ship, which we had to leave there and leave ourselves the next day. The sister of my uncle who lived in Whitley Bay, north of Newcastle, lived in Douglas and I knew from a map I had looked at that it was not far from the harbour. So during the evening I went along and rang the bell and she opened the door. To her surprise she saw a smart Naval officer in uniform standing at the door and had quite a shock, until I introduced myself and explained how I knew where she was. I was then invited in and we had a cup of tea or coffee, and I spent an hour or so with her, then departed. I seem to remember visiting her twice but that was all.

We also went up the west coast of Scotland and once had to go to Tobermory on the Isle of Mull. This was a training area in tactics and ship handling and various things like that. The headquarters ship was called the *Western Isles* and she was permanently moored in the harbour, and had the officer in charge of these operations on board. In order to ensure that we were adequately trained we would receive a signal at about 8 a.m. giving us our instructions for the day. For example, these might include carrying out some repair to the port engine, and this would be followed shortly afterwards by an order instructing us to go alongside the quay to pick something up. This with only one engine, which threw the ship's stern to one side, was a rather complicated business which we had to master.

Another time the order was that both engines were out of action. The officers were then instructed to go over to the *Western Isles* for some instruction on board. Shortly afterwards this was followed by an instruction to the ship which was received by the crew, that they were to come alongside the *Western Isles* without the use of engines.

Unknown to the people on the *Western Isles,* one of the Wrens in the office was known to one of the officers in our flotilla. The result was that we frequently knew the night before what signals were to be sent to us the following day, and this manoeuvre went through extremely well. The previous evening we had to borrow some ropes from the other ship that was with us and these were carefully smuggled on board. When the order came, our little rowing boat left the ship with two men on board, one of whom was paying out a rope attached to the bows of the ship, whilst the other was rowing towards the nearest buoy. When they got there, they secured the end of the rope to the buoy and signalled to the ship for the crew to start hauling in. It was then attached to the buoy with a short rope and the manoeuvre was repeated going to the next buoy and on to the ship's side, so we came through with flying colours for the ingenuity of the crew!

Just prior to going to Tobermory we had acquired three bottles of Drambuie duty free. The two captains had gone on Christmas leave for a few days and the first lieutenant of the other craft and I decided that we would have our evening meal together on board my ship. Half of it came from my ship and the other half came from his, and he brought it over in a large thermos jar which had a capacity of about a gallon or more. We had our meal together and it was very pleasant and enjoyable. I then opened a bottle of Drambuie and we started to drink it in small glasses with frequent refills. After a while the whole room was becoming rather hazy and I remember saying to him, 'There are four of you, how many of me are there?' He replied, 'There are four of you as well,' and so I said, 'I think it's about time we stopped drinking this and turned in.' We staggered up on deck and the four of him signalled across to the four ships lying opposite, asking them to send a boat. A variety of lights flashed in reply. In due course, the boats started to approach the ship and he managed to get in the right one and away he went. I got down below to my bunk where I slept solidly for the whole night.

My breakfast consisted largely of two or three cups of coffee, and very little else and my head was still throbbing violently. We both agreed that it would be a good idea to go for a walk around the inland side of the harbour. We got ashore and started walking around but the bang on our skulls every time a foot touched the ground was too much, and we had to sit down for a rest. Eventually, we managed to get back to the ship and collapse, as best we could. In case anybody should be worried about it I should like to add that Drambuie is still one of my favourite drinks but I now take it in moderation.

When we were escorting merchant ships we would have to take them into the Clyde and, having left them at their destination, we then had to find somewhere to spend the night. The easiest way of getting a berth was to go alongside any large ship we could find that was lying in the sheltered area to the north of the Clyde estuary. Permission would normally be granted and presented no problem. On one occasion, we saw HMS *Eagle* the aircraft carrier lying at anchor in one of the little inlets. We sent the usual signal and got a reply saying we were approved. We went along side, taking care to see that our Asdic dome under the ship did not hit the bulge which was built below the water line on aircraft carriers to protect them from torpedo attacks. At the same time we had to make sure that our mast did not hit the overhanging area of the flight deck. All this was achieved. We went on board and I went to see the doctor because I had an appalling sore throat. He pointed out to me that I was smoking a colossal number of cigarettes and this was the basic problem and the only way that I would get rid of it was to stop smoking.

I had for some time been smoking export woodbines which are larger than the normal English cigarette and are of totally different quality from the ones sold in this country. I was obliged to take his advice and from that day I did not smoke until the end of the war, having made a decision that I would give up smoking for the period of the war. It seemed a good resolution at the time but I have doubts about it since I did resume smoking then. But I have given it up several times since then and I don't think I've smoked for ten or fifteen years. As Mark Twain said, 'To give up smoking is the easiest thing in the world – I know – I do it every day.'

Another benefit of HMS *Eagle* was that we were invited over to the officers' mess to have a meal with them which we gladly accepted. From then on if ever we went into the Clyde and saw the *Eagle* we would go alongside for the evening and we were always received with great hospitality. I suppose that for a ship of that size it would be rare to get any visitors on board. It came as a very severe blow to all of us when later on in the war we saw that HMS *Eagle* had been sunk, with the loss of everybody, if I remember correctly.

Whilst plying up and down that area we would stand on the bridge with the binoculars looking longingly ashore, particularly at any attractive pub we saw or any interesting restaurant where we might fancy having a meal. The scenery was very attractive even if the facility to make the best of it did not occur. Fortunately, both the captain and I got some Christmas leave but not at the same time, of course. As we had a third officer on board this was relatively easy but when other ships were taking leave we had to pass him over to them for the period. It is interesting to reflect that after approximately eighteen months in the Royal Navy I had not served on any ship in a Naval port. Perhaps my wish to join Coastal Forces had some merit after all, although I was to discover that, although I would still not be going into any significant number of Naval ports, it was not quite as I had envisaged.

Chapter Seven

Foreign Service – the Mediterranean

It is difficult without any clear records of dates to know exactly when particular things happened. However, early in August 1942 we became aware that we were to have a refit, and it soon became clear that this was to be in respect of foreign service. The ship was to have five deck petrol tanks fitted which would carry approximately two and a half thousand gallons of fuel and this meant that we could reach somewhere like Gibraltar with a little petrol still in hand. We were well aware that we would sooner or later take part in a landing somewhere, although we knew not where. I expect it was quite a relief for us to know that it was not going to be across the Channel because the enemy resources there were so much more powerful than other parts of the world. It did, however, mean that we should be a long way from home and would not be seeing any of our relatives and friends for a long time.

We sailed south down the Cornish coast and had to head round Lands End to reach Falmouth. When we were approaching Lands End there was a violent storm blowing in from the Atlantic with waves several feet high, higher than the ship. After we rounded the end of the land the sea was on our stern, which is the worst possible position for maintaining the stability of the ship in really rough weather. Roughly every seventh wave was a big one and these we had to keep a lookout for very, very carefully. If one of them caught the stern of the ship and swung it round to one side, we had to decide quickly whether to fight the sea and put the helm over and try to straighten the ship up. If this was not possible the technique was to swing the helm over so that the ship swung round quickly and headed in the direction of the waves before the really big one hit it. Then, in a suitable lull in the weather, if there was one, we had to turn the ship round again quickly and head in the direction that we wanted to go. All very nerve racking, as these basically were the design of yachts which kept close in shore and hardly went to sea in really rough weather.

We reached our destination which was Falmouth and spent a night there when we were told that we had to move on to Fowey, where the majority of the work would be undertaken. Although nobody on board had ever been to Fowey we were well aware that it must be a very pleasant small place in which to be based when in the Navy. We arrived there in the daytime and at high tide and we sailed in and tied up alongside the quay. There was a very small Naval presence there with an officer in charge and we discovered that we would have to stay moored to a buoy in mid stream, except when it was necessary to come into the quay side for any particular purpose.

So, to get ashore, we used the ship's dinghy which could carry two passengers in addition to the oarsman. The round trip from the boat would be about ten minutes, so to get an entire watch ashore was a fairly lengthy process. However, the compensation was that there was a rather nice pub by the quayside which we frequented, and also another one a little way up the main road. We also took the opportunity of taking a walk around the district in order to stretch our legs and get a bit of exercise. At one stage we went up river towards Lostwithiel and on the left hand side of the estuary there was a small boatyard where we went up on the slip.

We realised that we were not going to raid the north coast of France, but were sad to think that we were going away from the country that we loved. Five tanks were fitted on the upper deck to carry the extra petrol, one on either side of the wheel house and another one on either side over the engine room just behind the bridge. The final one was across the ship just behind the entrance to the engine room. They had to have high guard rails to stop anybody being washed over board whilst going across them and there were steps put at each end of every tank so that the journey forward along the ship involved quite a bit of up and down work apart from that created by the waves. We were all convinced that the ship would capsize with all this extra deck weight but we were assured by the experts that this was not so and that it had all been worked out.

The main worry was that with the octane petrol we burnt and the quantity that was in the tanks at any time a certain amount of sand and fine grit would settle in the bottom of the tank and if one ran them too dry this was liable to get in the engines and cause engine failure, so the use of the tank had to be very, very carefully controlled. Our ship was also the first one in coastal forces to be camouflaged in a modern design which involved large areas of pastel colours: white, blue and green on the side of the ship in rather bizarre shapes. Everybody on board was quite convinced that this would make the ship far more visible than if it stayed its previously dull battleship grey. However, once again the experts assured us that this would ensure our safety because it was more difficult to be seen at sea. I must admit that previously I had never seen bright pastel colours at sea on a ship or anywhere else.

During this period, the personnel had to be billeted ashore because the ship could not be used whilst it was on the slip. The officers lived in the Riverside Hotel just below Lostwithiel, and being the holiday season Marjorie came down to spend her summer holiday with me in that area.

This was a happy interlude in what was otherwise a rather depressing situation. We took the opportunity of having walks in the surrounding countryside and looking at anything there was to see. We walked along the cliff road to the west of Fowey where we saw the house where Daphne du Maurier lived and wrote her novels. We were very envious of anybody who could live in such luxurious surroundings and work at home so to speak.

We had known for a while that we were all to be inoculated against Yellow Fever, even though it was unheard of in the Mediterranean, but was present in West Africa. We were pretty sure there was nowhere to invade other than in the Mediterranean. After my wife had left for home, I went with a party of about a dozen of the crew for an inoculation which was to be for me an unusual experience and for them no doubt, a frightening one. I went first, with sleeve rolled up, with a line of sailors behind me. I had the inoculation, and it felt as though my arm had been blown up like a balloon. I walked to the door and crumpled up in a heap just before I reached it. I knew no more until I realised hazily that I was on the doctor's examination couch, with him and the nurse treating me, the crew having hastily been sent outside. It seems I had to have a heart stimulant in the other arm. Then the problem came as to where I was to go to recover, and the Navy had no accommodation to offer.

I know not how, but the decision was reached that I was to go to the Wrens' quarters for the night. I was only partially aware of what was going on, and was taken to a single room and put to bed. I was wearing pyjamas, and not a night-dress! Every hour or so throughout the night one of the Wrens would come in to make sure that I was all right, and from time to time I was offered a cup of tea and something to eat. It must have been quite unusual for a Naval officer to spend a night or two in the Wrens' quarters, and not to take advantage of the situation. In any case, I am not that sort of person, even with Naval training! The rest of the men must have had quite a struggle to have their inoculations after seeing what happened to me.

A long, long time afterwards, I found out from the doctor in Malta, that the needle had gone into a nerve and not a vein, and that it took about four or five seconds to reach the brain and have its effect!

After a few weeks the work was finished and we set sail again to go round Lands End and back to Milford Haven. I seem to recall that the weather was somewhat better for this journey, than it had been on the outward one but it still was a long journey although the redeeming factor was to see the attractive countryside of Cornwall from the sea.

Back at Milford Haven we resumed our berth alongside the *Warrior*. Another vessel in our flotilla had similarly had a refit; and fully tanked up with petrol and loaded down with food, ammunition and everything, we set sail from Milford Haven on the 5th October, 1942 in a raging south-westerly gale coming in with full force from the Atlantic. We could not believe that anybody could send us to sea with such a colossal deck weight in such violent weather. However, they did and when we had been out of the harbour entrance for about two or three hundred yards, the signal light on the headland started to flash towards us. Every person on the ship who could read Morse was anxiously gazing at it completely convinced that it was about to say, 'Return to harbour.' It did not! It said simply, 'Goodbye and good luck.' The ship was laden down with swear words afterwards. Some people must have a very peculiar conception of luck.

We joined three or four other large Naval vessels, I cannot remember for certain whether they were destroyers or not, and set sail into the Atlantic. It was incredibly rough for about twenty-four hours and then the weather calmed down somewhat so that it was tolerable, even with the weight we were carrying. After about three or four days when we had seen no other signs of life, we eventually steamed into the Mediterranean and headed for Gibraltar. We entered the harbour and found a small berth, but the harbour was just about completely full of ships, obviously waiting to take part in an invasion. It was not possible to sail across the harbour owing to the lines of ships moored in the centre almost bow to stern, and to get around the harbour one had to go up to one end, around the nearside and down the other.

We were not in a very relaxed mood when we were in Gibraltar because we knew perfectly well that we'd gone there for a purpose. We didn't know what the purpose was but we assumed it would be a destination somewhere in the Mediterranean. As a result of this feeling within us we did not particularly enjoy the period there, although I went up to the border once to look over at Spain. But although some people went over, it didn't attract me sufficiently to go. I also went up on the rock to have a look around the area from a height and that was quite a pleasant view.

One scary incident was when I went to the hairdresser's in Gibraltar to have my hair trimmed. I sat down in the chair and he came towards me with his scissors, and in no time at all they were flashing around all over my head. I was really in serious danger, I thought, of having my ears removed. There was nothing I could do to slow him down because I couldn't speak any Spanish and one had the impression that he couldn't really understand much English. I hardly dared breath in case I moved and his scissors stabbed me somewhere. But in the end it was finished. I rather think my head looked more like it had been shaven than as though I'd had a hair cut, so I decided I'd never go to a Spanish hairdresser again!

We used to go ashore in the evening for a drink in one of the local bars, although I cannot remember now where it was or what exactly we drank – I suppose there was beer that we would normally drink but it may have been more in the line of spirits because they were duty free. The interesting experience, however, was returning to the ship at about 10 p.m. when the bodies of sailors would be laid more or less head to foot on either side of the road all the way back from the inhabited area to the dock entrance. They also had been killing their worries with drink and could not make it back to the ship and stayed where they lay. Any sailor found in this condition in England would have been carted off and put in the cells under supervision and would have been charged the next morning with being drunk and incapable in a public place. It was obvious that the numbers in this condition were far too many for the Naval police to deal with and all they could do was watch them and leave them where they were until they came round, where upon they would stagger back to their ships at any hour from two or three in the morning onwards. It would have been quite impossible to charge them because if they stayed on their ship there would be nowhere to put them into custody or give them the punishment which they required. At the same time, of course, if they were taken ashore it would deplete the ship which would then not be much good in the event of carrying out an invasion. That was something I never saw anywhere else whilst I was serving in the Navy. It was no doubt arranged by Hitler and his men to prevent the ships setting out to sea and carrying out an invasion, even though he did not know where it would be!

Shortly after reaching Gibraltar the captain of my ship went into hospital to have an operation, which was for the removal of his appendix. It was about at this time that the preliminary information which was secret had arrived regarding the invasion.

The official history of events says that the secret information was in a sealed packet which was given to ships but was not to be opened until they were at sea or on the way to the invasion. This is not entirely true because as my ship and one or two others had to lead the force into the invasion beach, we had to attend preliminary talks on how it was to take place. For this purpose we had to open the secret orders and read them through and understand them and this obviously fell to me as the person in charge of the ship at that time. I had to go up on the top of the rock with one or two other people, who were also due to lead troops into the beach, to see how this would be done. The guidance would be through an infra-red beam which was not visible to the naked eye but could be seen through a pair of binoculars specially made so that they could receive the infra-red and convert it into a visible signal. The signal would come from a small canoe with two men in it and these, I believe, were referred to as the 'cockle shell heroes'.

As far as I remember this all took place under the cover of darkness and looking out to sea I could see nothing at all, but when I put the infra-red binoculars to my eyes sure enough there was a bright light which I could see flashing.

The next stage was more complex. I had to take the ship to sea a few miles off Gibraltar into the Mediterranean and rendezvous with one of the submarines which would be operating off the beach area with the cockle shell heroes, before the landing party arrived. The submarine would have been submerged off the invasion area and the person who was to guide the forces in would have been observing the beach area through binoculars so that he would know exactly where the landing point was to be. We had to practise going alongside the submarine so that we could pick him up and he could come on board our ship to enable us to find the correct area to put the troops down, and to indicate that they must land. This was not quite as simple as it might sound because the submarine obviously was built of very tough steel whereas my ship was built of wooden planking one inch thick. If I was lucky and skilful enough I could perhaps take the ship in gradually beside the submarine so that where the bow of my ship overhung I could get it close enough to the catwalk on top of the submarine for this person to jump over, grab the guard-rails and get on board. He was accompanied by a signaller as well and it was a matter of fine judgement to get this just right, and it was possible in a flat calm. What would happen if there was a sea running is difficult to conjecture. They had a canoe with them and, if necessary, would have to put the canoe over the side and get in themselves somehow and paddle across to the ship. The canoe came with them, when we picked them up, so that they could lead the landing craft ashore.

We set sail for Algiers on the 4th or 5th November and the captain came out of hospital a day or two before that date. There was no possibility of him getting through the orders as we carried a complete set of all the information relating to the entire landing, whereas most ships had only what was relevant to them. The reason for this was that if one of the larger ships with one of the controlling officers was sunk it was most likely that it would be one of the small Coastal Force vessels that picked him up and he would have a complete set of the orders available straight away. It was interesting to note that the whole process was carried out with a great deal of care and forethought. I had to give the captain a run through, as quickly as I could, as to what the orders said and what we were to do and so on, so that he was familiar with them. I could point out to him any particular point which was of undue importance. It meant us both working closely together.

We had to take on enough stores to last us the period up to the landing and for some time afterwards because we would not know at this stage quite what the situation would be after that. This included taking on board the ship as much whisky, gin and sherry as we could carry. I remember particularly that we had three cases of sherry with twelve bottles in each stowed away in the bilges under the wardroom floor.

Chapter Eight
The Home Front

From letters received from Marjorie and from my family I was beginning to get an impression of what life was like in England and to realise that very few people were leading the ordinary life they had been accustomed to. My parents' house had an Anderson Shelter at the bottom of the garden which was built of corrugated iron sunk half way into the garden, and had sandbags and so on to protect it. When there was an air raid they were supposed to dash out of the house down the garden and get into the Anderson Shelter until the all clear went. I have no doubt this is what happened in the early stages of air raid warnings. I suspect that after a while people began to realise that Kettering was not a main target for the bombers which were more interested in the large industrial areas where their bombs would do damage wherever they landed. Life and death gambles took place both in the United Kingdom and at sea and in the army. The garden at the back of Marjorie's parents' house was not large enough for an Anderson Shelter and I can't remember quite what happened there. I believe that more communal shelters were provided in suitable areas and they had to run along the road until they got to one.

At Weetabix Marjorie was still looking after the financial affairs and producing a monthly statement for the proprietor of the company together with quarterly statements and the annual statement of financial affairs. These were audited by auditors who were situated in Leicester and came down periodically to check through her books and records.

She was secretary of the Weetabix sports and social club during the war and would arrange dances and tennis tournaments amongst the staff, relatives and friends. Along with other members of the office staff she would usually spend one, or possibly more, evenings a week working in the factory on the packing line as part of the war effort. I am not sure about payment but I believe they were paid the rate that was paid to the normal workers in the daytime.

As far as the civilian duties were concerned she was a member of the staff of the control centre headquarters which was situated in the cornmarket hall. I seem to remember that she was on night duty for one night a week when she would sleep on the premises, that is assuming she got an opportunity to sleep. I believe they would receive information about what was going on from regional headquarters and also from local observations around the area. They would then take appropriate action in calling out whatever units or services were required. These might be fire services, ambulance services etc. When she was not on duty she would be at home and sometimes would be on call-out duties. This meant that if the air raid warning went on one of these occasions she would have to get dressed hurriedly, fly downstairs, jump on her bicycle and cycle as fast as she could to the headquarters, a quarter of a mile away. This would be in the dark with what was, technically, a blacked out lamp on her bicycle which did no more, I believe, than light up the front wheel. She would leave her bicycle outside and dash in and man whatever section was required.

This was not all, however. She spent one evening a week in the WVS canteen serving meals to service personnel who came in feeling hungry and wanting some food. These would obviously be mainly army and airforce personnel and I assume at some stages in the war probably United States soldiers as well. The sort of service that I would experience in other parts of the country and, in due course, abroad. They were very welcome, not only for the service they gave, but for the change of atmosphere and for meeting different people. The only thing I can really remember about it is that she told me after the war that if somebody came in looking very hungry and thin they would get a rather large helping of the official allowance.

Whilst Marjorie was at Weetabix, a young lady called Pauline Mitchell joined the staff. She had come to the area with her parents, who had lived previously in the south. Her mother was French, and had married an English soldier at the end of the First World War. She was a nurse, who had nursed General de Gaulle when he was injured, and became a friend of his and his wife. She had also been awarded the *Croix de Guerre*, for her nursing services, in aiding the evacuation of wounded French soldiers, from the front line to Brittany, a journey which took fourteen days.

When she moved to Wellingborough she set up a nursing home for wounded French soldiers. Marjorie used to go there at the weekends when she could, to help with the wounded, and this is how she developed her interest in France, and led to both of us meeting many people who were well known in France.

My parents had evacuees billeted on them for quite a length of time, particularly in the earlier stages of the war.

They had no control or say in who came and they just had to accept whoever was allocated to them. The only thing I really know about it is that before the war my brother and I had quite a stamp collection which we had built up. After the war when we looked for it we could not find it anywhere and we were forced to the conclusion that it had gone back to London with an evacuee. That was a lot of effort we had made which came to nothing.

My father was sixty-five in 1942 and as far as I know, he retired round about that time with the national pension, whatever that was. Although by then he would have paid off the mortgage on his house, I don't suppose he was feeling particularly well off financially and, of course, he no longer had the use of the car he had whilst he was working. As it happened the NAAFI depot for that area was on the outskirts of the town reasonably close to our house. By then the evacuees had tailed off somewhat and my mother took in the manager of the NAAFI depot as a lodger. After that my father worked at the NAAFI depot assisting with various matters at the depot and looking after the stores and so on – something with which he would be quite accustomed following his previous jobs. That gave them a little extra money which made all the difference.

There is a tendency when one is in the forces to assume that you are having major dislocations in your life and that the people back home are very lucky to have a fairly normal existence. Things were not quite like that, and for the people at home there was also severe dislocation in their working life and to the standards they had been accustomed. My parents were fortunate in that in addition to their garden which had a greenhouse in it, in which they grew tomatoes, they had the allotment which was fenced and grew fruit. Altogether they did quite well. Also they had enclosed a small area of the garden behind the house where they kept hens so that they would get eggs and, periodically, a bird to eat. Meat, butter and other things were rationed and that required ingenuity; I have no doubt, from time to time, odd items would lose their way and end up somewhere they were really not supposed to be. We have to remember after all that we were all fighting for our own way of life and our standards of living.

Top left and right: Two of first leave.
Bottom: ML273 sea.

Top: Marjorie at Weetabix.
Bottom: Algiers - dry dock.

Top: Algiers - dry dock.
Bottom: Sicily - Avola Beach.

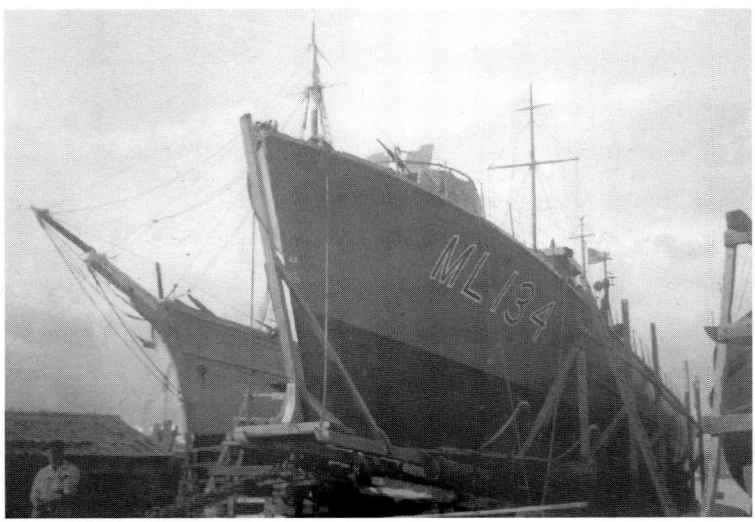

Top: ML134 on the slipway, at Augusta, Sicily.
Bottom: ML134 after refit.

Chapter Nine
North Africa and Algiers

By the time we were ready to sail from Gibraltar the British troops had been evacuated from Dunkirk and Hitler had overrun the northern part of France, which was totally under his control from Paris. The remainder of France was under the control of the Vichy government and, although there was some discontent in this area, it was basically under German control. The Allies had various agents in the south of France and probably in the north so that they had some idea of what was going on. The Vichy government was in control of such units of the French Navy as were in the Mediterranean and on the whole they were fairly dormant. It appeared that nobody really knew what reaction they would take if they were aware of an impending invasion force and if they came into contact with it. The people taking part in the force certainly had no idea what would happen and this was an added matter of worry for us all. I suppose we all hoped that Hitler would assume that the invasion force would be heading for the south of France. There can be no doubt that he was aware that it was forming in Gibraltar because the Spanish border was only a mile or two away from the centre of Gibraltar and from the harbour. Certain Spanish people were crossing the border daily to undertake various jobs they had in Gibraltar and they would pass on this information to people even if it was only as a matter of general gossip.

The voyage to Algiers would be approximately six hundred miles, assuming we sailed by the most direct route. We were clear of Gibraltar on the 4th or 5th of November and we were situated on the northern flank of the convoy together with one of our sister ships. In other words, although we were carrying the complete details of the landings along the north African coast, we were the nearest to the enemy. One would have expected that a ship that was so essential to getting the troops ashore would have been, perhaps, in the middle of the convoy so that it got the maximum protection. It felt rather as if the big boys in the convoy wanted the maximum amount of protection for themselves and that was why we were on the northern flank. If anything happened we would probably be opening fire and that would give them early warning of what was imminent. Well, that was how we saw it, rightly or wrongly.

On this voyage the captain and I would be on four hour watches alternately so that one or other of us was always on the bridge. This would be the case unless we were both there for some particular reason such as an air raid alarm or some incident which required the maximum degree of control from the bridge. Bearing in mind that this was the largest operation of its kind in the world up to then, there was plenty to worry about even if we didn't get that much time for worrying. Neither did we get that much time for sleep.

In these circumstances, one day was much the same as the next or the one before and even the hour before or after. We were progressively emptying our deck petrol tanks on the journey and we were supposed to drain them off, seal them and then fill them with water. We chose not to do either of these things, firstly because if we drained them off we would no doubt get a certain amount of sand and grit in the bottom of the tank getting down into the engines which could cause engine failure, and wouldn't be very healthy for us. Secondly, if we filled them with salt water there would be a risk of the salt water leaking down and that would cause problems with the engines. We preferred to risk the tanks blowing up to being without engines in these circumstances.

We were to lead the landing craft carrying the troops to the easternmost beach of the whole operation and their function was to head back towards Algiers on the cliff top and capture the fifteen inch gun battery on Cap Matifou, which was at the eastern end of Algiers harbour. The prospect of being further away from home than anybody else in the whole operation was not exactly a very attractive idea. We were to rendezvous with the submarine and pick up our pilot who was to guide us into the right area without any difficulty. Fortunately, the weather was calm so he didn't have a problem getting on board.

The landing point we were aiming for was to the east of Bordelaise Rock which was three or four hundred yards off the coast and was sticking up out of the water like a pinnacle. It could be seen dimly through the binoculars when we were approaching and, as required, we steered to the east of it. When we were just about opposite it there was an almighty shudder and a crash and obviously we had hit an uncharted rock which was a little way off it. We soon realised that we had damaged the starboard screw, and it was vibrating so much we had to take it out of gear although we kept the engine running. We then crept on towards the beach with one engine only, not the happiest situation to have in those circumstances.

At this time I was standing on the bow of the ship right as far forward as I could, gazing towards the shore and also looking out for any objects which might be causing us a problem in the water. I was protected by my tin hat which the Admiralty, presumably, thought was adequate protection for anybody approaching an invasion beach – it certainly did not feel like that to me because the chance of anybody who was firing a rifle at me of hitting the tin hat was just about zero. The biggest target of course was my body and that had no protection whatsoever.

Also I was the only person up there in that part of the ship and there could be anything up to a dozen people firing at me simultaneously. Fortunately, the heavens were with us and nobody fired. However, I then had another worry. Just as we were stopping and signalling the landing craft to go in on either side of us I could hear people talking ashore and there was also the sound of a dog barking. This was hardly what one expected at about 2 a.m. and that added to my worries. Since Hitler had a major influence in French affairs I had no reason to believe that this would be a welcome home party for us!

The landing craft passed down on both sides of the ship and beached ashore and the troops advanced. We didn't hear a single shot fired. We had to assume that they had landed safely but, of course, we did not know whether they would be walking into a trap a bit later on. War is always a very worrying business. After all the landing craft had gone in, the pilot who was on our bridge with the captain decided that he wanted to go ashore and join up with the party and see that they knew where their target was and how to get there. He had been observing the area at night, presumably from a canoe put over the side of the submarine, so he had some general idea of the situation ashore. He asked us if we could put him ashore, and so our little rowing boat went ashore with one of our seamen rowing and him sitting in the stern. He and the boat returned to the ship.

Now I think that our sailor must have been one of the first members of the Royal Navy to land on the beach. By this time we had no further duties to fulfil in that area so we turned around carefully, with one engine, and headed back out to sea to join up with the main ships of the force which were responsible for this area of the coast.

Later on in the night we were patrolling along the coastline to the west of the landing area we had been at, in other words to some extent towards Cap Matifou. As we were doing this they realised in the battery that something was going on at sea, and a search light came on and started sweeping round from the area of Algiers towards where we were. We could see clearly the beam of the search light lighting up the sea and there were no ships there at all which they could have seen and fired upon. We were very concerned because the beam was getting very close to us and we knew that if it did it could certainly light us up completely. A debate began to start as to whether they would fire a shell at us and whether we would blow up completely and disappear or whether it would blow straight through our wooden ship before it exploded. This was only an academic discussion, of course, because we knew that if it did fire at us the prospect of us knowing anything about it would be minimal. But the heavens were with us again and just before the beam was about to reach us it must have hit a hump on the hilltop and the beam went up one side of the ship, over the top of the mast, and came down on the other side. We remained in darkness all of the time. We could all have done with a few stiff whiskies at that time but I don't think we dared have them because we had to stay alert.

After that we moved a little further away from the shore to minimise the risk of being caught by the search light on a later occasion. By now the officer we had picked up in the night from the submarine had come back on board for us to return him to wherever he wanted to go. I don't know who was more surprised, he or I, when we realised the two of us had both gone through the officers' training course at HMS *King Alfred* together. In the dark when we could not see each other and everyone was talking in hushed voices we had no idea.

Later on in the day we moved away and joined a group of various ships which were conducting a patrol along the seaward side of the various ships that were still engaged in unloading troops. We were a mixed bag of about sixteen ships including trawlers and small vessels like our own all fitted with submarine detection equipment. We were steaming along in a large rectangle about two to three hundred yards apart and the orders were that if we got an echo on our anti submarine equipment we were to turn out of the group and investigate it. In the meantime, the ships ahead and astern were to close the gap, whilst the ship which had got the echo investigated it. When satisfied that the echo was not an enemy vessel, the ship had to rejoin the group in an appropriate position. The ships on either side would vary their speed in order to allow this to happen. This was when the next misfortune befell us – it was not caused by the enemy.

We were carrying on board a third officer who was not yet very experienced in the ways of Coastal Forces and the peculiar behaviour of the ships. We tossed up, in view of the fact that we'd all had no sleep for a long time, to determine who was to go on watch and who were the lucky two to go below. He lost so he became in charge of the ship whilst it was patrolling and listening for enemy submarines. We both lay down on our bunks still in our full uniform and were just about to drop off to sleep when I heard dimly three blasts on the ship's siren and realised that the vessel had signalled that it was going astern. This was a most dangerous situation for a ship in the middle of a group of vessels. I fell out of my bunk, shot to the ladder and started to climb up the ladder; as soon as my head was above deck level I saw the bows of a great trawler heading straight for me. I only paused to shout out, 'Look out, Gibby, there's a trawler heading for us.' I then made a dash to the bridge to try to rescue us from a highly dangerous situation. I was half way there when the bows of the trawler hit us astern, just aft of the wardroom, and cut a great hole in the ship's side. I was thrown against a hard angular piece of iron while I was half way to the bridge and had my knee very badly cut.

The captain down below had tumbled out of his bunk and was heading for the gangway to dash up and see what was going on when the bow of the ship hit us and the whole ship keeled right over to the port side. He was thrown across the wardroom flat and hit the door of the wash place, which flew open and he was then thrown across the room and ended up sitting on the toilet in full uniform. It would be difficult to say whether he was more annoyed about the damage to the ship or the damage to his dignity!

We both gave the officer who was on watch on the bridge a lecture on the way one got out of trouble in

Coastal Forces. This was to use the power of the engines to increase speed and get out of the way. In going astern the engines had, first of all, to stop the ship from going ahead and this took a matter of a minute or two, and then it slowly built up the power to start moving the ship astern. By this time you were too late to get out of trouble. We were suffering from the hazards of war. We were now in the position of having one engine we could only use in very severe emergencies and a hole in the starboard side of the stern with the water flushing in and out of the after compartment. We went down the hatch to get out anything important which would suffer too badly, the rest had to stay.

One consolation was that the party which we had led into the beach had apparently been successful because the gun battery on Cap Matifou did not start firing. No doubt there were problems in places, but the general impression we had was that the whole operation had proceeded reasonably satisfactorily, and most of the objectives seemed to have been achieved. After a while, and I am not sure whether this was the day of the invasion or the day after as I had lost all sense of time, a gale began to blow up severely and we had great difficulty in keeping the ship under control. We saw the headquarters ship steaming into Algiers harbour, accompanied by two destroyers. We flashed a signal to the ship saying that we had a damaged screw and also a hole in the starboard side which was letting in water, and requested permission to enter the harbour. To our relief we received a signal saying approved!

On the assumption that Algiers was now under our control, we adopted the correct procedure for entering the harbour of another country and trained all our guns fore and aft and had the crew standing on the forecastle in line, with the officers standing to attention on the bridge. It was quite a shock to find that, despite the headquarters ship being in the harbour, the guns on either side of the harbour entrance were trained on us as we were entering the harbour and continued to keep on us until we were inside. We carried out the correct procedure of having a man on the forecastle who blew on the boson's pipe the order for attention. So the crew were standing at attention and the officers were saluting as we passed the guns which fortunately did not open fire. Just another of the worrying moments we had during the last few days.

It was quite a shock when we got in to discover that the headquarters ship which seemed to be entering harbour so calmly had continued to steam ahead until it hit the quay and became embedded in the quay. Apparently, an enemy plane had dropped a bomb just astern of the ship which did not do any physical damage but put out of action the ship's telegraphs and controls which were all electrical, and when the captain rang down the order to stop, it was not conveyed to the engine room and the engines kept going ahead. I understand that when it hit the quay there was a resounding cheer from the French people who were around watching, because they assumed that this meant that the British had really come to stay.

We went alongside the ship and tied ourselves up for the night, secure in the knowledge that at least we would not sink due to the weather. It was also a relief to be able to get a bit of exercise on the deck of a larger ship instead of being limited to a walk of about five yards on ours. Needless to say, by this time the stock of duty free whisky which we had taken on board at Gibraltar had diminished significantly, as I am sure it had on every other ship which was taking part. After a day or so in the harbour the large ship was towed clear of the quay it had invaded and berthed more comfortably alongside so work could commence on restoring its electrical circuits and making it fit for sea again. We then moved alongside the quay which was the public quay and stayed there for a while. We were told that as it was a public quay we would have to have one man on duty on board as we would normally do in any dockyard, and, in addition, have a sentry on the shore patrolling by the ship. This was quite a strain on a ship which had a crew of only about twelve altogether.

We had only been there a few hours when a call came down the hatch to the wardroom saying that there was some top brass arriving. The captain and I went up on deck to greet the captain from the shore establishment of the Royal Navy who told us that we were to stand by to take an important person to sea at a minute's notice and this meant that either the captain or I had to be on board all the time. We were asked where he could be accommodated and we said that he could come on the bridge if he wished and that also the wardroom would be available to him. We were told that this would be no use because he would be under guard and was not coming voluntarily. We assumed he must be somebody from the French shore establishment. After a day or two, we were told we could stand down as the problem had now been resolved.

The following day we heard an announcement on the radio that the French ships in the Mediterranean had been authorised to co-operate with the Allies in the work that they were undertaking. From this we realised who the person we were to take to sea was; but there was no guarantee that the individual French ships would comply with the instructions that had been given. In fact, they might remain where they were and do nothing at all until the occasion required a firm decision one way or the other. Warfare can have some very peculiar twists at times.

Attention was now drawn to the need for our ship to be repaired. We had assumed that there would be a slipway somewhere in the region and we would be hauled up on it and be repaired in that way. However, this was not to be. We were told that we would have to go into the dry dock, and this was quite a shock. The dry dock was as large as any dry dock I had seen anywhere, although I had obviously not seen all the dry docks I might have done, and the thought of a ship our size going into a huge dock like that was quite horrifying. Neither we nor the headquarters ship could produce a plan of the keel of the ship to show exactly what it was like and how it could be berthed.

The dock had a row of large wooden blocks running from one end to the other and probably about four or five feet high from its base. These would then be adjusted according to the needs of the ship whether the keel was flat or not or any obstructions which had to be allowed for. We could tell them where our dome was approximately, and what the size was approximately, but this was not sufficiently accurate to allow for sitting the ship down in the bottom of the dock. It was decided that a diver would have to go down as the water was being drained out to make sure that the right blocks were removed to allow for the dome to lie between them. The dock then flooded and the outer gates opened, we sailed in to roughly the centre position in the dock. Two ropes were attached to the bow of the ship, one on either side, and two at the stern, and these were held ashore by dockyard workers who would adjust the position of the ship as instructed by pulling on them or letting them out. They closed the dock door and then started to pump out the water and slowly we disappeared below the surface of land.

Eventually, it was decided that we were in the right position to drain the water out completely and that we would then be sitting neatly on the blocks. At this stage, balks of timber were put on either side of the ship from the hull of the ship to the side of the dock and secured with wedges to make sure that the ship did not tip over sideways when the water went. I think it could be said that the docking of our ship, small as it was, was as elaborate as if it had been a major capital ship. By the time we had settled down on to the blocks and all of the water had gone, the top of the mast was just above ground level and we were sitting in the ship down at the bottom of the dock surrounded by concrete walls.

To add to our problems we were still living on board because there was no accommodation on shore to which we could go. All the washing facilities were out of order, together with toilets and, I think, we had a temporary water supply so that our galley could still be used to cook the meals for those people who were on board. It was certainly not the type of welcome to a foreign country which we had been expecting. By this time, Algiers had become sufficiently stable for ships which were in harbour to allow their crew to have some leave ashore but there was a curfew at 8 p.m. and everybody had to be back in the harbour area by then. The captain and I, being fully qualified drinkers, would go ashore to have a few drinks somewhere and wander around the town and we got to know the places that we liked and those that we didn't like quite so much. As far as I remember, we were largely drinking the local wines, probably the red one, and this required a certain amount of effort and adjustment to our sense of taste.

Now work had to proceed on getting the ship back into a fit state to put out to sea again. It was very fortunate that I had studied French at school. I had also brought a small French/English dictionary with me, although the speed of my French did not quite match that of everybody else. The French manager of the dockyard spoke English as well, so between the two of us we got on very well. He was François Caradec and lived with his wife and two sons at the Rue Ernst Zeys, Algiers. His home, where his parents lived, was at Kerfautras in Brittany. Between the two of us we began to get things moving and slowly progress was made.

From time to time the French workers would come to me speaking away in French and asking for particular things which, of course, I had not covered in my study of French. I would hand them my dictionary and in the French part they would find the article they wanted and point to it for me and then I knew what they were after. With the aid of a bit of questioning and sketches I was able to discover what it was they required. It might, for example, be two inch brass screws with a round head. It might be two and a half inch galvanised nails. If we did not have them on board I would then go to the headquarters ship and see if I could obtain them from there and get whatever was the nearest approximation they had. I cannot remember clearly now what happened about the starboard propeller which had suffered damage when it hit the rock. I think I succeeded in finding one on one of the supply ships which was carrying certain specialist spares for our particular vessels. Repairing the hole in the side of the wooden ship was much easier and more in their line of business.

We had to use the dockyard toilets, which were designed for Arabs. They were square sinks about six inches deep, with two foot pads, not easy to balance on. We then had to flush the lavatory; that was done by a lever at the back of the cubicle which one could not reach if one had got off the stepping stones on to safe territory, so we had to do this with the water flushing down before we got off and that could have disastrous consequences. There was nothing like this in our training as ordinary seaman at the beginning of our Naval career, I can assure you. Fortunately, by this time there were a few Naval ships berthed in Algiers beside the sea wall, and we took to scurrying along the quay finding the first ship we could and asking the sentry if we could go on board to use the officers' toilet which was readily agreed. No doubt the locals were used to these toilets but for us it was a matter of making a mountain out of a molehill. From time to time one of the ships, if we happened to meet one of the officers, would probably invite us on board to have a meal with them and that was like heaven.

By this time François had invited me to visit him at his house to meet his wife and his family. This was a really delightful deviation from the more sombre life I had been leading in the last week or two. I was invited to an evening meal with the family and this was really a pleasure although, with problems of rationing and so on, it required all her skills as a French cook to make a meal. But I have to say that she produced some marvellous and really enjoyable meals. I can't remember for certain the Christian name of Madame Caradec but I have the impression that we used to call her Mimi, which seemed to be acceptable. When I told her that I would like to buy some French perfume to send home to Marjorie she came with me around the shops and we ended up by buying two bottles of a very good quality French brand. It seemed that it was more readily available in Algiers than it was in most of France. I also bought one or two other things with her help and I posted home one of the bottles of perfume, the remainder of my purchases awaited my return to England in due course.

One day the captain and I had gone ashore to have a drink at our favourite bar which was on the corner of the steps leading up to the civic buildings, and we had been there some time and were becoming quite inebriated. Suddenly, two officers from our flotilla called out, 'Oh hello, Gibbie, thank goodness we have found you at last! We have been looking everywhere for you. Your ship is on fire and you must come back as quickly as you can.' Our reply was, 'Good show, we'll drink to that, come and join us.' It took some time for them to convince us that the ship really was on fire, so off we set and headed back to the quay.

The sight that met us was pretty horrible – the mast was charred half way up, there obviously had been flames coming out of the portholes on the starboard side of the ship, and there were signs of damage everywhere, not to mention water all over the place. It seemed that the cylinder that was beside the galley stove and provided the fuel which heated it, had sprung a leak and the stove had ignited the fuel and then the whole thing had exploded. Fortunately, the cook had managed to get out of the galley and escape to the upper deck at once and raise the alarm. The heavens were with us because the army fire service for the area was based on the quay beside the dry dock and almost opposite where the fire had taken place. They got it out but not before the whole ship was in a pretty depressing state. This added to the work for the French dockyard workers but caused further delays for us getting back to sea. We had to endure the hardships of living in a small ship in a dry dock with no facilities, for longer and longer.

The fire had burnt through a lot of electric cables on the sides of the ship and this caused further problems. The French electricians, equipped with a screwdriver and a large hammer, had no plan of the wiring at all and started to reconnect what they thought were the correct wires. This had some most unusual results – for example, if we rang the bell in the wardroom to call somebody from the crew to come and enquire what we wanted, they would not turn up because all that had happened was that the masthead light had come on. Alternatively, another switch somewhere would have the effect of ringing the ship's alarm buzzers. It took a long time before this was sorted out, particularly because we had no wiring diagrams whatsoever and the colours of the wires didn't necessarily give the right results.

Eventually, after several weeks, the day came for the dock to be flooded, so we could get out again. This was a day we had been looking forward to for a long time. Thankfully, as the water came into the dock and the ship floated up off the blocks, it did not sink and there were no leaks in the hull. The next stage was to try the engines. We gingerly crept out of the dock and moored alongside the quay for a while until we went out to have a sea trial to make sure that everything was still operating properly at sea. After what we had endured it was quite a pleasure to go back to war.

Two or three vessels of our flotilla would go to sea and do an anti-submarine patrol about a mile and a half off the coast, steaming along the coast and back on a set line. But after a while this was changed to what was called 'fruit patrols' and we were allocated a certain block area to patrol and these would vary according to the name of the fruit, to different positions along the coast. The idea was that if we had a general area to patrol instead of a set line, the enemy could never be sure where we would be, and adjust their movements accordingly. We enjoyed the sense of freedom which this gave, even if it was not of any great significance. There was one advantage, however – we would survey the coast with our binoculars and find a small harbour somewhere which looked deep enough to enter, taking into account the draft of the ships that we could see already in there. One of the ships would then suddenly develop a problem with one of the engines which would require stopping the engines for quarter of an hour or half an hour, to allow the motor mechanic to find the fault. That ship would sail into the harbour and tie up alongside the quay somewhere whilst the motor mechanic did his necessary work. We also had to survey the coastline to make sure that the coast road was visible from where the harbour was in case any staff cars should come along the coast. In this case, we would very quickly put to sea. In the meantime the officers and one or two members of the crew would go ashore to do a bit of shopping – after all it was a fruit patrol! We would pick up fresh vegetables and a bottle or two of local wine and return to the ship feeling that something useful had been achieved, then back to sea and rejoin the patrol. This procedure had its risks but, after all, what is war if there are no risks?

After a while, I transferred from ML273, the senior half flotilla ship, to ML338 which was also part of the group. There was no very clear reason for this but I had the uneasy feeling that the captain regarded me as being unlucky in view of all the accidents that had happened to us in the landing and subsequently. This did not entirely fit with the naval philosophy that the captain was responsible for everything that happened on his ship. I suppose, however, that it gave me a more relaxed approach to my job than I had had previously.

There was one occasion when I was on duty patrolling along, on the right hand flank of the three ships which were steaming in line abreast, when I picked up an echo on the anti-submarine detection equipment. I altered course to starboard (the right) and proceeded again and picked up the echo once again which indicated that the submarine was to the starboard side of the group of us. I swung round and switched to the bow transmitter until I picked up the echo once again and then knew roughly where the submarine was. By this time the captain was on deck and he left me to continue because if he had suddenly tried to take over in the middle it would only have caused confusion. We prepared three or four depth charges and fired them where we thought the submarine was.

As we continued over the spot and began to turn we saw a metal object breaking surface and steam coming out of it; we assumed the bow of the submarine was breaking surface and this was not exactly the sort of thing we had wished for, because if the submarine did break surface and used its gun we would disappear out of the water with the power of their guns. We promptly called the other ships in plain language saying, 'Submarine breaking surface, submarine breaking surface, close me at once, close me at once.' We saw two of them turning round immediately and start heading for us, the third one was very hesitant and I must not say what the occupation of the captain was, because it might be seen as criticising a whole branch of the community. A signal came back saying, 'Do you want me to close you?'

By this time we realised that it was not the submarine breaking surface, but a torpedo which had come up to the surface and was lying there. Its compressed air was blowing off because it had presumably been slightly damaged. That meant that we had dropped our charges sufficiently close to the submarine to cause damage and this would have been one of the spare torpedoes which they carried on the upper deck casing so that they could reload at sea when they had fired the torpedoes in the tubes already down below deck. We saw no more of the submarine and could not get any further response from our apparatus, so we never did know what happened to it, whether it sunk or whether it crept away.

Long after the war, I checked the records of German submarine losses in the Mediterranean and could find no evidence of one having been lost in that area or on that day. So what happened to it we have no idea. However, it brightened us up quite a lot to realise that the apparatus could work effectively, because we had always had some doubts about this. This was one of life's pleasanter interludes, although, of course, when we got back into harbour everybody was pulling our legs and saying there never had been a submarine and we had invented it all. How did anybody know that what we were saying was anything like the truth? This is typical Naval behaviour and I have no doubt that under similar circumstances our comments might well have been the same.

When we were lying in Algiers, off duty, an order came out that of the two or three ships that were there one must always be ready to proceed to sea at once in an emergency, if necessary taking officers and crew members from either of the other two. This happened once and I was the senior officer present and I decided to go to sea in my ship and I borrowed another officer from another ship and a few members of the crew. We had just taken on board a BBC reporter who was to go to sea with us for a few days to get a taste of what life was like. He was Norwegian by birth and a very entertaining person. The order to go to sea was to search for the survivors from an aeroplane that had come down in the sea somewhere to the south of Majorca and Minorca. We were instructed to return to harbour by dark which was about 10 p.m. and the time then was about 4 or 5 p.m. We set off and headed for the area at a reasonable speed. About half way there we saw a shadow or a reflection on the surface of the sea and we all shouted out at once, 'Submarine!' and headed for the spot. By the time we reached there it had disappeared and we all realised from previous experience that there had not been a submarine at all but that it was a sort of shadow effect from the sky which happened from time to time when the light was in a certain position. This did not impress our reporter who, when he subsequently reported on the radio said that we had bravely rushed in to attack an enemy submarine which realised we were coming and steamed away in a hurry.

On we went, heading for the spot where the aeroplane had ditched, and eventually reached there when it was getting fairly close to darkness. I then turned the ship and sailed in the direction of the wind keeping a sharp lookout for anything we could see. We went quite a way and saw nothing at all, but then saw a life raft floating in the sea. There was no sign of any life on it or around it and we picked it up and brought it on board. We continued a little further down wind and searched around the area, but there were no signs of anybody at all. We headed back for Algiers and arrived at about day break the following day. We staggered into harbour and almost fell asleep on the spot.

Our reporter was highly skilled in his job and sometime later we began to hear from home reports of a story on the radio in which he said that we had gone in single-handed, looking for an aeroplane in enemy waters, and had bravely spent a long time there, longer than we were supposed and picked up a life raft which he reported had nobody in it. On the way, we had attacked a submarine seen on the surface. Although he didn't mention any names or anything I was quite clearly identified by where I worked, the town where I lived, and other facts which he had picked up from my colleague. He was similarly identified by the town where he lived, the fact that he was a civil servant and the department where he worked in London. Much of this information he had picked up later on when he was with us for a period of a week or two.

We were using the port of Bougie further along the coast to the east of Algiers and would spend a night there from time to time. On a very early visit, myself and two other officers decided to go for a walk along the cliff path to the north west of Bougie which was set in really beautiful rural country. We got about two hundred yards along the path and all three of us were puffing and panting. We had to sit down for a rest. Even after the rest we decided we could not get any further and had to turn back towards the harbour. One of the hazards of serving in the Navy on a small ship is that after you've been at sea for a few weeks and you go ashore you discover that you can hardly walk at all because you've had no practice.

An amusing incident on one of our visits with the reporter still on board was when we went into a local café bar to have a bit of food and a drink. The drink turned into two drinks and three drinks, and so on, until we were all quite merry. Our reporter went out to the toilet, as we all did from time to time, and when he came back he was in a very unsteady state and managed to get through the door. He ended up on his hands and knees. Not to be outdone he started to crawl towards our table and in so doing passed under another table and ended up crawling towards us with this table on his back. This really was one of the most cheering sights I'd seen for ages. He eventually arrived to loud applause and we extracted him and got him sat down again!

We began to move further along the cost of North Africa for various duties, largely escorting one or two merchant ships into ports such as Djijelli, Philippeville and Bône. We enjoyed these visits to new ports but memory of them dims with time. We also had to escort a merchant ship into Bizerta harbour to anchor in the estuary. We all knew that Bizerta had been heavily bombed by our forces, principally the American element. We went alongside the quay to look at it and the whole place was just about flat with hardly a building standing above first floor level. We walked around for a while just to see what it really was like and there was absolutely no life at all apart from the few mad cats and dogs roaming the streets and searching for something to eat. We also visited Tunis which was more civilised and untouched. With the heat of the Mediterranean I would not wish to live in any of these places but it was very interesting to observe what life was like for the locals. We also went round Cap Bon which is opposite Sicily, and down the African coast into Susa. We went there two or three times and visited the ancient city of Monastir which is some little distance to the south of Susa but within walking distance. I still have a few pottery souvenirs from that area and also a rather attractive earthenware water chattie which is still in evidence in the house with its decorations.

On the 1st January, 1943 I made a New Year resolution, which was very unusual for me, to stop drinking whisky. I am not sure whether this was entirely out of consideration for my health or whether it was because our stock of duty free whisky was getting very low. However, I made it and the result was I started on the sherry which was in the bilges. It was not easy to drink enough sherry to be very effective, but I stuck it out, and as was said at the time, 'It's hard work drinking this stuff and I shan't half be glad when I've had enough of it.' Well I'd had enough of it in about four weeks when we returned to Algiers and I visited the doctor on the depot ship as I was feeling quite unwell. He looked at me and said, 'You know what's the matter with you, don't you?' He handed me a mirror and said, 'Go over to the porthole and look at yourself in the mirror.' He said, 'You've got jaundice and it's quite common in the Navy for people to have no idea they've got it because, in general, they only see themselves in electric light and their colleagues become so used to the gradual change that they don't notice anything in particular.' He then gave me three options. He said: 'You can stay on board your ship and be treated if you wish, or you can come into the sick bay on the depot ship and be treated here; the third possibility is that you go to the Ninety-Third General hospital of the army.' I knew this was at the back of Algiers on the top of the hill, looking out to the sea over the city. I said, I thought that I had better go to the hospital as that would give me the best chance of recovering within a reasonable time, and he told me he thought I was quite wise.

Within a couple of days I was trundled up to the hospital in a Navy truck together with a few of my belongings and occupied a bed in the ward. There were two Army officers who had jaundice also, and in the bed next to me there was a somewhat unusual character. In London he had been a superintendent dockie in the dockyard overseeing the loading and unloading of goods on merchant ships. In Algiers he was in charge of getting the goods ashore which had arrived on various cargo ships. I am not sure what was the matter with him, but I believe it was something internal, possibly a rupture. He was a very interesting character to have in the bed next to me as he used to tell me all sorts of stories about various bits of cargo which had been interfered with.

A consignment of champagne, designed for the Prince of Wales's yacht for one of his cruises, was one of the cases he explained to me. They turned the wooden cases upside down and took the bottom off. Then, with a square iron nail placed on the bottom of the 'punt' as it was called – the glass hollow in the bottom of the bottle which had a little bump in the middle; a sharp blow with a hammer and it penetrated the glass and the champagne bubbled up into the hollow – the first lot was drunk from the bottom of the bottle and then it was poured off into other containers so they could enjoy themselves at their leisure. They would empty every bottle in the case and then fill them all with water and plug the holes in the bottom with a small piece of wood similar in size to a match to stop the water coming out. The bottom went back on the case, turned right way up, and there was a case of champagne awaiting the Prince. I often wonder what he must have said when he came to treat his guests to champagne on board his yacht!

Whilst in hospital I was on a very strict low fat diet with plenty of fruit and fruit juice and so on, to which I stuck as fairly as I could, despite the temptations offered to me by my next door neighbour who seemed to have the ability, with his experience in the docks, of obtaining anything by any means. He would bribe one of the male nurses who was going ashore for the evening to come back with a bottle of whisky or brandy or something similar which we would all have access to if we wished it. I was very modest in my consumption of it and I also used to go out in the grounds and walk around. I came across an itinerant North African man coming around selling oranges. I used to buy about half a dozen large juicy eating oranges from him and these I would get through in a day, although I haven't the faintest idea how I managed it. It no doubt helped to speed up my recovery which was the main idea. He would from time to time have a small boy with him who was trailing along doing nothing much, and I asked him in French how many children he had. His reply was a bit surprising when he said, 'Six, four are still alive.' I spoke French as best I could and he spoke a mixture of French and Arabic which I managed to understand with a little difficulty. I said to him, 'Oh I am sorry to hear about that happening,' and he replied by saying, 'Why worry – plenty more where they came from.'

I had already discovered in Algiers that the attitude of the locals to their children was not what we were accustomed to in the West. There was one very badly crippled boy sitting huddled on the steps which led up to the city offices and he had his hat out begging for money. His legs were very badly deformed and he hadn't a hope of walking. To move he had to drag himself along with his arms and his legs, such as they were, would be trailing along behind him.

It was when I commented to François about this small boy he said to me, 'Oh, that is quite common in this area. It is not at all unusual for a family which is reasonably large to disable one of their children deliberately from birth in order to put them on the street to beg for money to help support the family.' It would appear that this boy had been disabled by having his legs tightly bound in a peculiar position when he was very small and those bindings were kept on for a year or so until it became a permanent feature. We don't always realise what goes on in other parts of the world that we never see.

One day when I was in a bad mood, the boy pestered me for money. In my best Arabic (I hope) I told him to get lost. He drew himself up to his full height, of two inches higher than he was normally, looked me straight in the eye and said in perfect English – 'And fuck you too, Jack!' I had to accept that whatever deformities had been imposed on him he had been very well taught!

At our berth in Algiers at some time an RAF pilot officer came on board to have a chat. It was not at all unusual for RAF or Army officers to come on board to meet somebody from their home country and to talk about things generally. It appeared that he was a night fighter pilot flying from Maison Blanche on the outskirts of Algiers. He invited me to go to lunch in the mess and have a look around the place. I accepted and went up a few days later. I seem to remember arranging Naval transport in view of the fact that it was an official visit in order to see what went on in the RAF.

We had an enjoyable lunch, after which he showed me around the place, took me to see the aeroplane which he flew and it was very interesting to see. He told me that he had to fly every afternoon to test fly it ready for the night operations, because all the work they did was at night. A few days later I arrived there at about two thirty and met him to be taken out to the aircraft. They are only single seater aircraft and I had to sit on an ammunition box behind the pilot. We took off with a roar of engines and flew up, circled the base, then set off for the interior doing a certain amount of flying over the countryside so that I could enjoy the views. He could only communicate with me by shouting behind to me and I could just pick it up. It was not very easy for him to get any replies from me. He decided to take me hedgehopping and indicated this either verbally or with hand signals.

We came to a field and he hedgehopped the hedge or wall at the beginning of the field and then we could see a farmer with a plough drawn by a horse, with his dog running along behind. I was rather worried and he flew straight towards them and when he was just before them up in the air he went and over the top and down the other side. I turned my head back to see what had happened to find the horse had bolted drawing the plough with it, the farmer was lying flat on his face on the ground and the dog had disappeared over the field as quickly as he could. Not the sort of thing I would have chosen for a living, but the pilot seemed to take it as a normal course of events.

Bearing in mind that they went out at night to fire at enemy targets anywhere they could find them, one had to remember the constant risk they were under. They were living their life one day at a time and that was all. This was, apparently, an explanation for this type of behaviour. When I met one of his colleagues a few days later, he told me that my pilot was blind drunk when he left the mess after lunch. I must have been blind stupid!

Whilst I was in hospital, air raids on Algiers would start relatively early in the evening as it was roughly the middle of winter. Those of us who were permitted to get out of bed and walk about would go outside and stand on the terrace outside our ward and watch what was going on. Generally speaking, the planes seemed to be attempting to bomb ships in the bay and possibly in the harbour, and from time to time there would be an explosion on land but there was no evidence of any tactical gain from this. The planes seemed to be concentrating on the harbour area below us and not bothering about the back and top of Algiers so we appeared to be relatively safe. There was no sign of any major successes in their attacks on the ships. They would sometimes secure a hit and this produced quite a spectacle for us to watch.

A little while after I had come out of hospital and was back on board my Coastal Force craft, we used to anchor at night at the far side of Algiers bay to be away from the main target areas. We regarded ourselves as being relatively safe from attack there and did not bother to man our guns or anything like that, having just one sentry on deck.

One night at about 10 p.m. there was a high pitched whistling in the area which we knew very well was a bomb heading for our area. There was a splash as it hit the water and we knew from the fountain of spray that landed on our ship that it was very, very close. We could not imagine how the plane had managed to see us and wondered whether it was just a lucky strike. The next day when we came to lift the anchor we had great difficulty getting it up and when the last bit of cable was approaching the ship it was thick with mud and sand and had to be hosed down before we could bring it in. It had been a very, very accurate aim. We realised that at night the moon had been shining and reflecting on the front window of the wheelhouse that sloped at about sixty degrees to the horizontal. Clearly, the pilot had picked up the reflection on the window and knew that there was a ship there so he let his bombs go. We learnt our lesson, and from then on we would cover the window of the wheelhouse with a canvas screen at night to prevent any reflection and we felt much safer when we went to sleep.

I left the hospital after about three weeks, being discharged with a caution about the type of food I ate and particularly my consumption of alcohol. It had been a very pleasant break from the Royal Navy and almost like a holiday. That evening I was back on my ship and we were at sea at night when we had a call to carry out some patrol duty lasting two or three days. On our journeys along the North African coast, if we saw an American merchant ship bringing stores and supplies, we would go alongside and ask them if we could have any fresh food as we hadn't had any for quite a time. They were very helpful and would let us have vegetables and, quite frequently, some form of meat, probably frozen, but it made a very good change for us. It was a real pleasure as well if we were able to get a sack of potatoes which would be far better than anything we'd had for a very long time. We always gave them a receipt for the goods we received which they were supposed to claim from the Admiralty, but I have no idea whether they ever did. Certainly the ship was never charged up with the cost of anything. It was a very good thing that the Americans came into the war to support us, and this benefit we felt in more ways than one.

Chapter Ten
Malta and Sicily

In due course we sailed for Malta and became part of the Third ML flotilla which had been based in Malta for some time. We escorted two merchant ships and sailed with them into Grand Harbour. They were instructed where to berth for the purpose of unloading and we went to a berth elsewhere in the harbour. To get to the town of Valetta, the capital of Malta and the largest centre of population, one had to get up a vertical cliff from the harbour which was the height from the quay of two houses at least. For this purpose there was a lift standing out from the cliff face and held in position by girders which went the whole distance up to the top. We embarked and this was a most peculiar experience and unlike anything else we had ever come across. The lift creaked and groaned as the wire hawser slowly lifted it up this framework of girders; and periodically, where it had suffered damage from a bomb blast, the lift would give a violent shudder and resume its journey. About half way up it gave a really violent shudder and then the lift moved sideways a few inches and continued its journey again. Eventually we reached the top with great relief that we had arrived safely. When we returned to the ship we went down the steps which was a very long descent but we felt it was preferable to risking one's life on the lift again.

Once again to be in a country where English was spoken was really something quite unusual and we found it very difficult to adapt to it at first. Although supplies in the shops were scarce it was a relief and a pleasure to see shops that looked very similar to the ones we had left behind us in England. Within a day or two we moved from the Grand Harbour to Sliema Creek next door, where the Coastal Force base was and the vessels spent the night. A major benefit was that we had got away from the thought of using the lift to get to civilisation. Everybody who had been to Malta had been telling us what a beautiful place it was, how relaxing and what a nice time we would have. When we were approaching the island it was a severe shock to see that it was almost entirely rock. There might be an occasional tree but hedges and grass seemed not to exist and the boundaries between fields were made of stone.

Enough of that, however, for when we got amongst other vessels like ourselves we began to pick up the threads of where to go and what to do. We soon discovered that beer was available on a very limited scale every evening but it was chemically brewed which meant that it didn't taste quite like the beer that we had been accustomed to. But anyway it looked like beer and was quite acceptable. The beer was released at various times by various establishments, the first being at 6 p.m. in the Union Club at Valetta. I was taken along by two or three officers from the base who knew the ropes and we all sat down with our first glass of beer. Those who were quick drinkers could get a second glass before the stocks ran out. We would then hurry on to Charley's Bar where the beer was released a little later on and again we would manage two glasses. The next stop was Auntie's Bar which was run by two elderly English ladies who had moved to Malta many years ago.

They started serving at approximately 7 p.m. so again one could manage one or two glasses. Three pints of beer in an hour and a half was pretty good going and compared well to what one might have done in England. The difference being this beer was not quite so strong and hadn't quite the taste. However, it was better than nothing. After several visits I could go into any of these places including the Union Club on my own and be served. From time to time I would have a meal at the Club also and it reached the stage when as I entered the doorman would say, 'Good evening sir.' I felt that I ought to join and become a formal member of the club but was rather worried as to what the reaction would be if I revealed that I had been going there for some time without being a member. I kept putting off taking a decision until, in the end, I was forced to leave the matter alone. Since I was not a member I never received a reminder that I had to pay for the next year and that added to my confusion. My gratitude goes out to the Union Club for my being an honorary member for quite a time.

A friend on one of the flotillas introduced me to two families in Malta and to the daughter of a third and we used to meet from time to time to have a talk and a drink. Now and again I visited them in their homes. This considerably improved the outlook and the social atmosphere for me, and was to be very useful when later on I spent some months in Malta when I was appointed to the base staff of Coastal Forces. I was lucky enough to have five days' leave in a rest camp at St Paul's Bay at the north of the island and opposite the island of Gozo. There was a sandy beach so I spent quite a time on the beach and in the water – this being one of the few places around the island where one could get into the sea because the rest of the coastline was so rocky. The camp was fairly isolated from anything else and there were no shops or cafés one could visit for a change. But the main place was very well worth while.

We had various seagoing duties to perform such as joining the escort of incoming convoys of merchant shipping and helping to escort them into harbour. In the meantime, whenever possible, we would have a quick run ashore doing a tour of the places where we could get a quick drop of beer. Generally speaking we were moored alongside pontoons in Msida Creek which was part of Sliema Creek, and having secured the ship we could walk along the pontoon to get on to the quay. There was a sentry on guard and having passed him we would walk up the hill and arrive at the opposite side of the main harbour. There was little to do other than drink but, from time to time, I would buy the odd souvenir of Malta from one of the shops.

We were aware that the Third ML flotilla of which we were now part had been fitted for minesweeping, a function it had carried out around Malta for some time. One day we were ordered into Malta dockyard to be fitted with minesweeping apparatus. We were rather apprehensive about this because nobody on board the ship had ever served on a minesweeper or knew anything about it other than the very elementary account we were given when we were first trained as seamen. A winch operated by hand was fitted on either side at the stern of the ship so that we could sweep to port of the ship, to starboard, or on both sides simultaneously. We were issued with all the apparatus which was fitted on board and also given a copy of the Admiralty minesweeping manual for this particular type of gear that we had. We were told, 'You are a minesweeper now – good luck!'

We would certainly need a lot more than luck to survive this peculiar introduction and we asked for an able seaman from one of the other ships, who was accustomed to minesweeping to come to sea with us for the day to show us how we worked it all. In tidal waters one had to lay mines so that they would not show on the surface at low tide. This meant that if there was a rise and fall in the tide of fourteen feet the mine could not be laid to less than fourteen feet below the water. It would have to be, in fact, something like twenty feet below so that it would not be showing to the ships. In the Mediterranean, with no tide, the mines could be laid very shallow and this was the normal procedure to make sure that they would hit the ships whatever size they were. So we would normally sweep to a depth of ten feet or more which would be pretty sure to cut any mines that were around.

We paid out a wire at the end of which was the 'otter', a square metal shape with blades which the sea pressed on and drew out sideways away from the ship. Then, there was a wire, ten or twelve feet long according to the depth we wished to sweep the mines, and this went upwards to a float which was cylindrical in shape, having very much the shape of a fat fish with blades at the stern to keep it steady and on top a flag on a pole about two feet above the water. The amount of wire paid out would determine the width to the side of the ship to which this could go. This was all very well but the other end of the wire was still up at deck level and to get this in the water we had to have a piece of apparatus similar to the otter which was called 'the kite'. The kite had a wire at each corner and these came together with a pulley fitted at the top. This was clipped over the wire to the sweeping apparatus and lowered over the stern on another wire. The amount of this wire that was paid out would determine the depth to which the kite went.

On the end of the sweep wire was a cutter so that when the sweep came into contact with the wire of a mine it would run across the wire mooring until it was caught in the cutter which had a device so that it was released suddenly, cutting the wire and the mine coming to the surface. One then steamed along happily at about eight knots and hoped to cut a mine. If one wanted to sweep on the port side of the ship instead of the starboard side of the ship the apparatus was used merely going out to the port side. If one wished to sweep on both sides which the leading ship in the sweep would normally do, the two had to be lowered together, port and starboard, and the kite had two pulleys on the top so they could both be clipped on.

I expect that by now the reader will find this totally incomprehensible and impossible to operate, which is precisely how we felt after we had a morning at sea with the able seaman who was quite expert at it. As I said, there wasn't a single person on our ship who had ever been involved in minesweeping before, although we had from time to time seen the occasional mine floating on the surface. As clear as mud, or should I say sand and shingle? In real life, when one was minesweeping and mines came up to the surface, either we or another vessel would have to go back and fire at them with rifles which had armour piercing bullets in order to let the water in and sink it to the bed of the sea where many of them will still be lying. As the reader will discover later, I was to gain ample experience of minesweeping and I still remember clearly the first mine I ever swept.

The next major operation was the invasion of Sicily which was to take place on 10th July, 1943. Our function was to be part of the escort for tank landing craft which were to beach at Avola at the southern end of the east coast of Sicily, which was separated further north from the mainland of Italy by a narrow strip of water at Messina. We escorted the craft from the north coast of Africa, from Tripoli or the immediate area of Tripoli. With the weight they had to carry and a landing ramp at the front these vessels and the convoy moved relatively slowly to its destination. Our function was to lead a group of them and signal to them when they were close enough to the beach of Avola to go in, land and discharge their tanks. This appeared to go reasonably well and we heard firing from time to time, but there didn't seem to be any violent opposition. When daylight came there was a rather depressing scene around us as troops who were carried on gliders towed by American aircraft from bases in north Africa were floating on the sea. The idea was that they could be released before they reached the beach and approach the landing area in silence. If they landed from aircraft they would have the noise of the aircraft and, in addition, descending by parachute would be seen from below and fired upon. Something went wrong with the system and about somewhere in the region of fifty soldiers didn't reach the beach because their gliders left too early to reach the beach, either because of a head wind, or an error in calculation, or because they were released too low or too far off the beach.

The result was that soldiers in full uniform were floating on the surface of the sea drowned because they had heavy equipment on them and could not do anything for themselves. Although our deck petrol tanks had been removed by now we could not pick them up because we had nowhere to put them except on deck and if they were on deck we would not have been able to get around the ship to man the guns and do anything else we were required to do. It was very depressing but we just had to leave them until they could be picked up by a larger ship and taken on board.

When daylight came we could see our tanks firing against enemy tanks to the south of the landing area – the nearest side to Africa. The captain of one of our sister ships decided that he would join in the battle and fired on one of the enemy tanks which he identified by its position. The tank immediately switched its fire to him and he promptly ceased fire and beat a hasty retreat out to sea leaving the tanks to get on with their own business. Around midday, the captain went down to the wardroom to have a rest whilst I was left in charge on the bridge. After twenty minutes or so I saw a plane which I identified as a bomber coming over the land from a northerly direction and I decided that it was an enemy plane, because I knew perfectly well that any of our bombing aircraft would keep well clear of an invasion area and there would be no need for them to fly over it. I ordered the gun crew forward on the ship to open fire on the aircraft which they did with the automatic anti-aircraft gun mounted on the fore-deck. Very shortly afterwards an urgent message came over the airways from the headquarters ship lying off the beach saying, 'Cease fire, cease fire, cease fire, you are firing on an enemy aircraft, you are firing on an enemy aircraft. Cease fire cease fire cease fire you are—'

By this time about six small black objects had appeared from under the plane and were heading down towards the invasion beach. My crew stopped firing because they had heard the message over the loud speaker which we had on board. The vibration had caused the captain to come running up to the bridge to see what was going on. I told him briefly and asked him what should I do. He said, 'You decide, I cannot take a decision without really knowing what's going on.' So I called out to the guns crew to re-open fire and they resumed the fire as did practically everything else in the anchorage. The plane quickly turned away and headed back towards Italy and I no longer had to consider the possibility of a court martial for firing on a friendly aircraft. On the other hand, I didn't receive any expression of gratitude either, such is the way of the Navy, particularly the ones higher up.

The landing went well and after about two days we entered Syracuse harbour and tied up alongside the quay, to take ashore a senior officer who had to perform some duty ashore. We all went ashore a few at a time to see what the effect of the bombing and gunfire on the little town was. One or two of our crew found the local post office which was damaged and went inside to have a look around only to find two large sacks of mail which were clearly identified as British and under international law should have been sent to Switzerland or another neutral country for redistribution. They had been sitting there for some time so the crew brought them on board so we could hand them over to the first Royal Naval mail office we came across. This caused so much fury among the crew.

We then visited one or two food shops which were also bomb damaged and picked up a certain amount of fresh food which we thoroughly enjoyed. Sometime later we discovered that the berth we had been moored at had been used by the Italians to dump their surplus ammunition in the water so we could not use it.

We had been sitting over a lot of ammunition, totally unaware that it was there because we never really bothered to look down other than to see how deep the water was. Subsequently, we went into Augusta, a little further to the north, where there was more in the nature of shipyards and slipways.

Chapter Eleven

Salerno, Sorrento and Northwards

We would have been quite happy to potter about Sicily for a time, enjoying ourselves in the fairly normal atmosphere. However, we realised that this was not going to be the future and that now that our troops were in Sicily they would want to move northwards into Italy. It would be impracticable to push forward from the south without some harbour available further north to keep supplies going.

The first harbour was Naples, on the southern promontory, which heads west and ends with the small island of Capri. On the southern side of the promontory there was also a bay which had the port of Salerno, and almost opposite it on the promontory was the well-known town called Sorrento. I suppose that at this point the headland is no more than ten to twenty miles across.

We calculated that the enemy would expect us to land in the bay of Naples, so we landed on the southern side at Salerno and the troops could easily travel overland to reach the Naples area. I cannot remember for certain where we sailed from escorting a variety of ships which were to beach and land troops, tanks and guns and so on, but I believe it was from Palermo on the northern coast of Sicily. I do not recall any particular incidents on the journey there, or of the landing itself, except that there was a great deal of gunfire and aircraft activity. We were not particularly close to the landing area which was on the beach to the west of the town.

Compared with the previous landings we had been involved in, this really was a major event with large numbers of good sized ships. The beachhead was established and then the port became available for use. We performed general activities around the area with no particular items outstanding.

In due course, our troops moved round the bay of Naples which came under allied control. Before long we entered Naples and endeavoured to berth to the west of the harbour as much as we could, away from the major activity so we could lead a reasonably quiet life. However, we were using the port of Castellamare which is on the eastern side of the bay, about half way from the landing area to Naples. This was quite pleasant because it was not so dominated by naval activity and one could walk into the town in a very short time and have a look around the shops, perhaps to buy a few odds and ends. In addition, the ruins of Pompeii were quite close and I remember visiting it with a colleague to have a look around. We found it fairly disappointing on the whole from the point of view of visual impact, as, very largely, it was stone walls only a few feet high, and there would sometimes be a roof structure, but that was very unusual. It was not possible to distinguish anything with a particular purpose, and without the plan and the signs that were there, one would not have known what was what, and could not really get any idea of what the town would have been like when it was fully built and occupied. One visit was quite enough.

The next stage was to move our troops and equipment slowly up the peninsula of Italy towards the next harbour which was Anzio. As the prelude to this operation, it was necessary to sweep the sea up towards that area so that ships capable of bombardment could get in and could assist the progress of the land forces.

For me the next event was the arrival of a signal, appointing me in command of ML134 which was then the ship of the senior officer of the Third ML flotilla and had been in the Mediterranean for some years. I was delighted about this and proceeded to Augusta where the ship was undergoing repairs alongside the harbour wall. This was a mixture of pleasure and work. It was a pleasure to be confined to port for a while so that I could potter around and see something of Sicily. At the same time, there was the responsibility of taking over the ship, making sure everything was in order and that there was nothing more required. This was a very pleasant period of relaxation compared with the previous activity. It was also improved by the fact that the proprietor of the shipyard would periodically bring me items of interest from the area such as a bottle of wine or some particularly attractive small item of food.

We went up on the slipway for repairs to be carried out to the hull of the ship and, at the same time, it had a Bofors gun fitted on the forecastle. It appeared that the commander in chief in the Mediterranean had asked the Royal Navy to authorise the supply of Bofors guns to be fitted to Coastal Forces. The reply they gave was that they were quite unsuitable and the ships were not strong enough to hold them and fire them. I don't know how it was done, but someone got in touch with one of the senior army commanders in the area, as a result of which he received three Bofors guns from the army. One was fitted on our forecastle and it was the first ship in Coastal Forces to be so fitted. I was proud to have something nobody else in Coastal Forces had.

All good things come to an end, and a signal arrived saying that the ship was to proceed to Maddalena in Sardinia as quickly as possible. We very soon had to come off the slipway and get prepared for sea, so that we could set out for our journey into the unknown. I set off for Maddalena which is on the northern tip of Sardinia and separated from Corsica by the straits. I could not imagine why I had to go there in such a hurry and sailed day and night until we got there. A ship from Coastal Forces passed us once and sent a signal saying, 'Goodbye and Good luck.' I was scratching my head wondering, *why goodbye* and also, *why good luck*? It sounded rather ominous. The next day this happened with another ship passing us. I decided I was going to find out what was going on and when the third ship turned up I signalled him to say, 'Please close with me I would like to discuss something with you.' He stopped and I went within hailing distance of him and asked, 'Have you any idea why I'm going to Maddalena?' His reply was rather disturbing. It had been decided to create a swept channel between Corsica and Sardinia so that ships could travel all the way round Sardinia and also so that any ship heading for Maddalena or the straits need not necessarily go round the southern tip but could cut across and shorten the journey. Apparently, four fleet minesweepers were sweeping through the channel to establish it, preceded by an Italian Maz Boat which encountered a mine and got it caught in its sweep. But, could not cut it, so it chopped the sweep wire and got off out of the way to leave the poor old minesweepers to it. The leading one hit a mine and was badly damaged with the result that the whole operation could not take place. Hence I and a sister ship of the flotilla were to sweep ahead of the minesweepers to get them through the channel. This would be the first occasion, I think, when I had been through a minefield knowing perfectly well that it was mined.

The two of us started off by going through the minefield on our own to clear a passage so that we should know better what we were doing when the real test came. My colleague was on a double sweep and I was following him on a starboard sweep. He got a mine in his starboard sweep and, unfortunately, his sweep wire did not cut it. He was there trying to drag away at it. By this time, I had got a mine in my starboard sweep and, as he was proceeding so slowly, I had to stop going ahead and I even had to keep going astern a little in order to wind the wire in so that I didn't get it round my screws. He realised I was getting into difficulty so he cut his sweep wire, pulled forward, and told me to continue on the previous bearing. By this time I had forgotten what the bearing was so I called down to the coxswain on the wheel, 'Carry on on the previous bearing, coxswain.' Up the voice pipe came the reply, 'I'm sorry, sir, I've forgotten what it was.' A pretty kettle of fish. So I looked across to Corsica and to Sardinia, decided what the appropriate course would be and called back, 'Steer 265 degrees.' We resumed our journey and cut the mine, fortunately, but then I was wondering how I would know where I'd been and how I would get back through it but my leader, being more experienced than me, promptly turned back and came round and dropped a marker buoy in my wake so that we knew where we'd got through. We then proceeded to widen out the channel and lay another buoy or two so that we could lead the fleet sweepers through in safety.

By this time I had been appointed a lieutenant RNVR as I had reached my twenty-fifth birthday, and this was the only way I could become a lieutenant by the rules of the Royal Navy. I had waited a very long time, particularly in view of my past experience. But that is life. No doubt we had a celebration ashore in Maddalena.

After a while I returned to Naples and spent the night in the harbour. Our troops were moving north from the area, further up Italy, and for this purpose it was necessary for them to have the support of capital ships off the west coast who could bombard troublesome targets ahead of the troops. This meant making sure that the area they would require to use was clear of mines and I was detailed to proceed to minesweeping up the coast with a half flotilla of fleet minesweepers. As they all had a draught at least twice that of my ship I had to sweep ahead on a double sweep so that the leading minesweeper could be sure that it was safe. From memory, no mines were swept but it was a job that needed to be done. We returned to Naples each night and the sweepers anchored on the southern side of the bay of Naples. I would go alongside the senior officers' ship for the night.

After about three or four trips up the coast, when we returned I received a signal from the senior officer that I was to go into the harbour of Sorrento and rescue the principal beach master whose landing craft had broken down there. This gave me a mixture of pleasure and anticipation because I had no idea quite what the problem was, and I was not at all sure why he was in there when the forces had all moved away. Possibly, he was going in to meet a contact ashore who gave him useful information and then his landing craft would not start up again. I was, however, anxious to see what Sorrento was like so that gave me some joyful anticipation.

I crept cautiously into the harbour because I had no chart to show what the depth was, and I conned the ship by standing on the bow and looking over the bow to see what depth of water I had, shouting my orders to the wheelhouse. We succeeded in getting alongside the harbour wall about fifty or a hundred yards from the beach master's landing craft which I could see ahead, and tied up there. I went along to him, and he was, fortunately, on his craft at the time. I told him I had come to rescue him for which he was grateful.

I went ashore with one watch and allowed them to go where they wished. I then set off for my own tour of Sorrento and it was a real delight to see a small town which just looked as it would normally and had seen nothing of the war at all. Everybody seemed happy to see me, particularly when I said to them, *'Buon giorno'* which is the Italian for 'good day'. I could see all sorts of things I would like to buy in the shops but by then it was about closing time so I could do nothing. I was particularly attracted to a shop where there were silk stockings displayed in the window. Something which was unheard of in England as most people never even saw them during the war. I felt that somehow I must get back to Sorrento with a little more time so that I could really enjoy the place.

I left there just after 7 p.m. with the principal beach master's landing craft in tow. First of all it was secured alongside until we got outside the harbour, then I dropped it astern on a long tow line so that we could travel at a more respectable speed. He then gave me the second bout of pleasure when he said that he was based in Ischia and would like me to tow him back into Ischia harbour. I had no objections whatever to this as a task to perform. In fact, I doubt if task is quite the right word. Ischia is a small island off the northern promontory of Naples bay and is in an almost equivalent position and of the same size, roughly, as Capri. I had a quick walk around and saw the thermal spring and other specialities of Ischia which is a really beautiful island. I returned to tie up alongside the senior officers' ship, with a degree of reluctance, and a vow to return as soon as I possibly could.

I went aboard to tell him about my journey. He was delighted to hear about Sorrento and asked me if there were any craft in the harbour. I said there were a number of trawlers which looked as though they had spent their time fishing. He said nothing but rang the bell and asked for his signalman to come in with his pad. He sent a signal to the senior officer of the area saying that he was remaining in harbour for the following day for engine overhaul and would take the opportunity of looking at Sorrento harbour where he had heard that there were craft that could possibly be minesweepers! He then said that he would get me to take him and his fellow captains ashore to investigate the situation and have a look at the town of Sorrento.

It was a Saturday and the captains of the four minesweepers came on board and I took them into Sorrento harbour, a journey of about five or ten minutes. We then climbed the steps to the top of the cliffs and they were overjoyed by the sight they saw before them. Such a peaceful and normal view and the Italian atmosphere was also conducive to relaxation. We wandered around for a time admiring the buildings and the scenery in general but I have no recollection of buying anything in particular in the shops. I think we had a cup of coffee somewhere but I cannot remember clearly where it was except that I feel that it was outside at tables in the square which is in the centre of the village.

I went into the ladies' shop to buy the silk stockings.

I went in and said, *'Vorrei!'* (I would like) whereupon four assistants all held a finger to their mouths and said, 'Sshh.' I thought to myself, *My goodness, are they going to call the Carabinieri?* the Italian equivalent of the police in England. One of the young ladies went out to the back of the shop and came back bearing a tray with a bottle of wine on it and a glass which was placed on the counter. A glass was poured and handed to me and I picked it up had a drink. Then one of them said to me in Italian, 'Now, what is it you would like?' In my best Italian I said I would like some silk stockings for my wife, although I have no idea how I succeeded in saying this now as my Italian has deteriorated badly. Out came the stockings and were displayed for me to look at and decide which I wanted. They were obviously delighted to see an English person come into the shop and particularly one who spoke some Italian.

After a very pleasant period with them and an empty glass I left with four to six pairs of silk stockings which I was planning to send home to my wife. I also purchased, in another shop, a small wooden casket, about six inches by four inches, with two compartments inside. It is about an inch and a quarter in depth. It is marquetry, which is beautiful wood with coloured wood inlaid to portray the Tarantella dancers of the area. It was only recently, when a marquetry exhibition was held in Winchester, that I discovered that Sorrento was renowned as the centre of marquetry work in Europe. So my casket was worth about five hundred pounds. Another addition to my memorabilia. And it still has the small sale label on the bottom.

The flotilla leader decided that we should have lunch in Sorrento before we returned to our ships and we decided upon the best hotel, which was on the west side of the town. I cannot remember what we had but we had an aperitif first, followed by the meal where we all sat around the table and were waited upon by the waitresses. I do not know how much my colleague enjoyed Italian food but I certainly did. They enjoyed the atmosphere which was very pleasant indeed and I remember a view from the windows of the bay of Naples. I have no recollection now of what it cost – that might be because I was stood the cost by the flotilla leader or the other captains together as a thank you for bringing them ashore and finding the place as well.

As we were finishing our meal and were at the coffee stage, a lady who was about forty years old, came up to the table and introduced herself as a countess. She told us her name and where she came from but these I have, regrettably, forgotten except that she lived somewhere near to Sorrento and a little way inland. She invited us all to return on the Sunday, to have lunch with her at the same hotel, which the flotilla leader accepted.

She spoke English quite well so there was no problem there, and I seem to remember that when she arrived at the table and spoke to us I welcomed her in Italian. After the meal was over, and after a further wander around the town looking at the shops, we returned to the ships with a feeling of elation – I think it was elation and nothing to do with all the alcohol we had consumed, but who knows.

The next day we went ashore somewhat later than before, just in time to stretch before lunch and we were all dressed in our Sunday best uniforms looking very smart indeed. We met the countess in the hotel a while before lunch and she treated us to a round of drinks. We went to the table and she sat at the head of it with the flotilla leader sitting at her left hand. She insisted that I sat at her right hand which I think did not entirely please some of the other captains. I am not quite sure whether it was because I spoke some Italian but I think it may well have been that I was a tall, handsome, young Naval Officer and possibly had more personality than some of my older colleagues! We had a very enjoyable and leisurely lunch with a certain amount of lubrication to help it on its way. Of course, Naval Officers are accustomed to heavy drinking, and it did not have quite as much effect on us as it would have done on people who were less well trained.

Although the words of the well known song say, 'Come back to Sorrento,' I have never managed to go back. I have, however, got the music to it and just before I wrote this I played on the piano the song from beginning to end (with one finger, needless to say, these days). I have never forgotten that episode of the three visits to Sorrento and it still lives in my memory as a time of great pleasure.

A recent travel programme on television visited Sorrento and I was horrified to see it. I had always dreamt of it as it was, and it has changed completely. High rise hotels, modernisation. There was no beach in the 1940s, just a rocky coast and high cliffs. Now it appears to be artificial beaches, probably concrete, laid out for sunbathing, swimming, and, of course, refreshment.

I do not wish to 'Come back to Sorrento' but prefer my collection of coloured postcards. Life does change!

Come the Monday morning and back to the grindstone once more. In other words, we set off up the coast of Italy again continuing the minesweeping operation, although we never found any mines. There was one unusual incident within a day or two, though. We were returning in the evening from the minesweeping back to Naples harbour when one of the ships broke down. It had an engine problem and whereas the three other ships continued on their own the captain of the one that was broken down sent a signal to me saying that he had an engine problem which would take about thirty minutes to put right. Would I mind standing by to protect him with a smoke screen if any of the enemy guns opened fire? I agreed, and to give him added confidence I went inshore between him and the guns, as far as I could judge where they were, and lay there stationary, with all my smoke-making equipment ready.

I could throw over two or three smoke floats which would remain in the water pumping out smoke and I also had a cylinder on the rear of the ship which would spray smoke if I sailed along. After a while, he signalled me to say that he had repaired the engine and he was ready to proceed, and he thanked me very much for my assistance.

We returned to Naples bay and I tied up alongside the senior officer as I usually did. By now, we must have checked the area for mines up to somewhere in the region of Rome, and the particular effort was over until the troops had reached further north. We dispersed to other duties and left the fleet minesweepers to other minesweeping jobs elsewhere. I then resumed doing various escort tasks around the area and after a few days I arrived in Maddalena where I did some minesweeping around the area and various escort duties. One of these took me into the port of Bonifacio in the southern tip of Corsica.

It was clear by now that the island of Sardinia which was Italian controlled had come over to our side without any fighting. I now began to realise that the island of Corsica must also have decided to accept our presence without any objection. One day I had to go into Bonifacio harbour, as far as I remember, either to deliver something or collect something. I had been advised by other people that the estuary leading up to the harbour was too narrow to turn around and it was advisable to go up stern first, which I did. This was the first time that I ever entered a harbour stern first but at least if anything went wrong I was pointing in the right direction to get away.

I tied up alongside the quay and carried out my duties. It was a very interesting old world place with old world buildings and so on. In one place there was a road going up the hillside at quite a steep angle. I went up it part of the way once when I was there. I was now beginning to see more attractive parts of the Mediterranean.

Chapter Twelve

Bastia, North Corsica and Northwards in Italy

Towards the end of November I sailed for Bastia, in north Corsica, escorting a tank landing craft. I was a bit mystified as to why anything should be going up there in a landing craft, but when I arrived at the harbour I realised that the reason was, there were no cranes or anything around the quay which could unload the cargo. So it was better to take a craft which could beach somewhere and run them ashore. It was two or three days before we got back to Maddalena and I had about a day in Bastia to have a look around. I suppose I was more in my element in a French speaking area than in an Italian one. and I quite enjoyed the atmosphere. I went into various shops and cafés etc. and I was really quite attracted to the place. Little was I to know then that I should see much more of it in the future.

Back in Maddalena I spent some time sweeping various channels into Maddalena and other harbours around the area. In the three or four days since I had returned from Bastia it appeared that the harbour entrance had been heavily mined by some small craft in the middle of the night and I had to go up and survey the minefield and advise on sweeping it. I had to approach at some four miles or so off the coast and then head in at a certain point where

I would be met by the pilot boat which would guide me into harbour. This was a very novel experience for me, and I would think, for anybody else in the Navy. The pilot boat was making a weird journey to the harbour turning to the left, to the right, and obviously going around various objects; and so I assumed he was steering me through the minefield. I was anxiously hoping that he knew what he was doing! Eventually after this very devious path and a wide sweep round the harbour entrance between the two sea walls, keeping quite close to the south and the west coast of the harbour, we entered harbour.

The pilot guided me to a berth towards the northern end of the harbour away from the harbour entrance. We had a chat about the general situation and my French was stretched to the limit and, in fact, beyond as he spoke no English at all. I asked him how he knew where the mines were and he showed me his chart which had a lot of crosses marked on it indicating the position of the mines. I said, 'Well, however do you know?' He said, 'Well I know where they are by taking two transits and where they cross is the position of the mines.' This meant that he took a bearing from above a mine, on two different points ashore, and marked them on the chart. I asked him how deep he thought the mines were. I realised they must be pretty shallow because he had identified them by looking over the side of the boat and that was how he fixed the positions. He said he would take me out the following day and show me a few of the mines and how the positions were fixed.

Off we went in his small boat which had one seaman on it in addition to ourselves. He stopped when he had two of the appropriate transits and that was the point where there should be a mine underneath. We knew very well we should have no difficulty in seeing it because in the Mediterranean one can, at times, see to a depth of fifty feet, and see the bottom of the sea if the water is calm. There it was, this mine, bobbing up and down, or so it appeared to be. But in fact it was the boat which was bobbing up and down, and as they got closer they looked larger, as they went down they looked smaller. In an unwise moment I asked him how deep he thought they were. He grabbed the boat hook and pushed it over the side probing away at the mine to find out where it was. I yelled out to him to stop. This did not really discourage him. He would touch the mine and then he would tell me they were about six to eight feet below the surface. In other words, if I sailed over one when I was sweeping I could probably just about hit it and get blown up. All very comforting for a minesweeper! He guided me back ashore and I think I needed a stiff drink by then.

We agreed that we would go out the following morning. He would guide me through and I would put out a double sweep so that I could sweep the width of some fifty to eighty feet, depending how well it ran. I sent a signal back to the base at Maddalena saying that the harbour entrance was very heavily mined with shallow mines and that I proposed to start sweeping in the morning, to try to establish a clear passage through them. I received a reply thanking me and expressing appreciation. I then enquired where the office of the French port commandant was and went to see him to see if I could obtain a chart of the harbour area. He was Commandant Du Porte Sticka. He was a very pleasant man who spoke some English, and between us we got on very well together.

He provided me with two charts, one of which was a large scale one of the area around the harbour. I have a tracing of this showing the mines I swept marked on it. It

BASTIA HARBOUR

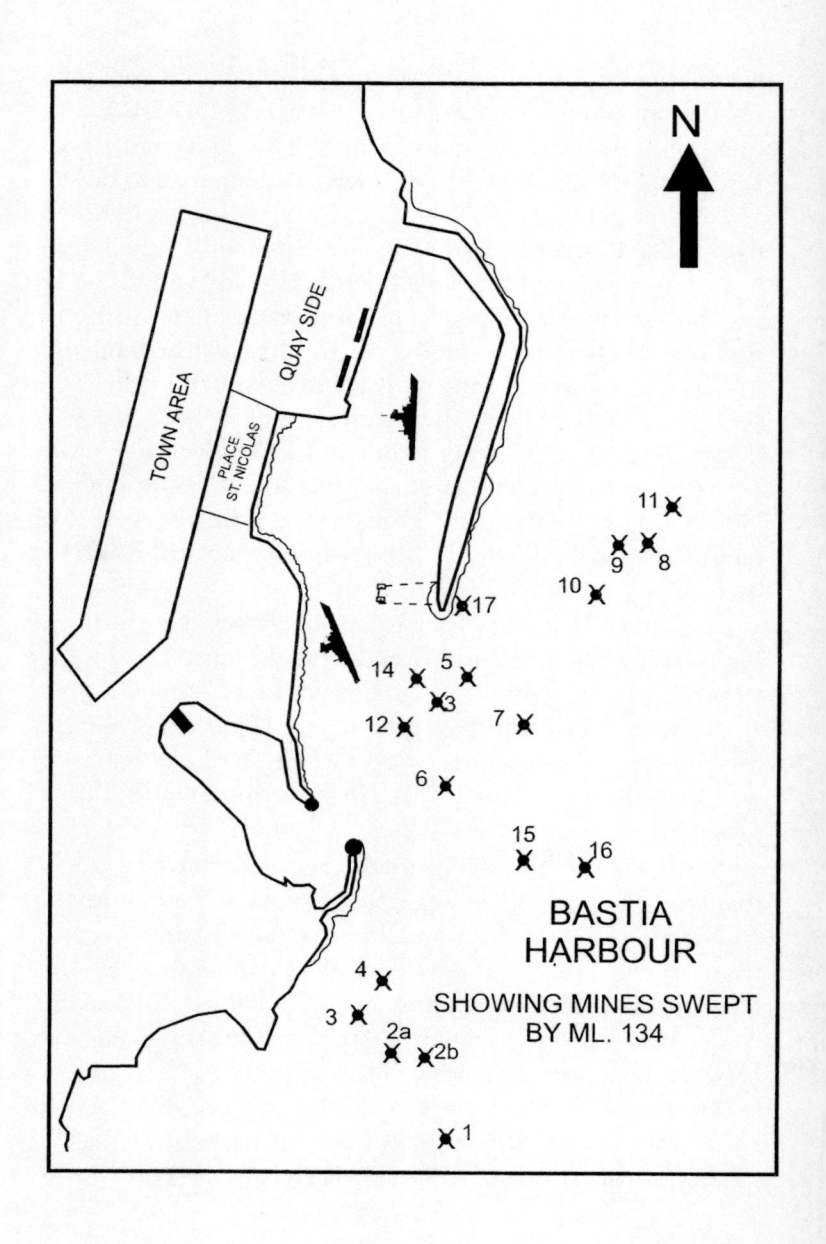

SHOWING MINES SWEPT BY ML. 134

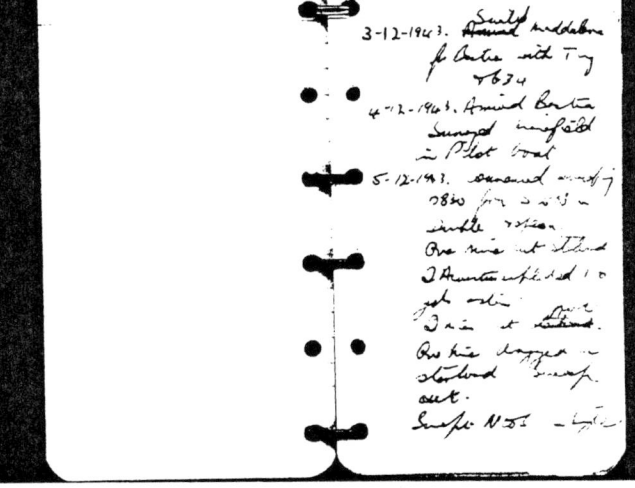

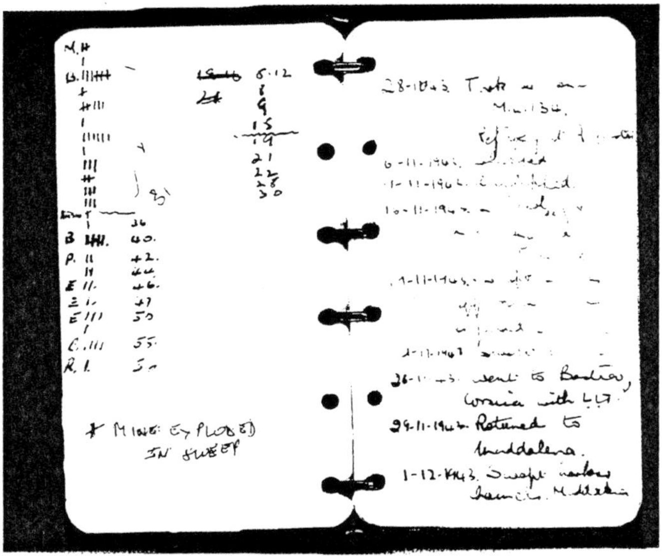

[Handwritten notebook pages - partially illegible]

```
M. H
I
W.IIIHH      Small  5.12
+            24      8
+III                 9
I                   15
IIIII               19
I                   21
III         }       22
++          } 3?    28
III                 30
B HH        36
            40.
P. II       +2.
   II       44
E II.       46.
   2 I.     47
E III       50
   I
C. III      55.
R. I        5 -

* MINES EXPLODED
  IN SWEEP
```

28-10-43 Took ... on
         M... 134.
         Ref...
6-11-1943. ...
1-11-1943. ...
10-11-1943. ...

...
1-11-1943. ...
...
...
2-11-1943 ...
26-11-43 went to Bastia,
         Corsica with LCT
24-11-1943 Returned to
           Maddalena.
1-12-1943. Swept harbour
           ... Maddalena

3-12-1943. Sailed Maddalena
           for Bastia with T.y
           +634
4-12-1943. Arrived Bastia
           Swept minefield
           in Pilot boat
5-12-1943. ...
           ...
           ...
           One mine ... ...
           I hunter exploded 1 ...
           ...
           I ... ...
           One mine dropped ...
           starboard sweep.
           out.
           Swept N5I - ...

really does look like a minefield. The pilot guided me out of the harbour and to the south, then I put my double sweep out and started to head northwards with him leading me.

It was not a completely straight line we went on as he would alter to starboard or to port to make sure I did not pass directly over a mine. One mine was cut to starboard and subsequently two acoustic mines exploded a hundred yards astern of the boat. These were mines which were set off by vibrations. Fortunately, the vibration was not enough when I passed over them to blow them up straight away, but presumably they were disturbed by the wake after the ship had gone past. Then two mines were cut in the port sweep and then I got another one in the starboard sweep which would not cut. It was dragged along so I had to cut the line. When we got clear of the minefield to the north we turned round and I put out one sweep to starboard as I could not put any more out to port in view of what had been blown up and lost. One mine was exploded and I had to cut the sweep wire. On the first day I had swept six mines.

The following day I swept from north to south on a single sweep to starboard as I was so short of gear that was all I could manage. One mine was caught in the starboard sweep and could not be cut, and I had to cut the sweep wire. As a result, the float obviously became clear of the mine and was very carefully recovered from the sea. When I reported the activities up to that stage to the base at Maddalena, I told them what had happened and asked whether they could send further gear by plane to the United States airforce base just south of Bastia so I could carry on. A reply came through saying they would be sent the following morning, and they were very quickly brought down to the ship. Within four days I had cut twenty mines up and down opposite the harbour. Once, I had been led through on a complete run north and south, off the harbour mouth; I laid two or three buoys in the water so that I knew exactly where I was and could continue without the pilot boat.

Every evening when I got into harbour I used to go and visit the port commandant to report to him on the day's activities. He almost invariably greeted me in the same way: 'Ah, Lootenant Denton, you have made today the beautiful work. I sit in my office and I hear boom, boom, and I say ooh, Lootenant Denton, he make the beautiful work. I get up, look out of my window, and I see your little ship sailing along cutting away at all the mines.' I think I usually was given a glass of wine but I cannot remember much about it. In six days the tally had reached thirty-one mines around the entrance to Bastia harbour. When I took over my ship it had cut twenty-seven mines over a given period and this was a record for any small sweeper cutting mines in non-tidal waters at that time. So the ship now held the record at about fifty-eight mines, which was really quite remarkable. After one of my sister ships in the flotilla, ML121, arrived and I had piloted it into the harbour, we could sweep with two sweepers instead of one which helped to get the area reasonably clear.

There were two or three mines right between the walls of the harbour entrance. They presented quite a problem. I tried entering the harbour, putting out a sweep without paying out too much wire so that it was not taught and then moving round, getting out towards seawards and then securing the wire on the ship and then this started a sweep so that it would tighten the wire and I hoped cut the mines or at least cut one of them. This succeeded with one mine and that was a good thing so I then tried to repeat it with another one. Unfortunately on this occasion the wire dropped down somehow and fouled my screw, i.e. the propeller, so that was not a very good idea. I had to cut the wire and eventually I think we managed to get a sweep around the mine with the aid of a motor launch or a rowing boat and tighten the sweep. Then we proceeded more along the usual lines and this one cut and exploded also. I then succeeded in getting my sweep back.

At about this time John Bridge arrived in Bastia, the well-known mine and bomb disposal officer in the Navy. He appeared in one of the services at the Cenotaph and was filmed and said a few words on television. He had come to Bastia after reports that a mine had been washed up on the shore further down the coast. He and I went down together by car to see it, and by the time we got there it had been rendered safe by the French mine disposal officer. He was showing it to us and he was demonstrating the inside. I asked him, 'Where was the detonator?' and he showed me. He had it in his hand and he thrust it into the top of the mine pulling it up and down. John Bridge and I didn't know whether to run or to overpower him but I said in my best French, 'For goodness sake, stop or you'll blow us all up,' whereupon he withdrew it with a look of disgust. We quickly thanked him very much and made our retreat. It is fortunate that our personnel who dealt with these matters had been better trained and taught than had the French ones.

It was now possible for ships to come into Bastia harbour from the east provided they were guided in by myself. At this time, when I used to visit the port commandant he used to say to me, 'I signal Ajaccio. Say send convoy?' I had to say, 'Not yet, I'm afraid. We're not quite ready to lead in a group of ships.'

The official approach to Bastia was coming in from the east for a distance of about six to eight miles and any incoming convoys would steam northwards to that point and then steam westwards to Bastia harbour. It became known from an aerial survey that the area had been mined so we started sweeping this area to clear it. By now I was accompanied by a motor minesweeper which carried out acoustic searches, and which could act as a buoy layer as channels were swept through. This was a big help but it was no comfort, when sweeping out there, to see fairly close the Isle of Elba which was Italian held. I was conscious of the fact that I was probably being kept under observation. Well, to be honest I knew that I was being kept under observation by a plane overhead circling me all day. It was Italian and could undoubtedly call for the area to be re-mined when it was clear.

By Christmas Day 1943 I was alone in Bastia harbour, the other ships having gone off on other duties. Everybody on the ship was thoroughly depressed as we had no particular meal for Christmas, probably only corned beef, and we had received no mail for some three or four weeks. Suddenly, the sentry on deck yelled down the hatchway, 'Launch entering the harbour from Maddalena, sir.' I shot up on deck. All the rest of the crew were on deck and we saw one of our sister ships sailing into the harbour with a turkey hanging by its legs from the mast and we knew then that Christmas Day was probably saved. They had brought us a turkey, a Christmas pudding and various other odds and ends, and also a large sack of back mail. We knew that we could celebrate Christmas in the proper manner and our dinner was obviously going to be later than normal. We thanked them sincerely and they had a drink with us and then we set about looking at the mail. I think it was about two thirty or three before anybody even started to think about the meal as the backlog of mail took quite a bit of reading. It was difficult to decide whether to look at the earlier ones first or the later ones first and, in the end, I think we all decided to look at the later ones and work backwards.

Eventually, our Christmas meal was ready and we all sat down together in the seaman's mess and thoroughly enjoyed it. I seem to remember we even had some paper hats. Whether they came along at the same time I really do not know. A good time was had by all. Some of us then went for a walk ashore to get a bit of exercise and help to get the food down.

I was then joined by MLs 121 and 563, working to widen the channel out to the east and to make sure it was completely cleared. I was never very happy about this approach – all the ships which were coming would be in eyesight from the island of Elba, without even the use of binoculars. Outside Bastia, on one occasion when I was sweeping to the south, I carried on sweeping right down a distance of fifteen miles or so with a double sweep and found no sign of mines whatsoever. I turned around and came back some little distance away and still no mines. My colleague on the motor minesweeper went down with his acoustic sweep lowered and checked: he came across no acoustic mines either so we regarded that as a far safer method of approach.

On the last day of 1943, a convoy was due from Maddalena of some five ships or so with an escort and I was to meet them, at the far end of the channel which had been cleared from the east into Bastia harbour, and guide them into harbour. I went out and lay there for some time with my engines switched off, as I was running very low on petrol, putting them on periodically to manoeuvre and I was really depending upon the arrival of a tanker to refuel and carry on the good work. Previously, to refuel meant sailing down to Maddalena, filling up the tanks, and coming back again. The gale which was running had pushed the ships coming up the coast further inshore than they wished, and one ship suddenly had an explosion and sank close to the shore. The convoy then turned back as it was obviously hopeless to get safely into Bastia harbour.

A day or two after this, in the evening I was sitting in the wardroom with Skipper Smith discussing the day's activities when a shout came down the hatchway from the sentry – 'Captain coming along quay, sir.' I didn't have time to get to the top of the ladder to meet him but he was coming down by the time I had got to the bottom. He entered the cabin, we welcomed him and he said, 'Boutwood.'

I immediately realised that he was the senior minesweeping officer for the Mediterranean. He said, 'Carry on talking, I know from my experience that as minesweeping captains you will be discussing the day's activities. I would like to listen and see what you have to say.' I replied that I was just saying to Skipper Smith that I would favour a channel coming into the harbour entrance from the south, not from the east, as this was vulnerable to re-mining. I told him that I had a reconnaissance aircraft circling overhead the whole time I was sweeping and I knew they would be able to see the mines and see when they were cut. When there was a clear channel I had little doubt that they would come and re-mine it. He said to me, 'What about the south – can't there be some mines there?' I said, 'When I've been sweeping, I've carried on down there on a double Oropesa and I have found nothing at all. I'm pretty sure that the area is clear.' He said to me, 'I don't know what to think about this. I will let you know.'

Two days later I received a signal that I was to meet him at a certain point to the south and lead four minesweepers in towards the coast on the bearing I had given. At the point of turning the vessel would lay a buoy to mark the point then turn on the appropriate course towards the harbour. This I did, and we encountered no mines at all anywhere on the route. They had laid a large buoy on the point of turning so that the route was secure. When we got to Bastia the minesweepers turned about and swept down on either side of the path we'd been on to make sure the channel was as wide as would be reasonably required. Within a day or two we were beginning to receive normal convoys into Bastia and I would meet them somewhere to the south and escort them in. The French port commandant was obviously delighted.

On one of my trips south to Maddalena I brought back two passengers – American Army officers in normal uniform but with no lapel badges or any indication as to what part of the service they were in. I asked them if they were going to the American airforce base just south of Bastia, to which they replied no – they were not anything to do with the airforce. I asked them if they were medical and they said no, and when I asked them what branch they were in one said, 'I'm afraid we cannot tell you.'

On one of my visits to the French port commandant I noticed a small door with a plate beside it saying OSS. Some time later, I was just passing this particular door when it opened and two people came out whom I immediately recognised as the two American officers I had taken up to Bastia. I greeted them and we exchanged greetings and then they said: 'Well, now you know why we could not tell you what we were doing.' OSS is the name of the American secret services or the equivalent of our MI5.

They would travel to the coast of France or to the coast of northern Italy and back in a small boat landing quietly at night somewhere remote. There were of course people in France who did not particularly favour the regime of Hitler and equally well people in Italy who were not favourable to Mussolini. They had contacts with these sorts of people and used to go over, sometimes just for the night, sometimes for a few days, and then return. Obviously, they never told me what they were doing and I never specifically asked, but when I met one of the officers the other one was not with him and I hadn't seen him for some days. I enquired where he was. He said, unfortunately he had injured his leg, I think that he had stood on a landmine or something, but they managed to get him back to the boat and bring him ashore where he went into hospital to have the leg amputated at the knee. The risks that some people took in performing for our side were really quite incredible.

Before this, and fairly soon after I had met them, I was taken to a restaurant in the evening for a meal. We went to the southern side of the harbour entrance and there was a very tall and dilapidated looking building which was a warehouse of some sort. We went up an obscure staircase at one end of it to the top floor, and went in what was obviously a luxury restaurant. Clearly a black market affair, but it didn't seem to matter because everybody of any significance in the Bastia area appeared to be there having a meal. It was very enjoyable to return to normal civilised living for one evening.

Some time later, the senior officer concerned asked me if I would like to pay a visit to the other coast of Corsica, to a small coastal town and harbour called Calvi. When he arrived in a truck to pick me up he said, 'Have you got your gun with you?' He opened his jacket and showed me his in a shoulder holster under his left arm and told me it would be wise to bring my revolver. I fetched it and put it in the right hand pocket of my greatcoat.

The main road across Corsica had been bombed and was out of action and we went by a secondary road, which was narrow and winding, through the countryside, alongside hills and valleys. But before we got to it, we arrived at a sentry post to discover that traffic was only allowed one way at a time, and that the next time for us to pass to the west would be in about three hours. After a certain amount of negotiation and bribing, we were allowed to continue on the strict understanding that whenever we saw a vehicle coming we were to get off the road to make way for it. My function as the passenger was to keep a sharp lookout ahead for any vehicles coming so that we had time to get off the road somewhere. Bearing in mind that some of the roads were cut into the mountainside, there was little opportunity, particularly on the bends, so I had to be looking one valley ahead to see what was coming to make sure we could perform our obligations. As far as I remember it happened once only with a fairly heavy army lorry and we managed to get on to a flat piece of verge somehow.

When we eventually arrived in Calvi, after about an hour, we had to go to a certain café, and sit outside at a table under a tree and order a drink or something of that sort so that we were not obvious. We would be joined shortly by a local agent who would come to discuss some matters with my colleague, the nature of which I was unaware. After an hour or more after the specified time, we realised that for some reason he was not going to turn up, so my partner decided that we would have to leave and go to visit somebody else he knew. We had had our lunch by then.

Off we set towards Bastia and, after a while, we turned left up into a hill village. This was quite an experience. It was little more than a narrow track and as we got up into the village there were houses indiscriminately on either side. We kept going until we reached a particular place and, I think, he had to go to a certain building to find the person he wanted. I waited around while he was there.

After a while he came back and we somehow succeeded in turning the vehicle around. It was quite hair-raising to be in a situation like this where one could hardly see above ten or twenty yards ahead. Eventually, we returned by the same route to Bastia and as far as I remember we had right of way and no bribes were necessary, so I enjoyed the scenery a little more than I had done before. To say that it was really beautiful would be an understatement – it was really quite fabulous. He took me back to my ship and we had a few celebratory drinks on our safe return. I hope that from his point of view it had been a successful trip.

Whenever I had a day to spare I would go up the coast of Bastia, sweeping, and go around the north to see if I could find any mines, and I did find one minefield and the mine which I swept was of an unusual design which I had never seen before. It was slightly smaller than usual and had one horn only on the top, whereas most of ours had three horns situated on the shoulders of the mine. The horns were about six inches high and an inch and a half in diameter, covered with lead. When a ship broke the lead it made the contact and the mine blew up. With a trusted member of the crew I got into the dinghy and we rowed up towards the mine, and when we were there he approached the mine, stern first.

We stopped about four feet from it, and I took a quick photograph and we retreated. We then sank it by rifle fire.

Interestingly, sometime later when we had progressed up the coast of Italy, I was in Leghorn where I had gone for some reason or other and, when I was secured for the night, I took a walk to the south of the town along the cliff road and came across the Italian school of mine laying. It was quite open, the gates, the doors and everything, and I went into the grounds rather gingerly wondering if it had all been booby trapped or whether they had just left in a terrible hurry. Various mines were standing on their weighted bases, which is the way they are laid at sea, and to my surprise one of them was an identical mine to the one I had found north of Corsica. I had reported the presence of this new type of mine to the captain minesweeping for the Mediterranean, so I then sent a further signal to say that a specimen of the mine was available for inspection at the school of mining south of Leghorn. I never heard any more about it though.

Whilst I was in Corsica I would go south, from time to time, escorting a ship or ships and going to a number of ports which I had visited in the past. On one occasion I went back to Malta, and whilst I was there I saw the Base Commander and had a chat with him. He told me that in about a week or two he was planning to move his base from Malta up to the Naples area so that he would be closer to the centre of activities, and be more able to cope with anything that came up. He asked me what the Naples harbour was like and whether there would be anywhere that was suitable for Coastal Forces. I told him that the best place was a quay to the outer edge of the main dock area, but I said it was not very attractive and that I didn't like it much. I didn't stop there unless I was forced to. I said there was a beautiful little island to the north of the bay of Naples, Ischia, and that the harbour was formed in the crater of an extinct volcano, one side of which was open to the sea. It was a beautiful little harbour, isolated from Naples, and had a good quay and buildings around it. I said the one difficulty was that it was away from the Naval hierarchy in Naples. He promptly said, 'That's no disadvantage, that's what I would like so that I can get on with things on my own. When I come up to Naples I will have a look at it.'

A week or two later he was installed in Ischia harbour very happily, and he had a building which he was using as his headquarters alongside the berth on the quay which I had used. As far as I remember he was living in the hotel Floridiana which I used to visit from time to time whenever I got into Ischia, and I went there for a meal if I possibly could. The proprietor and the waitress after the meal used to sing Italian songs to whoever was there and this was really a pleasure. I always had a question in the back of my mind as to what the relationship between the two was. They did not give me the impression that they were solely employer and employee.

The next significant operation was the landing at Anzio, further up the coast of Italy. I was not involved in the preliminary beach-finding operations and I have no idea how that took place, but I was escorting some tank landing craft which left us when we were on the fringe of the area in to land. My one major recollection of this particular operation was that a destroyer, further in shore than I was at the time, was hit by gun fire from the shore. There was an explosion and then it was on fire. As far as I am aware, it sank with quite a lot of the people on board. It probably keeled over and sank upside down. Later on, after the war, when I was visiting the dentist in my home town of Kettering, I was telling him what I had been doing during the war and he asked me if I knew Anzio. I told him that I was there at the landing and saw what was going on. He told me that a relative of his lost her husband when a destroyer sank off Anzio on the day of the landing. I told him that I had seen it and I had a photograph of the ship taken before it sank. He said his relative would be very pleased to hear of this and I let him have a copy of the photograph to give to her.

I, together with another Coastal Force sweeper and two fleet minesweepers, did a certain amount of minesweeping in the area and then I returned to Malta to have a refit which was very pleasant relaxation because it meant that I would not be able to go to sea for a while.

Once access to Bastia harbour had been firmly established I started to move around the Mediterranean more amongst my older ports of call, so I was getting more variety into my life. In the early days of arrival in Bastia the French port commandant informed me one day that he was making me and my ship honorary members of the Free French Navy. This gave me a feeling of pride and pleasure, although I have to confess I completely forgot to inform the Admiralty that their ship had now moved over to the Free French Navy. Perhaps I thought that this information might not meet with their approval. The main apparent benefit for us was that we became entitled to the daily ration of French wine and bread which all personnel in the French Navy had. Although the bread was quite welcome we soon found out that the ration of wine was not exactly to our taste. It was a fairly coarse French red wine which was not particularly easy for us to swallow. We did try, of course, but it was not until years later, when I was visiting

France after the war, that I realised that the custom in France was to add the low strength fizzy lemonade which was available in France, and that made it drinkable, even to the British. Unfortunately, when we were in Bastia we were not aware of this method of disposing of it.

Some time after the war I wrote to the French Admiralty in Paris enquiring if they had any records of who was serving in Corsica during the war. I rather wanted to see if my name appeared amongst the names and if my ship appeared in the lists. The reply, unfortunately, was that they had no records whatsoever of French personnel in Corsica during the war. This, presumably, was because the French Admiralty in Paris was under the control of the German invaders, and places like Corsica continued independently. Their records never got to the central organisation.

Early in February 1944, I returned to Malta for a refit. It made a great difference to have two families who I could visit and who I would go out with in the evening, something that didn't happen anywhere else in the Mediterranean as far as I was concerned. I could, of course, still call at the Union Club for my drop of beer in the evenings, and to avoid any problems on my first visits I would say, 'Hello, nice to see you, I've been away for some time,' so that they would not question my membership.

During the period of the refit I was more concerned with my visits to my old haunts and enjoying Malta than I was with what was happening to my ship. My impression was that some of the refit took place at the Coastal Force base in Sliema and some of it took place in the dockyard at Grand Harbour, but I am not very clear as to what exactly happened. I finally left the Malta area at the end of April 1944 and headed back up further north.

My first stopping place was at Augusta in Sicily, and then the next day I moved up the coast to Messina and had a meal ashore. I spent three days in Messina although I cannot remember why, except that I probably had no orders as to where to go next. I had lunch ashore and walked around the town, and in the evening I had an evening meal ashore in a club with two of my colleagues. On leaving I sailed for the Naples area and went into the base which was now established at Ischia and had dinner ashore in the mess. I then sailed for Maddalena and arrived on Friday, 5th May and went ashore into the naval mess to have dinner in the evening. After that I moved on to Bonifacio on the southern tip of Corsica and spent a day or two minesweeping around the area to check the areas already swept. In my spare time I went walking in the hills with one or two colleagues. I spent a few days in both Bonifacio in Corsica and Maddalena in the north of Sardinia.

Visits to these places had a little more social life now, as shore bases were becoming established. I could go ashore for a meal when I could find the time. There was a period of very bad weather in May and I had to go out on an air-sea rescue mission to look for a plane which had come down seven miles from the island of Elba. I found no survivors but one dinghy and the weather was very, very bad by the time I reached Bastia harbour. I spent the next few weeks around the general area of Corsica and Sardinia minesweeping, checking areas, having meals ashore, and drinking too much.

After the base in Ischia had become well established, I would spend the night there whenever possible, and sometimes a day or two if I was lucky. I would have an evening meal with the base staff and anyone else who happened to be present. One evening, I was commenting on what a beautiful island it was, and that I would like to have a run round the island to see the beauty from a little closer. The outcome was that the base engineer officer said that he would take me round in his truck. He took me and someone else for a run around, and when we were returning up the East coast we were all ready for a drink. We called in at a bar on the edge of the road. We had a bottle of Sorisso. We found that there was a terrace at the back, which owing to the lie of the land was effectively one storey up from the ground. We would sit there in the sunshine enjoying the drink and the view.

There was an area of cultivated land, irrigated by channels interlinked and about twenty feet apart. The water was from a well and could be pumped up by a donkey pulling round a long pole which worked the pump. The farmer was too poor for a donkey and his wife and two children pushed the pole round to provide the water. The farmer had a shovel and would close one channel, by putting the earth from another in to divert the water. This continued until everything was watered. What a life some people had! It was so relaxing that we went whenever possible!

Regrettably, I have never found the Sorisso wine other than on Ischia, and never in England. One day, I was talking to an Italian man who now lives in Winchester, and knows Ischia and brings some back on a visit whenever he can. He tells me there is one other man in Winchester who does the same.

In the middle of June I was in Bastia and the next target was landing on the island of Elba, which I had seen many times when I was sweeping to the east of Bastia. This was to be a particularly sad occasion for me, unfortunately. I was towing an assault landing craft to the area and had the two officers and the crew on board for the journey. We arrived off the island of Elba on Saturday, 17th June at 2 a.m. The target of the assault craft that was accompanying me was a small sheltered harbour to the west of the south coast which had a stone pier about fifty or a hundred feet long. There were heavy guns at the end of it.

The officer in charge told me that their plan was to go alongside the rocky outer wall of this harbour wall, their landing craft of course was silenced, and they would run right up to the rocks, scramble up the wrong side of the harbour wall, get over the top and take the people by surprise. There would be one person left in the landing craft to take it off again and pick them up in due course. Before they went the senior officer gave me a bundle of letters from his wife who lived in a town in Northamptonshire, my home county. He asked me if he did not return to pick them up, would I kindly take them ashore and burn them for him as he did not wish anyone else to see them. I asked him if he would like me to write to his wife to tell her what was going on. He said, 'No, don't do that, please, because the senior officer on the ship that I am on will cope with all of that for me.'

I could see later on when daylight came that the guns were not firing and everything appeared to be under control. I was expecting him to get in touch with me within the next few days to collect his letters again but nothing happened, and I heard nothing. After three or four days, I went alongside the headquarters ship he had come from, to see the officer in charge, and I discovered to my dismay that the pier had been mined and, unbeknown to them it was still mined. Somebody fired the mines off and they were all killed, except the one man who was at the shore end. I think this was the biggest tragedy I came across during the whole of the war, and I had in due course to go ashore with a bucket, sit down and keep dropping the letters into it, burning them until I had finished the whole lot. That situation was in my mind for quite a while.

Later on in the early morning another two minesweepers and myself swept in towards Pianosa further along the coast. We eventually returned to Porto Vecchio where we anchored in the dark with a howling gale and with both fingers crossed. Fortunately, the ship held its anchor and I slept well that night. The following day we had a little bit of a party and turned in at 11 p.m. feeling very weary, and possibly a little bit under the 'affluence of incohol'. For the next few weeks, I was largely in Bastia, sweeping around the area and in the area of Elba clearing various areas and beginning to move north from the island. Our forces ashore were progressing up Italy towards Leghorn and, correspondingly, we were sweeping further and further up the coast.

When I was in Ajaccio, on the west coast of Corsica, I and two other officers went for a walk in the town and ended up sitting on a bench in the park. A band was playing and it was all quite relaxing. Suddenly, it started to play the French National Anthem, so we all stood to attention and saluted, humming the tune. That was when I discovered there were three (or was it four) verses. We all collapsed exhausted – that day we all did our duty for our Allies!

Chapter Thirteen
The South of France

It was becoming clear that we were progressing very well up the coast of Italy and there was no significant opposition. It seemed that the Italians were probably more inclined to accept the British in their country than to risk any further advances from the German forces. I am not even sure if there were any significant German forces in Italy.

We were beginning to realise that the next target for landing was bound to be the south of France where we would be coming into more direct contact with the German enemy. None of us involved knew what the strength of the Germans was in the south of France, but we had no doubt that there would be some there. I do not know now how we heard that there was to be a landing in the south of France, or how long in advance of it we actually knew what was going to happen and what our function would be. At the time, I was operating somewhere in the area of Corsica and Sardinia, and received orders to proceed northwards.

I went up the east coast of Corsica and I realised why the captain of minesweeping had been interested in that area and had visited my ship in Bastia to enquire how I was getting on with the job in the area. He was interested in the area south of Bastia which was a very large open bay and with no mines there. In due course he sent the fleet minesweepers up to check the approach to Bastia from the south.

The area was now full of ships at anchor which, obviously, were the ships standing by with supplies to take to the south of France. There were four coastal minesweepers from our flotilla involved in the landing. Our landing was to be established somewhere in the vicinity of St Raphael.

We started off a few miles off the shore led by the senior officer of the four of us. Being junior officer, I was at the end of the four in line. The leader was going in on a double sweep; in other words, one sweep wire out to each side of the ship, and the rest of us were following with a single starboard sweep on the right hand side of the ship. Altogether we were sweeping a width of some two or three hundred feet. When we reached a certain position off the shore, the leading ship turned to port and returned to the point which he had reached previously, and started heading back on a reciprocal course. We were, therefore, establishing an area of swept water twice the width of our trip in towards the beach.

I had an uneasy feeling that the person who had planned it had not allowed for the fact that the sweepers would get closer to the coast as each one turned. I seriously thought that my float and minesweeping gear would end up on the beach and that I would have to cut the sweep wire. But, even worse, I feared that my ship had got so close to the coast, which I could see clearly, that I was in serious danger of running aground. This was not a position anybody would wish to be in at the beginning of a landing. However, I did clear and around we came.

As we were coming out, the tank landing ships were beginning to head towards the beach, and I was placed in a very difficult situation as I was travelling so close to them in the line that my sweep wire went under them. I made a quick decision to cut my sweep wire, because, if it got tangled up in the propellers of any of the landing ships, it would cause a real disaster. I thought it was better for them to go in water that possibly was mined than for me to cause them to break down close to the beach. Fortunately, no mines had been cut in the operation, which seemed to imply that the area was clear.

Later in the day, we swept into the bay of Rade d'Agay and again no mines were cut. Then we swept into the gulf of Frejus with some yard minesweepers as well. This was a bad day. One of our sister ships hit a mine, and so did one of the larger minesweepers. The next day another of the larger minesweepers was mined. All this took place in the gulf of Frejus which lies between St Tropez and to the west of Cannes. After that, we were sweeping generally in the area, and I dragged one mine to the surface which was sunk by gunfire. Altogether this was a very hectic period, relieved only by the pleasant view of the South of France from the sea.

After this we headed back towards Italy and our favourite areas which we knew well. The next special event was in the middle of September when we swept the channel up towards Leghorn. In fact, we went beyond Leghorn to make sure it was safe to enter the harbour. Everything was quite peaceful and we found nothing. The area had been captured by the army from the land, without any sea intervention. Before the port was captured the enemy had sunk a line of merchant ships across the harbour between the entrance and the main quay. The Americans, not to be foiled by this, had cut down, with oxyacetylene cutting gear, the superstructure of one of the ships in the centre of the line to a depth of about ten or twelve feet below the surface. This had all been removed so that it was possible for ships, which were not too deep, to sail over the line of merchant ships and get into the harbour. I went over and tied up alongside, and this is the occasion on which I found the Italian School of Mining to the south of the town when I was taking some exercise along the sea front. All soon began to come to life with ships carrying cargo and going over the line of the blockade and unloading on the harbour wharfs.

One of the officers in the flotilla had an aunt living at Florence. He wanted to go and see how she was as they had heard nothing from her since very early in the war. He, I and another officer got a car and arranged to be driven to Florence. I am not quite sure what our excuse was but I am sure we had a perfectly good one. It was a distance of sixty miles or more, but that could be fitted into a day quite easily. We did not know quite where the front line was, but we set off and along the way we stopped off at Pisa to have a look at the leaning tower and to make sure that it was safe. It is quite an impressive sight but I am not sure that many people would visit Pisa if it was not for the fact of the leaning tower. We had lunch on the way somewhere and we eventually located the house of his aunt.

We rang the bell and a very smart lady came to the door dressed in traditional English clothing. It was a most pleasant and relaxing experience. He had to tell her about all the people in England and what was going on and so on and she gave us all her memories up to date. We brought her some English tea, so we all had a cup and a snack, then we left her and decided to have a look at Florence and the cathedral whilst we were there. It was very impressive and we also went to look at the well-known and important bridge. In fact, we walked across it and back. We arrived back in Leghorn rather late in the evening having gained a very useful experience of life in Italy, if only brief.

After a few days, a signal arrived informing me that I was to be relieved of my command by one of the fellow officers and I was to return to report to the Coastal Force base in Malta. The 13th September was the day for me to leave my ship and head towards Naples. Transport was arranged for the following day. In the evening, as is the custom when the captain is leaving a ship, I sent a signal to the other Coastal Force vessels in the harbour inviting the officers to come for a farewell drink. The signal went on to say, 'Rig of the day – loin cloths and bow ties, optional sea boots and lanyards.' I had regarded this as a joke and I was dressed in my normal Naval uniform to fit the occasion. It came as rather a surprise when I saw a boat pulling across the harbour with one person rowing and the other sitting in the stern: they were both dressed in loin cloths with bow ties, wearing seaboots, and had lanyards round their necks. One of them had a dagger clutched in his teeth, like a real pirate! They had protective clothing under the loin cloths! In due course, there were six of them, all similarly dressed, and me in my full Naval uniform. However, we had a very enjoyable evening and one that I remember to this day.

I loaded all my belongings into the back of a truck and was joined by two other officers heading for the base in Naples. We were all sitting in the back of the truck and the driver was in the front and we carried on until we reached the half way point and stopped to spend the night. We took in what we needed for the night – pyjamas, toothbrush – and left the rest of our things in the back of the vehicle which was in a safe compound. Next morning, when we went to get on the truck we found that it had gone and the driver had not bothered to look for us or tell us that he was going. So, there we were in this remote place with only a night's clothing.

After searching around, we discovered a vehicle was due to leave for Rome in half an hour, so we made arrangements to travel on that. We went on and arrived in Rome to spend a night in Naval accommodation and that was about it. Despite the hardships, it was an opportunity to see Rome, which we would not have missed. And we had a good tour around and looked at all the special exhibits.

We went into St Peter's and had a good look around there. We even saw the Pope come on to the balcony and address the crowds, although we could not understand it. From memory, I think he repeated some of it in English and some other languages but it's a long time ago now. I enquired if it was possible to visit the Vatican City and found that the entrance was at the back of the place where the Pope addressed the crowd from.

We went there to enquire and were told that it was closed. No visitors were permitted on that day. With my usual ingenuity, I pulled out a note in my hand, I don't know what it was, probably fifty or one hundred lira, although I had no idea what that meant. I rustled this and asked if there was any possibility of getting inside. He said, 'I could open the door for you,' looking at the note, so I handed the note over and he opened the door.

We went in the Pope's robing room and all sorts of places like that, but the prime exhibit was, of course, the Sistine Chapel. We spent quite a time in there and the guide explained to us the significance of various items portrayed on the ceiling, so we felt we had really done well. When we came out of the last door into the open again, we totted up and found that it had cost each of us something like ten to fifteen pounds, but it was very much worth it.

We had not reported our arrival to the Naval authorities in Rome and we had a good look round the place for the next two or three days, going in to various restaurants for meals. We went in one for lunch, and the three of us sat down and ordered our meal. When the main course arrived the younger one said, 'I don't want any of that,' pointing to the main dish! Immediately, the proprietor came out (having heard what he said) clutching a dagger in his fist – and demanded, 'Who doesn't like my excellent cooking?' in Italian. The complainant was kicked on each shin and told to shut up and say he did not understand. Peace was restored, but we were aware of the need to be careful in an exclusive Italian restaurant!

When we were ready we went into the naval transport office and asked if we could get transport to Naples, implying that we had arrived the night before. This was arranged and, in due course, we arrived in Naples where we were then faced with the problem of finding our baggage. Mine was in the Coastal Force base. By this time, I had been four years in the Royal Navy and approximately two years abroad in the Mediterranean. I had no idea what I was returning to Malta for but I hoped it was either to return to England or to have another seagoing appointment. I flew back to Malta in an aircraft which was primarily carrying cargo but had two or three seats for passengers, and this was quite a pleasant trip as I was flying over much of the country I had known. We landed at the airport in Malta and I reported to the Coastal Force base where I was given accommodation for the night, or for the next few days, I should say.

Chapter Fourteen
HMS *Gregale* – Malta

I then had to go and report to the captain of Coastal Forces at his base in HMS *Gregale,* which was the Coastal Force base in Msida Creek. I was told that I would be appointed to the staff of the Coastal Force base in Malta, where my duties would be taking charge of the mess and all the accommodation arrangements. In addition, I would be divisional officer for the Roman Catholic Division comprising the Maltese who were serving in the base in the Navy.

This was about the last thing that I had expected, and I'm afraid I was pretty furious. I told him I had expected a better appointment than this and that I thought I ought still to remain at sea. I was told that I had spent a long time at sea and it was time I came ashore for a rest and to undertake some different work. He was patiently trying to calm me down but I'm afraid it was not altogether successful.

I realised later that he was considering that if I went on minesweeping any longer I would blow myself up and that would be my last appointment. So, I suppose in a way I was grateful that he brought me in from the sea. By this time I had swept fifty-six shallow draft mines in the Mediterranean. The ship had twenty-seven mines when I joined it and this made a total of eighty-three mines. This has never been given any form of recognition by the Navy, I was told that the mess was in a certain degree of chaos because of the unruly nature (politely put!) of many of the people who were serving in Coastal Forces, and the fact that they got out of control and caused trouble and damage. I was expected to keep this under control, with my vast experience of the Royal Navy and its ways! I retreated to the cabin I had been allocated, with all my gear and found I was sharing a two berth room with the Church of England padre. I'm not at all sure that this was a particularly well thought out match. However, he was a very pleasant person – we got on very well together and didn't have any arguments or disputes.

My predecessor had to show me all the functions I would have to undertake, which included controlling the mess room and approving the menus with the chief petty officer steward, who was in charge of the overall arrangements. It was in a fairly large house on the corner and had belonged, or probably still belonged, to the local cinema proprietor, who had had to hand it over as the area had been requisitioned by the Navy. There was a flight of what looked like marble steps, curving up to the front entrance – about eight or ten steps up to a very impressive entrance with a beautiful floor inside. The mess room where we ate our meals was in a room at the front, to the left of the entrance. There were two long tables where people sat and there was a servery at the back with a hand-worked lift to bring food up from the cellar below where all the cookers were situated. The cellar was not entirely underground but about a third of its height was underground, with some windows along the front for ventilation and light.

In another large area, further to the back, was a bar with a fair amount of room for sitting down, or standing up, and drinking. At the back of this room under the stairs was the wine store and this was quite a large area because the stairs were pretty luxurious.

The Captain Coastal Forces and the base commander had rooms up above as had two other influential people around the base. The medical officer was technically the wine caterer for the base, but in practice I had to exercise most of the day to day control and supervise the receipt of incoming liqueur. As far as I remember, the regular members of the base could book down their drinks and pay at the end of the month, whereas the casual visitors had to pay as they drank them.

I began to get used to the idea of having an appointment ashore and gradually got into the routine of things. It was also very helpful to be in a place where I knew a few of the local people, the bars and where everybody, or virtually everybody, spoke English. I began to pick up a few words of Maltese but not too many.

A notice was produced periodically which was entitled the *Daily State*. This was a list of all the Coastal Force vessels which were in the Malta area at the time. I soon realised that it also included all the ships of Coastal Forces which had been lost in the Mediterranean: these were listed at the end of the list of active participants. The officer whom I replaced was a member of the special section of the Royal Navy which was, I think, described as shore based, which meant that he could not take a seagoing appointment. These officers could only serve in base establishments.

Once a month it was his duty, and subsequently mine, to order the monthly ration of spirits which were strictly rationed. I soon found out that he was ordering the supply of whisky and gin on the basis of this signal which included two officers per ship, as well as for those who were no longer afloat. This meant that there was a considerable intake of spirits into the base every time, including probably twenty or more bottles in excess of what was strictly entitled. In addition, some of the people for whom it had been ordered would leave the base within a day or two, before they had been able to take up their allocation. People used their allocation in the bar and it was ticked off against them to show how much they'd had. I soon realised that in the cellar were many bottles which were now surplus to requirements. I also discovered that it had been the practice for people who particularly wanted a bottle of spirit to ask the mess man if they could have one. This would normally be agreed and he would pay for the bottle and take it away. Needless to say, I took advantage of this arrangement and always had one or two bottles in the bottom of my wardrobe, hidden behind a pile of clothes so I could entertain anybody in my room if I wanted to do so.

Other people, who included the doctor who was wine caterer, also took part in this procedure. Of course, the base commander was quite accustomed to ringing down and asking for a bottle of whisky or gin and it would be sent up to him. He would pay at the end of the month for it. All this made for a very happy existence, and I could begin to appreciate the joys of being ashore. It also meant that if I went for a dance anywhere, I could take a bottle with me, and put it on the table. We would all enjoy ourselves. It cost me very little but it added to the enjoyment of the evening and to my situation in society.

Dances were like something that we would very rarely see in England at the time. The dancers would sit at one end of the room around a table, with their refreshments on the table. They went to dance and, when they'd finished, went back to their table. All very high society, very sociable and interesting.

I could not criticise or comment on any activity of any nature in the host country, so I cheerfully joined in. I think there were somewhere around fifty officers in the base altogether who would, generally speaking, use the mess for their meals. Of these, probably ten or fifteen at any one time, might be in transit from the UK or somewhere else to join a ship. They would have to wait a few days until they found out where the ship was and how they could join it. It was, generally, these people who were in transit who were causing the problem in the mess, because they were probably fairly new to cheap drinks and would get rather rough after they'd had a few. It was not unusual for them to run at an armchair, throw their head down and do a somersault, tipping the chair with them on the way so that it ended up upside down on the floor. This sort of conduct didn't do the furniture any good and I was expected to smooth it out and get rid of it. Apparently, the shore-going officer was not very good at resolving these matters and kept out of the way.

My technique was somewhat different. When the situation was getting a bit lively I would say, 'Come on, let me show you all the bars, where they are and what you can get.' They thought this was a good idea and I would take them ashore, starting probably with Charlie's, then Auntie's bar, then a few more. With any luck, I could lose a couple of them in every place by taking the remainder out to go on to somewhere else while they were still busy drinking.

Eventually, with a little effort, I could probably succeed in losing virtually all of them and go back to the mess where they would trickle in slowly in a pretty bad state and no longer capable of doing any damage! It worked and they got used to the idea of going ashore to have their drinks as well as staying in the mess. Quite a simple solution if you only knew the ropes.

I could not claim expenses for this sort of trip, so it meant spending a bit of my own money. Fortunately, they would quite often insist on paying for a round, so I didn't have to spend that much on an evening out anyway.

My title amongst the stewards and cooks, was '*Il Secretario*' which is the Maltese expression for 'the secretary'. When I went into the mess and sat down at the table the mess man would call down to the stewards, '*Il Secretario – mulliktarfa*', which was Maltese for 'the secretary, get a move on'. I must say that on the whole they treated me with great respect.

I did not suffer too badly when one day I felt that the final course was cold when it came to the table. I got up and went down below to the galley to see why. All the fires had been drawn out and had been laid ready for lighting for the next meal. I asked for a box of matches and put a match to all the cookers and they blazed away again and that never happened again, fortunately.

The two principal friends on the base staff whom I used to go ashore with when we got an opportunity were the warrant officer in charge of wireless telegraphy and the warrant officer in charge of torpedoes. They were a little older than me but we got on very well together, and when we came back from our run ashore we would probably end up in my room, sitting on the bed and having a drop of whisky from the bottle hidden in my wardrobe.

My room was a very pleasant upstairs room in a building at the back of the mess, in a little side road. My room had a casement window almost down to the floor, both sides of which could be opened and I had a beautiful view out over

Malta. Unfortunately, in the foreground was only a rocky surface, but it was better than looking out on to a road. The bathroom was next door so I didn't have to go far for that and I could usually tell when it was empty because there would be no noises there. The roof of the building was flat, so I could go up and lie in the blazing sun and get even hotter. I had been long enough abroad – my skin could stand anything. In fact, when I came back to England my sun tan lasted about three years! I began to appreciate this life of relative luxury and began to wonder why I had been so keen to go back to sea again. I began to think that the Captain of Coastal Forces was probably quite right in stopping me going to sea for more minesweeping.

In Malta, in addition to my bedroom, I had an office in the main block on the right hand side of the ornate entrance towards the back of the building. This was where I was supposed to do all work connected with the mess and the base generally. After divisions on a Sunday, the Catholic priest would stay behind to conduct a brief service with the Catholics who fell out on parade. When he had finished he would come along to my office, and with the mess man we would sit down and have a cup of coffee and a chat. Since I always doubled off the parade ground with the Maltese on the order, 'Fall out the Roman Catholics', he was quite convinced I really was a Roman Catholic. He was constantly asking me to come to him and confess my sins. I could not succeed in persuading him that I really was Church of England and he was very persistent about this, unfortunately.

I mentioned earlier that at the back of the mess, on the left hand side under the stairs, was the wine store where we kept all our liquor. One evening the medical officer who was wine secretary, and I went in there and locked ourselves in to test some of the bottles to see if everything was all right. There were rather a lot of bottles to test, and the more we tested the more we wished to continue. There were frequent bangings on the door from people outside demanding to be let in and to join us, but we protested that we were very busy and could not meet their wishes. Before long, I think we were probably quite incapable of meeting their wishes anyway, and were not at all sure how we were going to get out. In the end, we did manage to stagger out and retire to our rooms and sleep the whole thing off. I have no doubt that our heads were still protesting the next morning as nobody could stand that sort of conduct without having some after effects.

There was an official base car with a driver and this was under the control of the first lieutenant of the base. I could use it from time to time by arrangement with him, but I had to have an official destination, otherwise it would be unreasonable of me to expect to use it. I could incorporate some other activity with the official purpose on which I was travelling, but this obviously had to be limited in terms of time and distance. However, it was very useful for reaching places which I could not easily get to by public transport. There was a place I visited on one occasion a little way north of Valetta. It was a large hole in the ground with fairly vertical sides which were some twenty or thirty feet deep. I believe there were some ruins of some buildings in the bottom of it. It was known as 'The Village of Sin' – the occupants were supposed to be quite evil, and one day God sought his retribution for all their evil ways by a sudden landslide or collapse of the earth. Quite a good story, but I'm not quite sure there was any truth in it as nobody had been present when it happened some thousand years previously. Everywhere in Malta seemed to have a historical story or a special feature of some sort. I had the impression it was designed to impress the visitors as much as the locals.

One social event which I enjoyed very much in Malta was a visit to a ballroom dance at the Union Club in Sliema on a Saturday evening with my friends from the area. I think this was reminiscent of some of my very early dancing days in England. Approximately half of the room was the dancing area and the other half, although I believe it was in a very large recess off the main hall, had tables in it with four chairs around each one, where the party who were visiting the place would sit, between dances, with a few bottles of wine or spirit and glasses. We had a thoroughly enjoyable time, chatting away and having a dance when we felt like it. I, of course, used to provide some of the bottles of whisky and gin. I have no recollection of paying but I presume we did, or it may have been just a privilege for members of the Union Club.

When I was abroad during the war I used to collect picture postcards of the places I went to, and in some places, such as Sorrento, I probably have twenty or thirty cards alone. Altogether I must have about a thousand postcards of places abroad which I have visited. I have a similar number of postcards of places in the United Kingdom which I have visited also. It is an excellent way of revising the memory. Unfortunately, when I was writing this book I knew I had them but I had put them in a safe place and there are so many safe places in the house that when I came to look for them I couldn't find them! The trouble is that in the average house one can't have everything handy. Regrettably, I seem to have very few postcards of Malta and I do not know why this is, possibly there were not many available while I was there. I do not know.

One of the places I visited was Rabat in the centre of Malta which I believe was the ancient capital of Malta before Valetta became the capital. I went there once or twice and I seem to remember there is a cathedral there, and various other old buildings of interest. I went particularly to visit a shop, the whereabouts of which was explained to me, to buy something which I was told I couldn't get anywhere else in Malta. Now, for the life of me I cannot remember what I bought or what happened to it, or whether it is still in the house. Unfortunately, I cannot even remember whether it was china, pottery, metalwork or anything else and so, consequently, I do not know what to look for.

Malta, with its rocky nature, and lack of vegetation and trees, was not a particularly interesting place from the point of view of countryside, but the old buildings were certainly very attractive. I never crossed the narrow strip of water to the island of Gozo but I could see it across there. It looked greener than Malta from my memory, but there were no simple means of getting there so I never went to have a look at it.

Towards the end of 1944 the mess fund had built up to a total of some three hundred pounds or more, which was a very large sum in those days. This was partly as a result of people paying for things in advance and then leaving the island and never coming back, and partly due to the profit margin on all the things we sold in the bar and otherwise. The general idea in the Royal Navy was that as these funds built up they would be distributed to the people in the mess periodically, but in this case the people in the mess at any one time were largely in transit as they were passing through from one place to another. We held a meeting and decided that rather than attempt to distribute it, which would be unfair, we would have a large party in December just before Christmas.

It was a large party when it took place and I think there were some two hundred or more people present. We issued invitations to every Naval officer who was in the area or in the base and who was connected with Coastal Forces. We also issued an invitation to every Wren in the island who could attend, and to all the nurses serving in the Navy in Malta, especially in the hospital which the Navy was running. It fell to the mess man to produce the appropriate buffet for the guests, and there certainly was a very wide range available. At the same time, we had what I can only describe as vast quantities of punch and other drinks. To make the punch and other drinks, the doc and I set off in an open-backed truck to visit the vineyards to collect some wine. Of course, we had to test all the wine before we could buy it, and the custom was to draw some wine off from a cask in a fairly large glass, about a half tumbler, and we would have one each to try and then decide our view on it. The rest was just thrown on to the floor, and we would move on to the next. Needless to say, this was a very merry occasion, and we were quite well inebriated by the time we had made our choices.

We headed back to the base with some twelve cases on the back of the truck, and the doc and I were sitting on top of them and singing our hearts out as we went along. We arrived outside the mess just as everybody was coming out from lunch. There we were, singing away merrily, and everybody was cheering and asking whatever had we been up to. Of course, they didn't get any replies and we got off the truck or fell off it, staggered into the mess to sit down and have a belated meal. The wine stewards took the wines in and put them in a safe place, probably so we couldn't get at them again, and my memory of the rest of the day is very, very dim. There were certainly times in the Royal Navy when being an officer and a gentleman, and carrying out his duty, required great stamina!

We had decided to have a Father Christmas and he was appropriately dressed over his uniform. We wanted a sledge so that he could enter the building in style, but this proved very difficult to find. All we could get was a torpedo trolley made of metal, on which torpedoes were wheeled around to get them to the ships that required them, and to say that they were very heavy would be an understatement. We had a team of reindeer officers pulling on two ropes and dragging this up the steps of the house with Father Christmas clinging on for dear life. The next day, the steps of the house looked a bit dilapidated after this load had come up it. However, Father Christmas arrived in the room to loud and vigorous cheers. I sometimes wonder how he ever survived some of the journeys he had to make and however he got down chimneys – I don't know!

The party was a huge success with singing and all manner of activities which I can no longer remember very clearly; in fact I am not sure that I remembered them very clearly at the time. The consumption of alcohol was high, even by Naval standards, and the food available in the buffet was really good. It included a whole bird or a ham carved as required. For a long time, I had a record of all this in detail, but like a lot of other things it's in a safe place somewhere.

The original plan had been to end the party with 'God save the King' at midnight or half past but I let it keep on going as everybody was enjoying themselves so much. There was dancing and singing, and there was still a lot of food and drink left. Eventually, at 3 a.m. I decided it really was time to bring things to a conclusion. In consultation with the other members of the mess committee, the end was called and we all sang 'God save the King', and staggered away. We had arranged quite a lot of transport outside to get the visitors back to wherever they had come from, rather than them having to stagger through the streets of Malta, which would not have done the Navy a great deal of good. We had about eight cases of beer for the staff and drivers – if they could still drive!

A few days later, the Base Commander asked me to go and see him in his office which I did. He had received a signal from the vice admiral, Malta, asking him to explain the high consumption of spirits at this function and he asked me where it all came from. I pointed out to him the practice of my predecessor had been to claim the ration on all ships in Coastal Forces shown on a daily state wherever they were. This explained the high availability of spirits in the mess, and I pointed out to the Base Commander that what my predecessor did, I had carried on, I thought that if it suddenly changed dramatically there would be a problem. He tried hard to blame me for this, and said I should not have done it. But I said that every month he countersigned the request for spirits so he was, in effect, as much involved in it as I was! He spoke to the Vice Admiral on the telephone and must have given him some explanation. Nothing further was said. Of course, from then on I had to request spirits only for people who were actually in Malta at the time when the request went in each month, so I did not suffer the fate I had feared; and we did not really suffer because there was an appreciable balance still in hand in the wine store.

I had two trips away from Malta during my stay there – various Italian ships under our control would come into the harbour bringing certain stores, and they would return loaded with stores for the Coastal Force bases in Messina and in Ischia. They were supposed to sail under the white ensign of Great Britain, and always spent the night in harbour rather than remaining at sea as they were only merchant vessels. They were normally quite small, about one hundred and thirty to one hundred and fifty feet long, like the small vessels one sees plying around the British Isles if one is on a visit to the seaside. I was asked if I would be prepared to accompany one on its visits, to supervise and see that everything was delivered properly. Most of the vessels I had seen previously were relatively comfortable, so I agreed.

When I came to get on the ship I discovered it was one of these ordinary old fishing trawlers, or something of that type. I was offered a berth in the captain's cabin but, having viewed it, I decided I didn't particularly want to sleep there, and I arranged to sleep in the hold, on top of the cargo, where our two seamen, who accompanied the ship, were to sleep. Much of the cargo was wood and the top of the hold was relatively level. We put three primitive camp beds, which were very low, on top, and lay on those with blankets. The cover was left off the hold as there was not likely to be any rain, so we were sleeping under the stars, although I am not sure that we slept particularly well.

On the first visit we called in at Messina in Sicily. We berthed in the harbour and arranged transport to unload the various things we had taken for Messina. We were then required to spend the night in Messina, so I and my two men walked ashore and had a look around.

It is quite an attractive place along the sea front and around the town area generally but then we decided to walk towards the outskirts and look at the countryside a bit. We were heading along a road to the north of the town and as we progressed we realised we were being followed by quite a crowd of young people who were spread out completely across the road. They were chanting all sorts of calls in Italian which we did not fully understand but we got the general idea that they did not regard us as very popular. It was interesting to note, when we were in Messina, that many of the painted slogans on walls saying, 'Yanks go home' had been replaced in some places by, 'Yanks come back'. This was because although they did not like the Yanks, they liked their money and the profits it brought to them. I think at that point we were bracketed with the Yanks and they did not see any particular good in us, so we were rather concerned about what would happen when we reached the edge of the town which was a hundred yards away. When we were just about there I said to the two men with me, 'I don't fancy going down with a knife in my back, and I'm afraid that's what might happen if we go out into the countryside. I suggest we turn about and face them, and, if we do go down, at least we will go down fighting.' They both agreed. I was on the left hand side with the two men on my right hand side. I said, 'One, two, three, *about turn*,' and we all turned about to the right, and walked straight towards the crowd who were then about eight or ten feet from us. To our amazement, the crowd parted to allow us through, and we passed through although we were virtually brushing the crowd on either side. When we had gone through they all turned round and followed us back into the town. We heaved a great sigh of relief to think that we had got away with it. I think that is probably the closest to death that I have felt.

The next time I went north was in early April on the vessel *San Antonio*. This was somewhat better than the previous one and I slept in a small cabin under the wheelhouse where the two crewmen also had their accommodation. Our first stop was towards the southern end of Sicily, between Sicily and Italy, in a small bay where there was virtually nothing. But the captain knew it was a safe anchorage.

When we had had a meal on board I asked the captain in Italian if there was anywhere we could get a drink. He replied, 'Oh, I expect so, come on let's try.' He, the other crewmen and I, got into a small boat, and rowed ashore. We started to walk inland through the varying plantations, trees and bushes. Before long we could hear voices of people talking, so we headed for them. There was a circle of about four people sitting down on the ground with two or three bottles, drinking wine. We enquired if we could join them and they replied that we certainly could. So we all sat there drinking wine and chatting away for an hour or two and then we headed back to the ship on a somewhat more unsteady course. We rowed back to the ship and had a good night's sleep. I have no recollection of any of us paying for anything and I gather that some of the wine came from one of the vineyards where they worked.

After leaving our anchorage in the bay we headed north. I mentioned to the captain that I had a bag of old clothing which I wished to get rid of, and asked if he had any ideas where it could be taken. He said Catania would be the best place. We sailed into the small harbour of Catania a bit later in the day and tied up on the quay to the north of the harbour. By this time, it was late afternoon or early evening. The captain and I went ashore and he found a small boy who was given the task of carrying the bag on his shoulder and coming with us. We walked along the quay and passed two policemen who were on duty on the gate, and we walked through with no comment about the bag. We headed along towards the house that he was going to take me to through the streets of the town. After a while, I looked back and saw that the two policemen were following us some fifty yards behind. I pointed this out to him and he said, 'Oh, we'll have to deal with that.' We came to a corner and turned round it, he grabbed the bag from the boy and told him to disappear, and we started to run along the road looking back periodically to see that we weren't caught up.

After turning two corners we were running along the road when suddenly he stopped at a door and rang the bell. To my surprise the door opened almost immediately and inside there was a flight of stairs going upwards with no other room accessible on the ground floor. Up the stairs we went, and as I looked back the door closed and I could see the whole thing was operated by wires going through the ceiling. One would pull a lever on the latch to release it, another would open the door catch, and then there was a wire with a pulley which would be used to open the door and close it again. I thought it all rather peculiar. We went upstairs and turned into a room at the front with a bay window, and I could see there was a young lady sitting in the bay and looking out of the window. She had all the controls available to her. And no doubt it was she who let us in and closed the door after us.

We were welcomed by two men and sat down with a drink. The captain started to empty the bag and they went through it pricing it all to tot up what it was worth. I was allowed a sum of money which was very favourable to me, as it was far more than I would have got anywhere else. I then proceeded to empty my pockets and piled up ten or twenty packets of duty free cigarettes: all their eyes lit up more than ever at the sight of these, and again a good price was negotiated. I was, of course, concerned that the two Carabinieri would know where we had gone and might well come to catch us red handed. Nothing happened, however, and they may well have got their rake-off as well.

We were invited to stay for a meal but I thought this would be testing fate rather too much, because this would mean probably two hours and we would be heading back to the ship well after dark – a thought that did not appeal to me. I was a bit concerned about going back with all the money on me, but there you are, we had to do it. One cannot become wealthy without taking a few risks! We walked back to the ship and the two Carabinieri were on the entrance again. We said good night to them and carried on our way.

Next day, we headed on for Messina and the captain told me that he would like to get some olive oil which was obtainable relatively cheaply in the south of Italy, and which we could dispose of when we got up to the Naples area. He suggested that we should have half shares in it to which I agreed; but it gave me the problem that if we sailed into Messina harbour with a British flag we would be directed where to berth, where to go and where to sail. So we could not just cross straight from Messina to a small port on the southern part of Italy. I resolved this problem by hoisting down the white ensign and telling him to raise the Italian flag. I said we would sail into Messina under the Italian flag, and I asked him if that would cause any consternation. He replied, 'No, that would be perfectly acceptable,' so in we went under the Italian flag. I looked around the harbour until I could see somewhere where Naval vessels would berth, and we went there and tied up alongside them. I then walked along the quay until I found a telephone. I got through to the Naval base and said I was lying in a position which I described and had certain engineering stores for the Coastal Force base – could they please arrange for them to be picked up because we had to sail again as soon as possible. This happened without question and the mechanical parts were picked up and taken away.

We sailed out again and across the straits to the destination we were seeking. The captain went ashore, negotiated the purchase of the olive oil and duly came back on board. I am not sure now, but I feel the oil was in three or four casks and I don't really know how much there was, but I would think there were ten or twelve gallons altogether. This was stowed away and we spent the night there before we sailed away the next day up the Italian coast. It would not have been much help to take the oil with us to Ischia which was our destination, and we had to get it somewhere on or near to the mainland. There was nowhere suitable on the way to Naples, and we spent the night at sea, arriving in the area sometime the next day. We berthed in Capri, which I was very pleased to visit having seen it so many times, and the captain was quite sure that the olive oil would be welcome there. He went ashore and negotiated a sale and it all went off the ship. I am not too certain now but my recollection is that we both made about twenty pounds out of the deal, which was very welcome. I was delighted to have a wander around Capri and to look at various shops.

We went on to Ischia, and after a few days looking around my old haunts and going out with some friends from Coastal Forces who were there, and having drinks and hot meals, I eventually returned to Malta from the mainland.

I was, in general, enjoying my social life in Malta which was very varied and relaxing, but also I was becoming increasingly concerned about still being in the Mediterranean after two years. I had been in the Mediterranean two years and a month since moving to the Coastal Force base. I was anxiously awaiting my return to the United Kingdom and seeing my wife, family and friends once more, quite apart from seeing England again.

One enjoyable, if somewhat unusual, experience in Malta, was when some of my Maltese friends took me to a social gathering in Sliema which was, if not officially Roman Catholic, of strong Roman Catholic presence and tradition. I met quite a number of pleasant people, some of whom I had met before, some of whom I had not. One person who I met and was talking to was the priest who visited the base to deal with the Catholic personnel, who were part of my responsibility. We were chatting away quite a while and then he introduced me to two young ladies who he described as being his nieces. I was told quite openly that they were unmarried and were looking for husbands, and he suggested to me that I might like to marry one of them. I protested that I was already married and that I could not marry again. He said, 'What Church were you married in?' and I told him that it was a Congregational Church. He said, 'Oh well, that isn't recognised in the Roman Catholic faith, so as far as the Roman Catholic faith is concerned you are not married. I would quite willingly marry you in a Roman Catholic church.' I found this a rather unusual interpretation of religion – something I had never experienced before and never expected to. As I said earlier, he has always been convinced that as I fell out with the Roman Catholic division in the Sunday morning parade, I must be Roman Catholic, because if I had been

Church of England I would have stayed behind for the service. I had assured him many times that I was not Catholic, and although we were married in a Congregational Church, basically my wife and I attended the Church of England whenever we felt inclined to do so.

I found this approach to religion rather peculiar although I think it may well have been more normal in Malta than we would have expected to find elsewhere. It left me wondering how he had two nieces all of marriageable age, but I was not given any explanation as to who their parents were and did not meet them. I left there, eventually, feeling somewhat more depressed than I had been earlier in the proceedings. I have to say that I do not hold it against the Catholic Church in general, with which I have had reasonable relations both before and since.

At this time I was beginning to see various people relieved and sent home who had served in the Mediterranean for a shorter time than I had; but every time I enquired about it, the base commander told me that the Admiralty had not sent my relief yet, and it was a matter for them to decide when to send my relief out for me. I could not really believe that the Admiralty knew every person in the Navy in the Mediterranean, what their appointment was, what they were doing, and whether it was reasonable for them to come home or to stay in the Mediterranean. I hardly thought that they would regard the job of mess secretary in the Coastal Force base at Malta of paramount importance and that there must be some other explanation. It was most unlikely that they were aware that I was managing the mess and its affairs well, and there were no significant problems that I did not deal with.

I was forced to the conclusion that the base commander was keeping me back and releasing other people before me because he did not want to have any upset in the mess and its general arrangements whilst he was there. My expressions of concern to him had no effect, though, and by this time my father was sixty-seven and I hadn't seen him since I came abroad. I was a bit concerned about seeing him, quite apart from returning to my wife. We had been married since 1941 and seen very, very little of each other since then. One consolation was that the exchange of mail between myself, my wife and family was more reliable than it had been for a long time. I think we had post in both ways roughly in two weeks, although this would vary from time to time if the ship carrying the mail diverted to somewhere else rather than its original destination. The mail could have a circuitous route.

In June 1945 when I had been abroad for two years and eight months, I received a letter from my wife. The handwriting on the envelope was rather shaky and it told me that she had been cycling home from work towards Kettering, down a road from Islip, which we both knew very well, when an American soldier on a bicycle accompanied by his lady friend, went past. He ran into her, she was thrown over the handlebars and landed in the road. She was picked up and, eventually, taken to hospital, I believe, by a passing car. She had concussion from which she was recovering. She assured me that she was now feeling much better and quite well. This was not very convincing because the letter was written diagonally across the note paper with a very shaky hand, and was only just legible.

I promptly took this to the base commander and told him that she was obviously worse than she said, that she was in hospital, and that I wanted to get home to see her as soon as I possibly could. I asked to be given a flight home as quickly as possible. I knew that there was a plane which left twice a week for the United Kingdom, and it was due to leave the following day.

I was booked on the next flight home on a Liberator bomber which had been converted as a mail plane, and could carry three passengers. I went up to the aerodrome on the following morning to catch the plane which was due to take off at 10.30 a.m. Unfortunately, it did not take off because the weather was too bad, so I had to return to the base and come back to the plane the next day. The following day, I went back in the base car taking one or two suitcases and nothing else. I had to make arrangements for my belongings to be sent home to me, and I had had a large wooden chest made earlier which contained virtually everything and this was locked and tied with rope. I had painted my address on the top of the box hoping that somehow it would get back. The theory was that it would be sent back on a destroyer or any other Naval vessel which was heading for the United Kingdom. Of course, there was a risk that if the ship got sank I should lose everything, but there you are, what could I do?

I got to the aerodrome and we got on to the plane. The three passengers were a senior Army officer, a senior RAF officer and myself, a lieutenant RNVR. At least I had succeeded in my objective of obtaining a concession, which must have been pretty rare.

There were three seats in the mail-carrying hold, each one by a porthole so that the three of us could look out. If I wanted to look out of the other side of the plane I had to get up and go across to the other side. I believe we all wore a harness to keep us in our seats in the event of trouble, but it went well and we each had a meal.

Lunch, of course, was in thermos containers, and there was one container for each passenger and for the members of the crew. The courses were each in a container and were put on to a plate and brought to us. We took off from Malta, flew non-stop and landed at Stoney Cross, in the New Forest the same day – a journey time of eight hours. The advantage was that we had a good view of everything as we went and I saw places from the air which I had only seen from the sea before. We passed over the South of France, headed up the Rhone Valley, then turned across to Brittany; and I'm not sure where we passed over the coast but the weather was good and we could see the ground the whole way. Across the channel, we flew over the Isle of Wight and landed at Stoney Cross on a temporary wartime airfield. We staggered ashore with our baggage, our legs having had no real exercise for eight hours – walking or even standing was not easy.

We passed through customs and it was no use trying to hide anything as there were three people and one customs officer. I think I paid some eight pounds in duty, including roughly four pounds on a watch I was bringing home for a friend of mine with a promise that I would post it to his wife.

Chapter Fifteen
England – at Last

The next stage was to get home as soon as we possibly could and we got a train from somewhere fairly close to Stoney Cross, having been taken to the station by one of the airforce cars. I took a taxi across London to St Pancras, and by the time I got there, the last train for Kettering had gone. All that was left was the mail train which would be leaving at about 10.30 p.m. stopping at various places en route. Somehow I managed to tell my hard luck story to the postman in charge. I was allowed to travel on board, although it would not normally carry passengers. I have no recollection of meals although I think I had a quick meal in London when I was hanging around St Pancras station.

I arrived in Kettering well after midnight, and I wanted to get home. There was I with two bags and no taxis or anything at all, but there was of course the van picking up the mail for Kettering. I had a word with the driver and told him that I had three brothers in the post office, so quite illegally I was allowed to travel on the van with my cases. He dropped me outside my mother's house, and said he could not divert his journey out of his normal route to take me to Marjorie's house.

I woke them up, went in and had a cup of coffee. I left some bags there but I carried on with a bag of overnight things, walking down to Marjorie's house and I arrived there very early in the morning. I have forgotten to say that after I had shown the base commander my letter I had received another one from her the following day when she was at home and said she was feeling very much better and had recovered from the shock of her accident. As you will have guessed, I completely forgot to show this to the base commander, otherwise I might very well still have been in Malta. Who knows?

After I had knocked on the front door of the house she came down and I was fitted up in the lounge, sleeping for the night on the couch. In the morning, after breakfast, I began to sort myself out, still feeling rather sleepy. We then decided that the best thing to do would be to go and have a room in my parents' house, where there was a spare room with a double bed. I had to transfer my few belongings there, and Marjorie came along with whatever she required. I don't know how we got there, whether it was by bus, or whether we managed to get a taxi – I have no idea. The main thing that was in our minds was that we were together at last.

I can hardly describe the pleasure of being back in my home town after nearly three years – going round the places I knew, meeting people I knew, and having a generally relaxing time. We would go into the town and visit some of our old haunts, have a cup of coffee and a drink here and there; it was so enjoyable, it felt almost unbelievable. She was away from work for three weeks or so, on a medical certificate, but eventually had to go back because she hadn't given notice. She could not at that stage decide upon giving up her employment until she knew a little more about what my future was. It was not easy to settle down to normal existence in a peaceful society. Being a professional worrier, I had to contemplate the possibility that I might be posted to the Far East and this was the last thing I wanted. I had doubts as to whether I could survive two major battle fronts and get away with it.

Another major concern was whether my sea chest with all my bits and pieces in it would safely arrive home. I was anxiously waiting to see it or to hear something, but I had a fear in the back of my mind that there might be a massive bill from customs for all the things I was importing. After about two or three weeks, to my surprise a railway wagon pulled up outside the door, and the man asked me to help him unload a large wooden box, which I did. It was my large chest, apparently untouched and not even opened. There was no indication as to any examination by the customs. He gave me the impression that it had been taken off the destroyer when it arrived at Devonport, and had been taken to the railway station. When it came off it looked like a chest full of something to do with the Navy and nobody had questioned it, I imagine. This was a great relief, because I didn't particularly want anybody rummaging through it, and because I feared for the safety of all the things that might be in it. However, I need not have worried.

Somehow we carried it into the shed, which my father and I had built just after we had moved into the house. By some stroke of luck it went through the doorway and then I spent a week or two rummaging through it, sorting things out, separating the clothing from all the other delights I had brought home. It reminded me of the many places I had been to and the happy times I had there.

There are, at times, major advantages to being in the Navy compared with the RAF or the Army. At least there is normally a reasonable cargo carrying capacity on a ship which does not exist in the Airforce or in the Army.

My father had lost the use of his car when he retired, and that was quite a handicap, although in wartime with petrol rationing I don't suppose there was much benefit in having it. However, by now Marjorie's bicycle had been put back in normal working order, and mine was all right when the tyres were blown up and it had been generally examined. We would go off for cycle rides in the country whenever we got the opportunity and the weather was respectable. We visited some of the village pubs and tea rooms we used to know, and found them much the same as they had been before the war. I think I tended to keep away from anything connected with work, in case people started pestering me to go in and help them with some difficult situation they had. I remember at one stage we lived for a few weeks with one of Marjorie's brothers who worked in the post office. That was quite a change. The two children had grown up and were no longer at home and that gave us a more relaxed time.

Approximately two months after arriving back in the United Kingdom, I discovered the Royal Navy had not forgotten me after all. I received instructions to proceed to Tobermory for a course, which was to be in the use of radar. This involved a return trip to the Isle of Mull, off the west coast of Scotland, crossing over on a ferry. I cannot remember clearly where I was accommodated, but I have a vague recollection of a building ashore close to the harbour. This looked like being a very interesting experience although it was clear that the Admiralty still had designs on sending me back to sea again.

I think we started off with a talk on the principles of radar and how it was operated, what it was capable of doing, and then we had to go out on a ship which was specially equipped for the purpose. I cannot remember exactly what it was, but I would say it was about the size of a Corvette and it could be controlled either from the bridge on the upper deck, or from the wheelhouse which was below the bridge.

First of all, I had to be in the wheelhouse, handling the ship normally in and out of harbour and up the straits between the island and the mainland, and back again. Then, having got used to handling the ship, the next stage was to do this from the wheelhouse with the windows blacked out so that I couldn't see out, using the radar screen. It seemed virtually impossible. By this time, I was beginning to get the hang of the harbour entrance, the route in and out, and what other vessels were likely to be around. I had an advantage over many of the other people who were taking the course at the same time, and I think there were probably about six of us. I had had a lot of experience over the years in handling ships in difficult circumstances and in sudden situations, whereas many of the others had not had the same intensity of use as I had.

It was done by watching the chart of the area and knowing what was on the coast line and identifying these on the radar screen so one could judge where one was in the sea without actually being on deck to look. I can remember towards the end of the period bringing the ship into the harbour at Tobermory under the radar control. I spotted the ferry ahead of me and reduced speed until it had passed in front of me; then I went back to my normal speed and continued in to the harbour. I identified where I was by various things I knew, such as a buoy or a headland. Eventually, I brought the ship to within a matter of fifty feet or so of where it had to berth, and then handed it over to the people on deck to bring it alongside with normal vision. It went off well and I passed the course with satisfactory results.

As it happened, I was never to put them into practice as I didn't go to sea again after that, before I was discharged from the Royal Navy. Tobermory was a pleasant place to be, but one could not get far on the island because there were no bus services or anything of that nature, and there was a limit as to how far one could walk. There were plenty of more interesting places to be. I was there for approximately a month and I returned home on leave again in September 1945.

This period of leave lasted just over three months, which was again a period of uncertainty, not knowing what one could plan or what was going to happen, or when it was going to happen. I spent quite a bit of time helping my father look after his garden; and he had an allotment too, so there was quite a bit to do. The allotment was fenced and had fruit trees on it, so there was the fruit to pick and take back to the house to put into store. There was a certain amount of tension through not feeling able to plan anything or look ahead further than a few days.

Regrettably, near Christmas, my father suddenly had violent pains in his stomach. We managed to get him up to bed. I phoned the doctor to ask her if she would come round, and I said I thought he had got a perforated duodenal ulcer.

She arrived shortly afterwards and said to me as she went upstairs, 'How can you know that he's got a perforated duodenal ulcer?'

She came down shortly afterwards and said to me, 'You were quite right after all, it is a perforated duodenal ulcer. However did you know?'

I told her that before the war I was with him on the allotment and suddenly he had collapsed and said he couldn't do anything. He had had a violent pain in his stomach, and he couldn't walk. I had looked and there hadn't been a single person in sight anywhere on the allotment, and I hadn't known what to do.

I left him for a minute to go to the end of the allotment where the pathway led down towards the entrance. When I got there I sprang on my bicycle, flew off home at high speed and found my mother was out. I then went across the road to a man who had been in St John's ambulance, and he came back with me. We found my father bent double trying to walk down the path. With one of us on either side supporting him, we got him home, and as soon as the doctor came, he diagnosed a perforated duodenal ulcer. He was taken straight off to hospital. The lady doctor was suitably impressed.

This time my mother and I went to hospital in the ambulance with him and stayed for some time while he was assessed. We were told he would have his operation within a matter of two or three hours. We telephoned later to be told that his operation had been carried out satisfactorily and he was now resting in his bed. The hospital was on our side of the town and we went round later in the day to see how he was and stayed for a while and then came back again.

Visiting was officially in the evening and we both went for the first two nights. On the third night for some reason I didn't go. I think I had to go somewhere else, I'm not sure. My mother went and while she was there he suddenly fell backwards flat on his bed.

The doctor came and said he'd had a heart attack and died instantly, so I didn't see him alive again. It was a very sad end to the war and something from which my mother never really recovered. Immediately after this I received a notice appointing me from the 3rd January to HMS *Ferret*, the naval base in Londonderry.

Top: Ship's company of 134 in Bastia.
Bottom: Floating mine north of Corsica - -sunk by rifle fire.

Top: Roundhay Park - demob leave.
Bottom: Gouffre de Padirac.

Top: The author photographed in Londonderry.
Bottom: Tramcars lined up in Princess Street, Edinburgh.

Top: Invasion of Anzio.
Bottom: VE Day at HMS *Gregale* - Malta.

Chapter Sixteen
HMS *Ferret* – Londonderry

Towards the end of 1945 I received orders to report to HMS *Ferret*, the naval base at Londonderry, on the 3rd January, 1946. By then I had been just over three months at home with no appointment and was wondering quite what was going to happen next. It was a relief in a way, to know that I was being appointed to a shore post in the United Kingdom, and this was certainly preferable to being posted to the Far East where there was still enough activity for anybody to get closely involved. I set off from Kettering, my home town in Northamptonshire, the day before, intending to spend the night in Stranraer. This was quite a long journey and it took the best part of a day because I had to change several times. I was pretty exhausted by the time I got there, taking two large cases with me, and was relieved to have a bed in a hotel that night together with a meal and breakfast.

The next day I caught the first ferry to Larne, a distance of about two hundred miles and then proceeded by train to Londonderry. I arrived at the base at about lunch time or early in the afternoon, and took a taxi from the station with my bags. I was received at the gate by the guards, and after reporting to the duty officer I was told where my cabin would be. I went there to put my things in.

I was also told that I would be duty officer that night, which was a bit of a shock as I had not expected to have any serious duty quite so quickly after my arrival. However, that is the way of the Navy. Worse was to come though, as I was told that the night before the sentry at the gate had had a knife stuck in his back. I do not know whether he was killed or whether he was just wounded and I did not feel inclined to ask. This meant that if the IRA were operating as close to the base as that, the routine for night rounds which I would have to carry out had been changed. Previously, I believe that the officer on night duty conducted rounds with the Petty Officer of the guard and two other soldiers at midnight and at four o'clock; and they followed the same routine every night. It was decided on my first night that rounds would be conducted three times, and that the officer in charge would not announce to anybody in advance when this would be. I set my alarm clock in the duty officer's cabin in the guard house. I had then turned out the guard to come with me. Worse was to come, as I had to vary my route and go by any method I chose around the base, so nobody would know when and where the guards would suddenly turn up. This was rather eerie, particularly for me, as I did not know the place. I would go between two buildings, turn left, turn right and so on, and wander around the place with the guards with me. I didn't feel I could ask their guidance on where to go otherwise it might have given a biased route. Of course, occasionally we ended up in a dead end and would have to turn back and take another route. I think we all had the feeling that at any minute people with knives might suddenly spring up behind us, but fortunately nothing happened and I got through my first night satisfactorily.

Before I left Kettering, my wife and I had agreed that if I felt I could get suitable accommodation ashore and be allowed to live ashore she would join me, after giving notice to her employer. I soon found out that people did sleep ashore in a flat or whatever accommodation they could get, and sometimes if a relative came to visit them temporarily they would take a room in a hotel for a few nights. It was confirmed to me by the senior staff at the base that I could sleep ashore if I wished provided that I was in the base for all my duties at the proper time in the daytime, and was in the base sleeping in the duty cabin when I was on night duty. I was aware of the problems of finding suitable accommodation in a town which was divided between Protestants and Catholics and I had no knowledge, and most other people did not, of exactly where they were living and what relations were like. I put an advert in the local paper saying, 'Naval officer seeks accommodation in Londonderry whilst serving in the area,' and awaited replies. I got about fourteen letters of response offering me accommodation at what appeared to be reasonable prices, so, when I got an opportunity, I started to go around looking at them, and I must say that some of them were pretty grim from my point of view.

I was aware of which areas were predominantly Catholic and looked at one or two of those and came away rather depressed. Other areas were not so clearly defined. I went to one which was quite close to the city centre already knowing the road because I had been along it before. I rang the doorbell, and was taken in by the lady who lived there. I could immediately see the house was of a different standard from anything else I had seen, and when she took me further inside, to put it mildly I was astounded. The lounge could only be described as luxurious, and was a room at the front with a bay window looking out on to what was called 'The Square'. There was a glass cabinet full of exquisite china and there were drawers with high quality cutlery in them. Beautiful pictures on the walls, everything anybody could wish for. I cannot remember now whether the table was mahogany or oak but it was probably mahogany.

The room next door was originally the dining room and that was the room she would occupy leaving us to have the front room. Next was the kitchen which we would share but it appeared there would not be any real conflict because her requirements as to meals were fairly simple. Behind that was a scullery with the wash-boiler, a sink, and a solid fuel cooking stove and so on, but in addition there was a gas stove and she had an electric kettle also. Upstairs our bedroom was on the front above the lounge and again this was quite luxurious. Her bedroom was further back and the bathroom was more or less over the kitchen as far as I remember. There was a small garden in the front of the house probably about five feet or so from the edge of the pathway.

Behind there was a small garden the width of the house which was terraced, and the plot at the back of the house was about twenty feet or twenty-five feet long and at the bottom was a high wall. This, I was told, was the wall of Londonderry prison. This was a bit of a shock, but apart from this everything was very satisfactory. I made a provisional reservation for it and told her my wife would be coming over within a few days and she would come to have a look at it and see what she thought.

I telephoned Marjorie and made arrangements for her to come to Stranraer where I would meet her at the station. Again I had arranged for a night in a hotel there rather than go on any further in one journey. Next day, we crossed on the ferry to Larne and arrived in Londonderry towards the end of the afternoon. I had booked a room in a hotel looking out on to the river just about in the centre of the town. I had to arrange the appropriate days off to do this, and that presented no trouble.

The next day she decided she would look at one or two of the other places which I had been offered before coming with me to visit the house which I thought was the ideal one. When I saw her later in the day, she had been to look at a few of them and very quickly came away deciding that they were not the sort of place she would wish to stay in. Towards the end of the day, we went to see the house that I had chosen and she immediately fell in love with it. We arranged to move in the following day. When we were in there the next day we asked about what we should use for meals and she said, 'Use the lounge at the front and have your meals in there and use anything you wish from the china cabinet or anywhere else.' Although it gave us great pleasure to use the items of such quality or value, at the same time it created a worry in case we broke anything. We were almost afraid to open the doors of the china cabinet and get something out for a meal, but I very much doubt if she would have worried if anything had been broken. She was a very, very nice person to get on with. We discovered that her brother was the proprietor of one of the successful shops in Londonderry and from what we heard, he was quite a wealthy person. We had been extraordinarily lucky to end up there: we were in such comfort and felt so relaxed.

Of course, everything is not always quite as perfect as one assumes, and on the second or third night I said to her, 'Shall I lock the back door now that we're all going to bed?' She replied, that the house was the 'official' escape route from Londonderry jail. They would come over the wall at the bottom of our garden, drop down, come along, and open the back door and let themselves in. They came straight through the house and went out of the front door. 'You hardly knew that anybody had been,' she said. 'If, on the other hand, the door is locked, they will smash it down and they will come in and they will smash up everything in the house they can get hold of, and smash up the occupants as well.' So, as I say, there was a slight cloud on the horizon. I had to make sure always that the back door was unlocked. There never was an escape while we were there, fortunately, so we didn't have to find out if the story was true or false. I gather that if they made a mistake and came over one of the houses on either side the same thing applied.

We also began to realise that the situation in Northern Ireland was rather tense to say the least of it. We also realised that the road we were living in which was more like a square was largely Catholic. When we walked along the road we had the sense of being kept under observation the whole time. The houses all seemed to have net curtains downstairs and one was conscious of people behind them keeping a watch on us. You could see the curtains moving occasionally with a little twitch, which indicated that there was someone behind them very close to the curtains. We soon got used to this sort of thing and accepted it. I think the tension all round was rather more intense than it should have been. I know of nowhere where everyone is in agreement and there are no problems.

I was on duty every fourth night but this was no particular trouble, and Marjorie was quite happy in the house on her own, at least on her own with the lady who owned it. I had various duties in the barracks which I had to pay attention to, and one somewhat unusual one: I was divisional officer for the Wrens. This was because there was no Wrens' officer in the barracks, and I believe the most senior person was a petty officer Wren. I was also responsible for the upkeep of all the barracks which meant that, amongst other things, I would, from time to time, have to visit the Wrens' quarters to check that everything was in order. I did this when I thought there would be no Wrens in the building, particularly none of them in bed, and to the best of my recollection I succeeded in this aim.

I was also responsible for some of the Naval personnel in the barracks but now I cannot remember what part of the organisation it was. Life was quite easy compared to what I had been used to in the past, as far as my Naval duties were concerned.

I was told that I was entitled to an afternoon off periodically and I would have to ask the base commander for his permission when I proposed to take the afternoon off. Within a few days, I had discovered by talking to other people that the base commander was never in the base in the afternoon as he took every afternoon off himself. I gathered that he went off to spend the afternoon with a certain friend of his who lived in Londonderry. Nod nod, wink wink! I realised that if I waited until he left the barracks and never asked him for the afternoon off I could say that I had looked for him but couldn't find him. By this means I could take off more than one afternoon per week which was my allowance, and nobody seemed to miss me if I wasn't there.

The result was that I took two or three afternoons a week off and we went off on our own journeys around the place. In the Navy one is expected to show initiative! We soon exhausted the things to do in Londonderry so had to look further afield. Londonderry has a city wall running round the centre of the city on the high ground and it is around this wall that the Apprentice Boys traditionally take their march one day a year with a band and everything else. Below the wall on one side, was a long road called the Bogside which was entirely Catholic, and we were advised not to walk along it. However, after five years in the Navy one could not give way to this sort of conduct, and we used to walk along it. Although we were conscious of people watching us, nobody seemed to worry, and we hoped that they would assume because we were going along there we were of their religion.

On one occasion, I had asked the landlady whether the chimney needed sweeping and she said, 'Oh no, you cannot get a chimney swept in Londonderry because there are no chimney sweeps.' She said, 'When the Apprentice Boys have their march, assuming the wind is in the right direction, all the Roman Catholics will set fire to their chimneys to try to smoke the Apprentice Boys out.' Religious differences can have some unusual effects.

Londonderry is situated at the landward end of Lough Foyle. One of our favourite trips was along the coast on the north west side of Lough Foyle. I believe we used to take a bus part of the way along, then walk on further to Moville, have afternoon tea, and then come back. I think we could get on a bus more or less anywhere we wanted on the coast when we felt like it. The two principal urban areas along there were Moville and Greencastle. I think we must have got there by bus because the bus services around the area were pretty good, and we could travel there some of the way, and get off, walk a bit in the country, then go into the town and possibly move on a bit further. We didn't experience any major difficulty in getting about when we wanted to take an afternoon off and part of the evening.

Life generally in Northern Ireland was quite different from anything we had experienced in England; and this does not only relate to the difference between the two communities but to all sorts of other things as well. Meat was rationed as in England, the only difference being that in Londonderry the rationing system meant that one could only visit the butcher once a day, which was what people would normally do anyway. Needless to say, the animals came across the border in the night so there was no real shortage of meat, and we ate very well in Northern Ireland as did everyone else.

After my first night on duty, walking around the base and wondering when we were going to be jumped by terrorists, I went to the guard house just in time to see a horse and cart arrive outside with a load of hay which, of course, mystified me. I asked the petty officer of the guard what it was doing, because I had a suspicion it might be full of explosives or something, but the answer was much more simple – 'Oh, that is the egg supply just arrived.' Apparently, the hay was merely a cover for a load of eggs which had been smuggled over the border to Londonderry to be disposed of, which presented no problem whatsoever. I went out and bought a dozen or two, although I have no recollection of what I put them in, probably my hat to get them back into the base; however, my wife was very surprised and delighted when I arrived home in the evening with a consignment of fresh eggs. Further enquiry revealed that in Londonderry one could buy extra strong egg boxes for people to post eggs home to England. I acquired four or six of these. I would send a box home every week to my mother and a couple of boxes to Marjorie's family which was much larger than mine. A few days later they would post the boxes back to me empty, but there might be a few odd sweets, chocolates and things in them, as the size of the compartments for the eggs didn't allow anybody to put anything else in. So, with six or eight boxes I was able to keep the supply going quite well at a reasonably low cost. We certainly had no difficulty with our meals and eating out was just as easy.

In Londonderry there was what was known as the 'toy railway' and this ran in either direction and the coaches were just high enough for me to sit down inside. Each compartment would hold about four people and no more. The train was a miniature one in comparison to normal standards, and it would go rattling along the track. We went on it to Strabane and had a good look around there, then we decided to cross the river which was still the Foyle, to Lifford on the other side, and we walked across the bridge.

I have no recollection of any border controls or customs or anything like that. We were walking around the town which was not particularly large and we decided we wanted a meal so we kept a look out and saw a sign somewhere saying that meals were available and went in. It was really a rather large ordinary house and the front room was where meals were served. We looked at what was available and decided upon a steak, grilled or fried, I cannot remember which. In due course, this arrived. We each got a steak which virtually covered the whole plate and vegetables were piled on top of it including chipped potatoes and some form of greens. We slaved away for quite a time doing our best to get through it, and although it was very delicious it was just about impossible to eat the whole lot.

Just an example of how easy supplies were in that part of the world. I cannot remember what the rest of the meal was, but I have no doubt that the sweet was equally massive and when we'd finished the price was relatively normal. We never went there again and I suspect we were afraid of collapsing under the strain.

From time to time, we would go across one of the bridges to the other side of the river and walk down or walk up and admire the view of Londonderry from across the river. It is a very impressive sight. It is dominated by the city wall and the cathedral with its spire. The wall is not just a wall, it is a wall with a walkway behind it which, obviously, is wide enough to take the Apprentice Boys marching around, although clearly it was not built for that purpose, because it must have been built long before they had been thought of. Presumably, the object when it was built was to allow a body of soldiers to march around, although who they would be defending it against was not included in the history I was taught in my younger days. We would walk around the wall periodically to get a view of the countryside from the high ground, and in addition we went in the cathedral sometimes. We would sit down for a quiet thought and rest and say a few words in memory of all the people we knew back in England. We had on a few occasions been to a Sunday morning service there which was much the same, I suppose, as any we would have gone to in England.

One rather more unusual experience, however, was when I was duty officer on a Sunday and had to take a parade of men to the cathedral as it was a special service, possibly in commemoration of the forces – I don't know now. I marched them round and dismissed them outside the cathedral so they could go in as they wished and take a seat. The custom was that I would sit at the front and they would occupy approximately two rows of pews behind me;

and on this occasion I was there with Marjorie. It came as quite a surprise to us to discover that although they would go through the motions of complying with the service in terms of standing up and sitting down when appropriate, when it came to the hymns not a word came from any one of them at all.

I have no idea what the reason for this was, but it seemed to have been planned and certainly they were not all Roman Catholics, and I doubt whether more than two or three of them could have been. In any case, if they were Catholics and asked to be exempt they would have been exempt from attendance. I suppose we all had the feeling that there were tensions in the area and one always wondered what the end product of all this would be.

It took me back to my school days, and if any of my fellow students asked me to go to their church with them on a Sunday to take part in the worship I would agree. On occasions, this would include visiting them at their home and having a meal with them. This was not the main attraction, but I thought it was worth investigating different religions to see how they behaved and see what they had to offer. My religion was Church of England and my father was a sidesman in the church we attended. I had attended Confirmation classes and so on whilst I was attending services there. I have to say that I was not tempted to move to any other religion by this experience. I have no recollection of anybody asking me to attend a spiritualist service because I doubt if there was anybody of that ilk in the class, but I attended various other religions such as the Salvation Army, Methodists, Congregationals and Wesleyans.

Later in life, I can only say I developed the philosophy – if there is only one God, why is he fighting himself all over the world? As the years passed and I have grown older I find this more of a question than ever. It could lead to the question: what is the point of religion? In life, many of the people I have met who have been most friendly and helpful have been the ones who do not have a particular religion.

We continued our journeys around Northern Ireland since I had virtually every afternoon off except when I was on duty, without ever being booked out officially. We only travelled on each of the toy railways once for the experience, but from the point of view of getting somewhere else it was simpler and quicker to go by bus.

On one occasion, we visited the Giant's Causeway and we had to walk the last two or three miles to reach it. It is very impressive as a feature and it seemed quite remarkable that nature could have produced something like this all made up of six sided columns of stone, vertical and mostly of a different height sloping downwards from the inshore end to where they disappeared under the sea. Going down required great care to avoid missing one's footing and falling over, because it would be very unpleasant to go rolling down that sort of slope. Coming up was somewhat easier because we could see where we were putting our feet, whereas going down it was not always possible. It was very impressive but one visit was quite enough, especially since when we got to the top there was nowhere one could get a cup of tea without walking a similar distance again to the nearest tea shop.

Once at the weekend we went to Belfast to stay overnight. I had been once before on my own, but I cannot remember what the purpose was now. I think I must have gone to conduct some official business for the Royal Navy. Anyway, we stayed at the Grand Central Hotel in Belfast and to describe it as luxurious is an understatement. One particular memory is the ornate staircase going from the entrance hall up to the first floor. The carpet was so thick one had to hold the handrail to ensure one was getting on a step. When you trod on the carpet it seemed that the step sank down so that without holding on one could never be quite sure where one was standing and whether one was taking off from firm ground.

The bedrooms were luxurious, as was the dining room, the lounge and everything else, and it was, I suppose, the best hotel I have ever stayed in. Of course, I had made sure first that they gave the fifty per cent discount to Naval personnel before I booked in.

We walked around Belfast looking at the shops and various other things and we also walked along some of the well known roads which we hear rather more about these days. We would see the great signs painted up everywhere indicating the dispute between the two main religions. One had an uneasy feeling walking around, but nothing happened to us, so that was all right. It struck me afterwards and this particularly applied to the Bogside. I suppose that when we walked down there and I was in uniform they probably would not be sure whether I was Church of England or Roman Catholic, because they must have known that quite a number of people were Roman Catholic, even in England.

From Londonderry, we went all over the countryside around there, walking quite a lot and getting a bus periodically to move to somewhere else or to get back to Londonderry. One outstanding memory is that we would often be walking through the countryside and felt that we could do with a meal. If we went to a farmhouse and asked if they provided meals for visitors almost invariably the answer was, 'Well we don't normally, but come in, certainly we can give you a meal.' What we had would vary according to what they had available and was reasonably easy to prepare and get on the table; but I have to say that we came away every time much fuller than we had been before, and walking wasn't quite so easy afterwards. The people of Northern Ireland were particularly friendly and it seemed such a pity that there has been this dispute going on for so long.

This time last century, of course, Ireland was all one country as part of Great Britain. The Irish Free State was formed, as far as I'm aware, in about 1917 towards the end of the First World War. I always understood from people there that the real aim of establishing Northern Ireland was to keep the shipyards and industrial areas of the north, around Belfast. The southern part of Ireland was largely agricultural with nothing much of an industrial nature. Great Britain could not do much about it because it was busily engaged fighting Germany in the First World War, and, as far as I'm aware, it was not until about 1922 that Eire was finally recognised by Great Britain. As everyone knows they did not gain their main objective of acquiring an industrial area, because eventually that was not included in their area. I am never sure what is gained throughout the world by quarrels and disputes between countries or factions, and I often feel that the situation generally ends up worse as a result of the disputes than it was before.

My account of Northern Ireland makes it sound like a marvellous holiday at the expense of the Royal Navy. It certainly seems more like a holiday than my period in the Mediterranean when one would constantly be on full alert at a few seconds notice. However, I still had my duties in the barracks to perform, including being officer of the guard one night in four, and all the various duties in the base. As far as I remember, I was responsible for the repair and maintenance of all the buildings. I had to deal with various personnel matters, with the people under me and I was still acting as the duty officer every few days. On top of all this, I had the very onerous duty of posting eggs home to Great Britain from time to time! My period of duty in Londonderry was approximately two and a half months only, and we certainly seemed to have packed a great deal into that period.

Early in March I was informed that I was about to be discharged from the Royal Navy. It appears that I was due for approximately two months' or eight weeks' leave and this seemed quite an attractive proposition. I had to go to Belfast for the formal discharge and paperwork to be carried out, and again we stayed in the Grand Central Hotel. I went to the discharge centre which was situated some miles from the city centre. I walked there on my own. I was, of course, entitled to a period of leave on discharge.

Chapter Seventeen

Discharge from the Royal Navy: the Long Journey Back to Civilian Life

My final release from Naval service class A was on the 20th May, 1946 about seven weeks from the date when I attended the centre in Belfast. I had to go through the appropriate paperwork, although by now my memory of what took place is very vague. The problem arose when I went to the room where I had to be kitted out for civilian life. I don't recall being given a bowler hat but there was trouble when it came to fitting me out with a suit. As I am six feet tall, they had nothing that would fit me, and this caused some consternation. I assured them that I had a civilian suit with me and could wear that for the time being, and arrangements were made for me to be visited on my return home by a tailor who was responsible for kitting out problem cases. I did not get home for quite a long time after this and a date was made for me to inform him when I was back at home, and, in due course, he turned up from somewhere near Sheffield.

He measured me up and showed me a few patterns which he could make up for me, and I chose a pale grey, pinstripe suit, double breasted with trousers with turn-ups.

This arrived in about two weeks and really was quite marvellous. It was a beautiful soft wool and I was wearing it for a long time as my number one suit. I cannot remember exactly what happened about shoes but I don't suppose they had any to fit me and these probably had to follow by some means or other.

I returned to the hotel and greeted Marjorie as a civilian. We spent three days in Belfast, looking around at various things, having meals and so on, and we had decided that it would be nice to visit my uncle Harry who lived in Dublin. I telephoned him to see if it would be feasible to come, and I was assured that I would be very welcome and they would be very pleased to accommodate both of us. Arrangements were made for me to arrive in Dublin railway station on a certain train and I would be met at the station. I had met him before but a long time ago, and I was not at all sure whether I would recognise him or whether he would recognise me.

I had to wear my civilian clothes to go into Eire and, in due course, we arrived at the station, and waited around for somebody to meet us. But we could see no signs of anybody who looked likely to be waiting for us. When we were beginning to wonder what to do the station loudspeaker came on, and said, 'Would Mr and Mrs Denton please go to the reception area where somebody is awaiting to welcome them.' We went and to our surprise were met by a person who was probably five or ten years older than me – this was not what we were expecting. He made us feel very welcome and told us that he was married to Harry Denton's eldest daughter, Sheila, and they lived in a house some distance from where he was. His name was Thornton and he worked for Dublin City Council and his position was, I believe, chief scientist, or what we would call in England a public health officer. He took us to his home by car, and we were introduced to his wife, unloaded our baggage and were shown a very attractive double bedroom which would be ours for our stay. We chatted away, and had an evening meal with them. They had two young sons and a young daughter, but I cannot remember their Christian names now.

On the next day we went into Dublin to see various sights and features and, of course, look at the Liffey and cross over it. We had a quick visit to Phoenix Park, although a visit to look at it from one side was quite enough as it was so large and fairly plain and did not encourage us to feel like walking round it.

One memorable event was going to lunch on one of the main roads in Dublin, although I cannot remember what it was now. We went into a high quality looking restaurant or hotel and had a meal which was beautifully served and very attractive. No doubt we had some wine with it, and when we came at the end to the coffee, the coffee was poured into both cups and we added sugar and stirred it up. The waiter was about to pour some cream into it and I said to him, 'Do you mind if I do that?' and he handed me the cream jug. I turned the spoon upside down and gently poured the cream on top, so that it flowed down the spoon and over the surface of the coffee where it remained, and I did this with both cups. He looked at me in surprise and said, 'Well, that's the first time I've ever seen that,' and he seemed to be quite impressed with it. I had come across it somewhere in the Mediterranean but only in one place and I haven't the faintest idea now where it was. I just wonder who it was who thought of Irish coffee.

The next day we were due to visit my uncle and aunt for tea in the early evening. We had made a rather unfortunate calculation, however, in visiting the Guinness brewery that afternoon, quite early in the afternoon. After we had looked around, we went into the tasting room where there were, altogether, about a dozen people who had come to taste the Guinness. Each man had a one pint tankard, and each lady a half pint tankard, and first of all we tried porter which is a weakened version of stout. This was quite pleasant but it appeared they expected us to drink the whole tankard full which we found very difficult, even with my Naval training, and I had to help Marjorie get through hers. Next came Guinness Stout, and this again was a full measure, despite our protests. Again, somehow, we got through it, and then we were confronted with Guinness Extra which is the export version of Guinness. Even stronger than the one we are normally accustomed to in the British Isles. By this time even tasting it was a real problem and I think we had to leave in the end with some of it still in the tankards.

We staggered out under the 'affluence of incohol' and then made our way to my uncle's residence. I'm not quite sure how we managed to keep awake through the meal, but somehow we managed it and hoped that we didn't appear to them to be too inebriated. We hoped that in Dublin everybody would be used to drinking large quantities of this product. We got through a couple of hours and left them to return to our hotel where we had a good night's sleep!

The next day, we planned to go on our journey, and this time we went back to Belfast and from there on to Larne to catch the ferry for Stranraer with the intention then of going to spend a few days in Glasgow.

We spent some time looking around Stranraer planning to get to Glasgow towards tea time in order to get into the St Enoch's Station Hotel which I had used several times in the past. Unfortunately, something went wrong with the train we were on and I think it broke down; we were very slow getting there and in the end we didn't get to Glasgow until something like nine o'clock in the evening. So we got a taxi straight to St Enoch's Hotel, only to find it was fully booked and they had no room at all. By the time we found this out we had unloaded all our baggage into the hall, only to discover there was no point in it. After the night porter had given us a cup of coffee, I went outside and found a taxi which picked us up, and I asked if he would try to find us a hotel for the night. Every hotel we tried was fully booked for some reason, and by about midnight we had got nowhere. In the end, he took us to a place where he thought we might get a bed for the night and they were able to offer us one so we went upstairs without baggage into a small single room with a double bed. We were too late to get a meal. By the time we had got ourselves in, we both realised it was not the sort of place we would wish to spend the night, and presumably it was designed for people who were unmarried. Hush Hush! Wink Wink! So we both went outside on the pretext of getting some food and found a taxi, and asked him if he would pick up our luggage and take us back to St Enoch's where I was going to ask the night porter if we could spend the night in the lounge until we could do something else.

We got to St Enoch's this time around midnight and the night porter was quite sympathetic and said we could spend the night in the lounge, if we didn't mind being on a settee. He brought us some food which was very welcome. After about half an hour, he came to us, and said there was a room booked for the night and the people were supposed to arrive by eight o'clock; they still hadn't turned up, so he would let us go there for the night. Up we went with our baggage, to be shown into a luxurious bedroom with everything you could think of: I had the impression that it was normally used for newly weds. It really was luxurious, and before he left we gave him a tip. I said, 'What do we do in the morning, go to the reception and see if they can book us in for two or three days?' He said to me, 'No – just sit tight and say nothing and I expect you'll be allowed to stay.' Whether he pulled a few strings with the receptionist I don't know, but we stayed there quite happily and in luxury for about three days, whilst I showed Marjorie around the city and all the things I knew about it. We also went on one or two excursions around the area to look at a bit of the countryside, travelled down the river and had a very enjoyable time. In a few days with all our baggage we made the short train journey to Edinburgh and booked into a hotel which was quite convenient to Princes Street.

The most outstanding place in Edinburgh is Princes Street, with all the monuments and ancient buildings on one side and the high quality shops on the other. We started off by walking along the street. There were small shops selling speciality items and also a few larger stores and we went in most of them and had a look around. I remember we bought something in one shop but for the life of me I cannot remember whether it was clothing or a souvenir or what it was.

The other attraction of this side of Princes Street is to get the wonderful view of all the historic buildings which are on the other side. In addition to the buildings, there are trees and gardens to add to the pleasure of it. We crossed over when we had reached, more or less, the end of the shops and went through the gardens. On the way, we saw the Scott monument and then we went to view the castle and the National War Memorial, both of which occupy high ground, and give a very good view of the city generally. We also went round inside and then we came back towards Princes Street visiting the Royal Scottish Academy and the National Gallery. Eventually, having walked through the gardens, we decided it was time to return to the other end and look for a meal.

The classic method of transport in Edinburgh was the tram unless one wanted a taxi. We got in a tram and proceeded back to our original point of departure which was a bit of a rattly ride but quite interesting. When we were getting towards our destination it stopped quite suddenly, and we could see there was a row of trams in front of us held up by some traffic problem. Within a matter of ten minutes or so, there were also trams queued up behind us until the whole length of Princes Street seemed to be blocked with them. At this stage, we got off to complete our journey on foot. I took a photograph of all the trams lined up the street and I should think there were fifty or more within a matter or ten or fifteen minutes. So, I suppose, Princes Street is the place in Edinburgh which remained in our minds for a very long time.

After that, we went and had lunch, although I have no recollection of what we had or where it was. After two or three days we decided to move on to our next destination, which was to visit my uncle and two aunts in Monkseaton, just north of Newcastle. We telephoned first to make sure they could accommodate us for a few nights. They were delighted to meet Marjorie and me, and we had a very pleasant stay there. We walked along the sea front from Monkseaton to Whitley Bay and then on to Cullercoats and, eventually, to Tynemouth. A distance of some four or five miles. Needless to say, we paused for refreshment periodically, and also had lunch on the way; and eventually returned to the house by bus.

Another day, we went to the north of the bay in which Whitley Bay stands, and where there is Holy Island with a lighthouse on top of it. One had to fit this journey in with tides, because it was only accessible on foot at low tide. We had time to have a quick look around the lighthouse and admire the view from it, and then return before getting wet feet!

One day, Marjorie and I went to Newcastle by travelling on the electric railway which ran from Monkseaton Station into Newcastle, and returned by a loop which went through the surrounding countryside. When the time came to return we went on the longer way round so that we could have a look at the countryside inland from the coastal towns, and it was very attractive and peaceful. I expect now it is all covered by developments and so on, and the beauty may well have disappeared like so many other places in the United Kingdom. It is an inevitable result of industrial, commercial and residential development and people's expectations.

The area which once would have housed four families with a small back yard each would now provide the land for one modern house and garden. This requires more land, roads and everything else that goes with it and it is an inevitable consequence of prosperity. Now they require a car to get into the country where previously they just walked a short distance.

I have never been greatly impressed with Newcastle and this visit was not significantly different from any other. My uncle was the manager of a large wholesale warehouse in Newcastle, and was a director of the firm of which it was a branch: their main establishment was in Manchester. It offered household goods and, although it was good to see it, we were not in a situation to buy anything significant, because we didn't know where we were going to end up. We went out and had lunch with him somewhere in Newcastle but I have no recollection of where it was except that the meal was very enjoyable.

After a few days here we headed south to the Leeds area where we had telephoned in advance and arranged to stay with my mother's sister at Horsforth. Her husband worked in Bradford, so he had a train journey every day to and from work. I had not seen them since before the war so it made a very pleasant change to visit them once again. Their daughter worked in the Income Tax Office and, as far as I can remember, the office had been evacuated to Wales. I cannot remember very clearly whether we met her at that time or not. However, she now lives on the outskirts of Worthing and we have been in touch ever since and she visited me for a day within the last few weeks. She spent most of her time with the Inland Revenue working on Super Tax, which is a welcome speciality for people who work in it, if not for the people who pay it.

We spent a day in Roundhay Park. A very attractive area not too far from the centre of Leeds, where we walked enjoying the atmosphere.

On another day we took the train to a station (or did it take us?) where we got off and walked across Ilkley Moor towards the Cow and Calf and climbed those two rock boulders. I have a photograph of myself standing on top of one of the large boulders, unfortunately with my head cut off, and one of Marjorie, who had taken it, sitting on the smaller rock at the bottom later on. We then moved on to Otley where I had relatives, who I used to visit pre-war; we enjoyed the area very much. I found the house where they lived and we went in to visit them, and I recognised the familiar scenes straight away. Unfortunately, the parents whom I had known had departed, and other members of the family, whom I had met before, were occupying the house then; nevertheless it was a very enjoyable occasion.

On a more recent visit to Leeds in the last few years we stayed north of Leeds and visited various places which were familiar to me and, to some extent, to Marjorie. In particular, I wanted to identify a painting I had – I thought it was a house but it turned out to be a mill since demolished. I have now succeeded in identifying where it was, with the aid of the Leeds city tourist office.

I am not quite sure why we did all this touring, except that it created a very welcome break from all the years of separation during the war, and was a period of relaxation before getting back to civilian life. However, all good things come to an end and eventually we had to get on a train and return to Kettering. By the time we got back to Kettering, my Naval service was over in about two weeks, so I had to start thinking about the return to civilian life, which was a matter that aroused many doubts in my mind.

There was quite a lot to be done to get ourselves established back in the community, partly because we were unaccustomed to living any normal life in the community, and also because of the strains of war, the separation and all the other by-products of war. First of all, we had to get our belongings together. We had a bedroom in my mother's house, and used the room in the front of the house with a bay window as our normal living quarters, although by no means was the house divided into two. There was a certain amount of working together and doing whatever we could to fit in comfortably without causing too much trouble. The bedroom we were in could not house very many of our belongings and some of these had to go to Marjorie's parents' house, and some to other members of her family who could provide a bit of spare room for us. They were all sympathetic to the problems of people coming back after a long period of war.

Within a week we were getting ourselves sorted out and reasonably under control, although it was not particularly easy. I went to visit the education office in Kettering where I had been working before the war, and was surprised to receive a reprimand from the education officer. He said, 'We have been expecting you back for weeks, why didn't you come straight home and report to the office when you were demobilised?' He totally overlooked the fact that it required a period to get oneself back into a normal point of view. The government, when passing the National Service Act before the war, had stipulated that everybody's post before the war would be guaranteed them when they returned after the war was over. This sounded very impressive, but bear in mind that people who were subject to the National Service Act were the younger element of the population, aged from about twenty upwards. Obviously, when they went into the forces they were in relatively junior positions, but in a period of six years would have hoped to have moved up the scale to a higher post and higher salary in civilian life. I had taken my intermediate examination in public and local government prior to the war and passed that with credit.

I immediately started to look for posts elsewhere, although I did not really wish to leave my home town quite so quickly after the war, and would have stayed longer if the post that I was offered had entailed some promotion rather than a lowering of my duties. I decided that if I was going to move it would be useful to gain experience of a more industrial area than Kettering, which was primarily a market town with some industry. I watched the educational press for vacancies, and applied for one or two. My duties in the Kettering office were less onerous than when I left, and I was only doing routine work, with little responsibility, and no links with schools or external visits.

Fortunately, Staffordshire were reorganising their educational system after the war and creating under the county office three divisional offices with more or less direct responsibility for the establishments under their charge. I applied for a post of administrative assistant in the southern divisional office which was based at Brownhills in Staffordshire, on the edge of the Cannock Chase coalfield. I made out an application for it and I cannot remember who I gave as referees, but certainly one of them was not in Kettering education office, and was as far as I remember one of the Councillors who was chairman of the education committee. He lived fairly close to my parents in my earlier days. I was invited to interview, went along and was offered the appointment.

Although I had had no experience of educational administration for approximately six years, I was rather surprised that I had succeeded and I assumed that probably all the other people who were applying had no experience. They might have been influenced by the fact that I had held a commission in the Royal Navy during the war, but it may have been also that not many people had applied for the post because the area was not a particularly attractive one. The next problem was finding somewhere to live, but my only means of transport at that time was my bicycle or public transport, which in practice generally speaking meant buses. As far as I remember, the lodgings I obtained were in Brownhills, not a great distance from the office. I then set about finding some accommodation where Marjorie could join me, put an advert in the local paper, and went round to look at the various places which I had been offered.

I finally settled on a house in Hammerwich occupied by a retired builder and his wife who was president of the local Women's Institute. It was a large house in the centre of the village; we shared it between us and we had a very pleasant downstairs room looking out from the front of the house, and they had the one on the other side of the entrance hall. The kitchen was shared but on the whole there was no conflict over the times when Marjorie required it, and when the owner did.

We had a very pleasant bedroom upstairs and the bathroom was quite large. We were in reasonable distance of Lichfield which was a very attractive small town, and when Marjorie went shopping there she was given a lift by car to do her shopping and came back by car also, so that was not too great a strain.

There were no shops in Hammerwich of any help. I used to cycle about two miles or so to the office and this was quite pleasant in fine weather, but when it poured with rain it was another matter entirely. I was completely equipped with weather-proof gear so I survived that all right, but it was very, very different from my previous years in the Navy.

It seemed at times that, although we had been fighting the Germans during the war, we were now fighting everybody to get ourselves established in society. It was not easy! During the winter, we had some heavy snow and, although it looked very beautiful, it really did create a problem, because on occasion there would be only one road out of Hammerwich open, and that of course was in the wrong direction for me. I remember once when it was particularly bad I walked to work about two miles or so, and I got through quite well. But when it came to returning home in the evening the drifts were getting really high and I was struggling up the road when I met the local roadman coming back with his shovel on his shoulder. He was using it to shovel his way through the snow where it was too deep to walk safely.

He was most concerned about me going in the other direction and said I'd never get through on the road. He told me to get through the hedge on to the field at the side, walk up the middle of the field where the snow was quite shallow and find a suitable place to get through the hedge into the next field, and so on until I got to Hammerwich, which was about three or four fields away. He also cut for me from the hedge, a stick about five feet long with a fork top, and chopped it to the appropriate condition he required, and gave that to me. He told me to take it with me, and to use it to lever myself through the snow where I couldn't avoid going through some which was fairly deep.

Fortunately, I got back to Hammerwich safely, and I still have a photograph of Marjorie standing in a passage cut through a snow drift six feet deep The interesting thing is that the snow had frozen and one could walk over the top of the snowdrift in that condition, with the footpath cut through beneath and to one side. Life could be most difficult at times!

Fortunately, in the office the caretaker cooked a midday meal for those people who wanted to have one in the office because they didn't live near enough to get home. This would be eaten in the committee room which was on the ground floor, so that worked out pretty well. Getting established after the war and getting sorted out was not easy, however.

I had got my capital sum and gratuity from the Royal Navy and also, to my surprise I received prize money. I had assumed that this was only paid to the personnel of ships which actually captured an enemy ship, but I discovered that all the enemy ships captured during the war were valued and the proceeds were allocated to all the people serving in the Royal Navy according to their rank and length of service. I am not sure now, but in total I seem to remember I had about three hundred pounds which was a very good sum to have available for housing. I had decided that the best place to live in the area would be in Chasetown which was about as close to Brownhills as I could get, and the town was more attractive and pleasant on the whole. There was a good range of shops quite close to where we hoped to live.

We found a house for sale in Chasetown and as we knew nothing whatever about the builder or the quality of it, I decided to ask the young lady in the office who was my typist and lived in Chasetown. She came back the next day and said she had asked her next door neighbour who was a builder, and the answer was, 'Don't buy that house, he's a Jerry builder.' He added, however, that he would build one for me for one thousand two hundred pounds. I could buy the plot of land for one hundred pounds. This sounded like heaven but I asked about a building licence. She replied, 'It appears that Lichfield City Council have three building licences to issue, and no applicants.' Within a few days I had a building licence issued, and we had agreed for him to build the house. It took about four months to build and was of extremely good quality, and we could make no complaints at all about it. It was built mostly in the evenings, as apparently he had the contract to build about fifty council houses in Brownhills. He put his men on working on my house in the evenings because it encouraged them to get some extra money, and he was not allowed to pay overtime in the building contract.

Perhaps the heavens were shining on us after all, despite all the hardships and separation of war. The house had a very attractive view, from the front bay window upstairs, of some three or four miles looking across a large reservoir which fed the canal system. Also we could see the parish church, with colliery winding gear close by! From the back bedroom window we could see some eight miles across country including a well-known landmark in the area, and we had a farmer's field at the bottom of the garden with cows in it. There was, however, to be a great deal of hard work in getting the garden and the site under control.

My next door neighbour's brother was a miner working in a four foot coal seam, and I gathered that he was willing to come and do some gardening for me. I asked if he could come and dig and level the front of the house for a lawn. He did this and to my surprise he did the whole lot on his knees, as this was the only way he could work after spending all his working life kneeling in the shallow drift of the mine where he was cutting coal. His strength appeared to be enormous.

Chapter Eighteen

Victory after Six Years: Frustration and Hard Work Ahead

The war was over and I had ended up much better than I had expected and much safer as well. I had been enrolled into the Royal Navy with the assumption that I would become a writer, but I became an ordinary seaman in June 1940. I was on a depot ship at Scapa after two months followed by the North Atlantic in December 1940. I became a sub-lieutenant RNVR just over a year after joining the Navy. I had seen three years service at sea mostly in the Mediterranean and, in addition, I saw very many parts of the world which I would not otherwise have seen.

At the same time my wife had been on the staff of Weetabix throughout the war and I think she probably worked as hard as I did in various ways. She was looking after the finances of Weetabix and submitting reports periodically to the director, and at the same time doing a lot of other things. She was secretary of the Weetabix sports and social club. She did a certain amount of work voluntarily on the production line to help the war effort. She also did voluntary work at the Kettering Control Centre and at a

WVS canteen and whatever else she could to help the war effort. She used to visit Wellingborough where the mother of one of her staff ran a convalescent home for free French soldiers and she used to help with the work there. This gave her a great interest in French which I had also developed, and this was going to be invaluable later, in terms of learning French better than she had learnt it at school, and giving us a strong link with France when the people she knew moved back home after the war. It led to many visits to us by French families and friends, and to our many visits to France.

We also had the task of rebuilding our lives after the war and getting our feet back on the ladder. After all the responsibilities of a Naval officer and captain of a ship, I had returned to a job which was far less responsible than I had before the war. I moved very quickly to working in one of the divisional offices of the Staffordshire Educational Committee and we settled down in the area, building our own house in Chasetown, or rather having it built in Chasetown, with a few modifications which we wanted to the standard design. In addition to my small payment from the Royal Navy which was in the form of a gratuity, I had Naval prize money. Marjorie had an allowance as the wife of a Naval officer which she built up to quite a useful saving. Since also she was working and getting a salary, she was able to save quite a bit of her monthly pay and build up many possessions ready for the end of the war. Amongst other things, we had bought furniture and put it into store with a removal firm. Without this financial stability, we would not have been able to afford the deposit on a house or to get the grounds laid out and fully equipped.

All we had was the front hedge which was trimmed to a reasonable height and a wire fence around the garden. We planted a hedge and built a shed, and I built a terrace across the back of the house with a footpath down to the hedge planted across to divide the flower part of the garden from the vegetable part. Hard work but welcome and enjoyable. Our transport was two bicycles which did not help a great deal, but were useful in that I could cycle to work and I also could cycle to a number of schools within a reasonable distance. We were on the edge of the coal mining area and from the front bedroom window we could see the parish church with the colliery winding gear beside it.

While there we had some lovely walks across the area and could see some eight or ten miles across the fields at the back of the house. We had a dog which was good exercise when we went walking, and the person in the end cottage close to us would look after it when we were away. My pay had improved but was not what I had aimed at. However, the chairman of the Education Committee for the area was a member of the County Education Committee, and various other people who I knew well were also on the committee. One member had a shop across the road from the Education Office. I cannot remember exactly what he sold but it was generally small items of furniture and household articles.

We had our first daughter in 1948, approximately two years after we had moved there, but we would really have liked to have moved to somewhere away from the dirt of the black country. After I had picked up the threads again of the education service after a gap of about six years, I began to feel that I wanted to move somewhere else with rather more responsibility. I also realised that having passed my intermediate exam before the war I had to study and get my finals as quickly as I could. This meant that I had to deliberately shut myself away for an hour or two every day to carry on my studies, and this did not make life particularly easy for Marjorie with a daughter to care for. We got through it with a struggle and by 1950 I had taken my examination and I became an Associate of the Chartered Institute of Secretaries; I specialised in local and central government, and gained a distinction which was very gratifying. I started applying for various posts in parts of the country but never got an interview.

I applied for a post in Hampshire where they were advertising for four administrative assistants in the County Education office. One for primary education, one for secondary education, one for further education and one for sites and buildings.

I got an interview and came down to Winchester for it. Quite a number of people were being interviewed for the four posts and they took more or less all day. My turn came around by about twelve o'clock and I went in, and felt the interview was going reasonably well, when the County Education officer said to me, 'Which post would you opt for Denton? Primary education or secondary education?' the two which I had applied for. To my amazement, I heard my mouth say, 'Further education, sir,' and I wondered whatever had come over me. They thumbed through my application and he said, 'But you didn't apply for further education.' We all returned home while they considered the matter and I was living very anxiously for a time until about ten days later I received a letter offering me the post in further education.

It is surprising in life how a sudden impulse becomes the factor which determines one's whole future.

Picking up the threads of civilian life and establishing a home and a career were by no means easy, as I had lost six years of progression up the ladder. Although we were extremely lucky to get a building licence and have a house built for us in Chasetown, it involved a great deal of effort in establishing the home and garden. I was also studying for my final examinations. This inevitably created a severe emotional strain on both of us and I have no doubt that this became transferred to our daughter indirectly, as I virtually had to shut myself off from the family to carry on with my studies and get my qualifications. I think that most people think that when war is over that is the finish, and they do not realise that for the people involved there is still a great deal of hard work in getting back to normal and getting established. Instead of living our lives as a whole, we had to live them in bits and pieces. Fortunately eventually we got over it and got established but not without effort and strain.

My appointment in Hampshire began on the 1st January, 1951 and I had to make the journey by train as at the time I was still dependent upon public transport and my bicycle. I obtained lodgings in St Paul's Hill just beside the church but I cannot remember now how I obtained them. I imagine that somebody at the castle or in Winchester, must have suggested to me where I could live. When I got there I found two other lodgers in the house. One of whom worked in the county treasurer's department and the other at a car sales garage in Winchester. None of us particularly liked living in lodgings and all of us used to go out quite a lot in the evenings, walking around the town, and calling in a pub for a drink on the way home. I think in that period I must have gone into virtually every pub and hotel bar in Winchester.

Going home to visit Marjorie and Susan was quite an effort because I had to travel by train and had to change at least twice, and finish the journey from Birmingham by bus. All this was a considerable strain and, with hindsight, this must have obviously fed through on to our daughter, Susan, who I am sure did not understand why sometimes I was there and sometimes I was not.

In about February I had a very bad attack of flu and was in bed; the landlady called the doctor who gave me tablets and told me to remain in bed. I then received an urgent message from Marjorie telling me to come home at once because Susan had been admitted to Lichfield hospital with a problem in her stomach. The flu obviously was not going to stop me and I got a taxi to the station and travelled by train to arrive at Birmingham. Apparently, Marjorie had arranged, although I did not know this, for the person who lived in the little cottage close to us and who was a taxi driver, to meet me at the end of the platform, and he said he was going to run me home. I very much doubt whether I would have got home on two feet without this wonderful help. The next day we went to Lichfield to see her and I was just about on my feet and wandering around in a bit of a daze. Susan had improved a little by then and began to improve much more when she saw Marjorie and me together. I am not at all sure whether we understand the reactions of young children to dislocations in their routine. I sent a medical certificate to the County Education office with an explanation as to what had happened. I got back to Winchester and resumed my previous routine of going home at the weekend whenever I could.

I found out that the Council had various flats for occupation temporarily by new staff moving into the area, and I put my name down for one. By about the end of March I was informed that I could have a flat in Park Road. In view of the fact that we had a young baby, it was a ground floor flat which they allocated to me. Although this was very good, it was not all that convenient with a young child because the two flats above had access through the hall and stairs to reach their flats, so we could never be certain when anybody would be coming or going, although they were very considerate and helped as much as they could. It meant also that our accommodation was divided by the hallway, with the kitchen on one side and the lounge dining room on the other, with the bedrooms at the back of the house. Our bedroom was quite large, so we put Susan's sleeping quarters in the corner of it. I had to arrange an alarm system over the cot and leading to the lounge so that we could hear if she woke up and cried.

I had decided by this time to buy a car and although I placed an order for a new one I did not really hope to get it. In the end I had to buy a second hand one, which cost me the same money or a little more than a new one. Such is life after a war! We were in the flat for nearly a year, and having a car made a great deal of difference to our ability to get about and particularly to return to our home town of Kettering to visit our relatives and stay for a few days. Being able to get into the countryside of Hampshire and to have an occasional visit to the seaside certainly improved life no end.

All this time we were looking for another house but without any great success. Eventually, we heard of one which was for sale and which had been built in 1951; and in those days the building licence system and the controls on prices were still in operation. We managed to negotiate a deal and moved in early in 1952. At last, almost six years after I was discharged from the Royal Navy, we felt we were beginning to get settled in life, although there was a great deal to be done to the house and the garden. I did most of the work myself with help from visitors from Kettering who would come from time to time and do a certain amount for me. As a reminder of the times, the house had two fifteen amp power points in it, one downstairs and one upstairs and the hot water was produced by an anthracite or coke fired stove in the kitchen, which we succeeded in keeping alight all night. There were no radiators whatever and no double glazing, so the house could be extremely chilly in the winter. I can remember occasions when we would be sitting in the lounge in the evening with our overcoats on even with a coal fire – this seems quite incredible these days. When we moved in the weather didn't even work on our side. I was standing in the porch wiping the snow off the top of all the furniture that came in. We did have an electric convector heater which we used to put in the hall at nights and we had an electric radiator which we could put in the lounge when we were not lighting a fire. (After I had put a power point in the lounge!)

Our second daughter, Angela, was born in 1952 in Winchester, which meant Marjorie had quite enough to do. We had our first car by then, which cost me second-hand as much as a new one, for which the waiting time would be several years. I taught Marjorie to drive and she passed her test at the first attempt. Usually, she used it in the morning, and it was used by me usually in the afternoon and evenings.

As far as work was concerned obviously I had quite a lot to learn. In terms of further education we had one small technical college with approximately six teaching spaces – a technical evening institute at Farnborough which met in the evenings in the premises of the RAE technical college. We had the Hampshire Farm Institute and the Winchester School of Art which met in part of the library building in North Walls. There were also some thirty-five or forty evening institutes spread over the county, and I also looked after community centres, village halls and youth clubs of which there would not be many at that time. I visited them all as soon as I could to get an idea of what they were like, and I also used to attend the governors' meetings of those bodies that had governors.

One difficult task was to submit proposals to the Board of Education for the building of new colleges and the extension and improvement of the facilities that existed. Looking through the files as to what had taken place before I arrived, I discovered that nothing had been approved, and I came to the conclusion that the submissions that were being made were mere requests for something rather than statements of justification. I spoke to my opposite numbers in Dorset and in the Isle of Wight and they kindly sent me copies of the submissions they had made recently: I could see that ours needed improvement. After this experience, I began to get approval for various projects. It was not easy to persuade the officials in London that there was a need for a college where one did not exist previously. I dealt with this to some extent by inviting the appropriate official down for the day, and taking him around to show him the situation and then for a respectable meal somewhere, at Hampshire's expense of course. When he went back to London he was rather more sympathetic. Approvals gradually came through and, in the end, when Hampshire took over the colleges of Portsmouth and Southampton I was looking after fourteen colleges of further and higher education. There had also been improvements for schools, in the building of youth wings or youth buildings at various secondary schools where there were no facilities for young people at all. I didn't get much spare time and I was frequently out till late in the evening. Theoretically, I could take time off later on to compensate for this, but it was very, very rare for me to obtain any, and I only took advantage of this when I particularly needed to do something for myself in the daytime.

I used to attend regional meetings in Reading and also from time to time as far away as Somerset. That involved a very long day away from home. In addition, I also overlooked the County Library Service and the Museum Service for the whole county. This involved about five museums in Hampshire and I had to attend regional meetings relating to museums. Needless to say, this was a very different world from anything else I was used to and the people I used to meet were quite different from anybody else I had ever met before.

At that time, the County Library Service was entirely in North Walls where the Winchester School of Art also had some teaching capacity upstairs. There were a few small units around the county as well which we looked after. I was involved with the county librarian and the chief mechanical engineer in the County Surveyor's Department, in the design and building of the first mobile library in Hampshire at Waterlooville. At the time it was regarded as a great success, and now of course there are very, very many more than there were at that time. So, altogether I was moving in a very different world to my six years in the Royal Navy. We were, of course, fighting for what we believed in, and what we wanted, just the same as in the Royal Navy, but the procedure was vastly different. And, in a funny sort of way, I enjoyed it all as it was a severe challenge.

Chapter Nineteen

France, the French Language and the French Way of Life

Both Marjorie and I had learnt French at school, although it had little use afterwards and consequently lay dormant. It came back to life with her visits to the convalescent home at Wellingborough, and her understanding of the French way of life began to develop. I expect that virtually all of the French soldiers who were recuperating there had no knowledge or understanding of English. Although Mrs Mitchell was born in France she had married her husband as an English soldier serving in France in the First World War and they lived in England afterwards somewhere in the region of the Thames. Their two daughters Pauline and Thérèse spoke English as their first language. There was, however, a lot of French conversation there, particularly in the presence of the wounded French soldiers. During the war, in about 1942, Pauline married Camille Genu who had by then recovered from his wartime experiences, except that he was left with a right hand and wrist which were damaged, and he had difficulty in holding anything or using his right hand to any great extent. Her sister, Thérèse, married Jean Simon. During the war, Pauline had a daughter called Claudine, and later moved with her husband to London where they lived in a flat: he became chauffeur to the Duke of Luxembourg. I can remember that at some time in London, Marjorie and I visited them in their flat – I assume it must have been after I returned to England from the Mediterranean. Naturally, when one knew a French family, and a family who spoke quite a lot of French, understanding of the country and the people became much clearer.

My knowledge of the French language and customs became much improved through living, shopping and drinking in French North Africa where, although there was a local language, there were many French people and French was the predominant language. I had known and visited the French family in Algiers, and when one became a fairly regular visitor to certain establishments one got more involved in the language and the customs. My main use and interest in French, of course, developed in Corsica where I spent quite a lot of time, and got to know many people very well.

When the Mitchell family lived in England there were two sons as well, one of whom lived in the north of England. This meant that after the war Madame Mitchell and Pauline would come over to England periodically on visits, and they always included us in their itinerary. Being in Winchester, we were handy and there were occasions when we would meet whoever was coming over on the ferry and bring them to us; after a stay of a night or two I would often take either or both of them on to Oxford, where we would meet the brother from the north who came down to Oxford. We would have a meal and then she would move on northwards and the same thing would be repeated on her trip back south again.

This generated our interest in France, especially as they would bring over gifts of French food and wine. In the early years after the war, with two young children we could hardly go to France. However, in the mid 1960s, when they were both around sixteen years of age, we paid our first visit to France together with them. We sailed on the ferry to Cherbourg and had a good crossing – this was quite interesting to all of us. We set off on the road south to Avranches and spent the first night at Coutances. The hotel provided bed and breakfast, but did not have a restaurant or provide any other food. This suited us quite well, because we had a large case of food which we could eat satisfactorily, and we had a little stove on which we could boil water. We did not wish to go headlong into French food until we had been in the country a little longer.

We had a walk around and a look at the shops, many of which were still open, and I believe we went into the church to see what that was like. We were heading for Camille and Pauline's house in St Molf. She had arranged to meet us on the approach to a certain town. She said she would then guide and lead us on to St Molf. Unfortunately, when we were approaching the town we could see no sign of her at all, so we stopped and awaited developments but after about half an hour or so we came to the conclusion that something had gone wrong, and we would have to press on ourselves. We carried on and got through the town, but as we were heading out to the south of the town we saw her somewhat impatiently waiting at the edge of the road. This was due to a French form of speech which we had not anticipated. She was talking about *her* approach to the town, whereas we had taken it for granted that it was *our* approach to the town where we would be met.

It was fortunate we did meet her, and she guided us to St Molf, to park right outside the door, which we would certainly have had much more difficulty in finding if we had been on our own. We went in, had a light lunch and a more normal meal during the evening. We had a look around St Molf which is quite a small village but the surrounding countryside is rather attractive. The Mitchell parents had moved back to France as soon as possible after the liberation of France and Madame Mitchell was running a restaurant called La Petite Cremiare at Guerande which is a walled city and a very attractive place. We visited the well-known resort of La Baule and other places around, including Vannes, and we began to get the feel of France. By now we were doing a certain amount of shopping and getting to know the whole area.

We stopped once or twice on the way back to Cherbourg but eventually it was all over, and we returned to the south coast on the ferry. We came back with a certain amount of French food, wine and various bits and pieces which we had bought and which still decorate the home. Our feeling for France had well and truly arrived, although it was some eight or more years before we got down to another visit. We were, however, getting people from France visiting us for varying periods after which they would move on around the country.

As our daughters got older, I found it convenient to remain in the County Education office during August while all the people who were tied to school term times would be taking their holidays. I was then able to take my holiday in June which made visiting France easier, and at a period when there were not so many visitors from this country. We began travelling much further afield and heading south to visit various places which we were interested in. Our first visit on our own was in June 1971 when we again headed for St Molf to visit Pauline and Camille.

We spent our first night at Avranches in what was the French equivalent of an English motel. They did not serve meals and we had a meal in a nearby restaurant or café. We learned a very important lesson there, which was not to speak English in a restaurant or anywhere like that, because once we were chatting to each other at the table and a rather pompous looking man came in to the room and sat down at a table about three tables away from us. As soon as he heard us speaking English he was shouting across the room asking us what something was on the menu, for example – then he would ask us where we going to and so on. We quite expected that the restaurant would empty within a few minutes, because everybody was so fed up and annoyed with him. As a result of this we decided in future that we were going to speak French whenever we were in the presence of French people, and this became more important later on. We found that if we were visiting some ancient building with a guide, and spoke to each other in English, somebody very soon afterwards would be asking us what the guide had just said because they didn't understand it. This meant that by the time we had translated his remarks into English we had missed the next bit. We pretended that we were French and hoped that we looked reasonably appropriate for the part.

We soon got to know the area where Pauline and Camille lived and they would invite people in for a meal in the evening for us to meet. Our knowledge of French people was growing rapidly. Two visitors whom we saw quite regularly, and they visited us two or three times in Great Britain, were Georges and Anne-Marie. He was the garage proprietor in St Molf and they lived in a very nice house a little way inland from La Baule. These meals were very happy occasions and would last two hours or so, although in France we were to discover that it was quite a common practice for everybody to get up in between the courses in the middle of the meal and wander off in the garden and come back after ten or fifteen minutes. On some occasions, the hostess would be getting the next course ready; on other occasions she would come with us so that there could be quite a significant gap between the courses, which is quite unusual in England. Needless to say, the guests did not stop drinking during this interval. Nor did the housewife, who would take her glass of wine with her. We spent a day in La Baule and also went up the coast visiting other places.

Our next stop was at Rennes where Jean and Thérèse Simon had settled. We spent a few nights with them at their house in Rennes, although later they moved out to a rather more ornate house south of the town with a small flat in the town for occasions when they required it. This small flat would be used by Madame Mitchell when she wished to stay in Rennes.

Our next call was Paris, and I had considerable trepidation about taking the car into the city – although I felt quite happy in other places in the country. On the way, we were passing through Versailles so we parked the car and visited the palace which was very attractive and impressive, as were the grounds at the back. We came out and then walked along the main road to have a cup of coffee and look at the shops. Unfortunately, when we returned, we could not find the car and in the end we had to find the entrance to the chateâu again, and retrace our steps to the car.

We then headed for Paris on a busy motorway with some worries. We knew that we had to turn right on the *boulevard périférique*, which is a great ring road that runs within Paris. Fortunately, we had to go round to the right, and as traffic is on the right we just went straight in and turned right. It was no good staying in this lane because this would be the one for traffic turning off at the next junction, so we had to keep moving to the left in one of the reasonably fast lanes. By the time we were approaching the exit we had to take, I realised that the trick was that one had to cross progressively into different lanes. In the end, at the exit before the one required, we got into the right-hand lane and turned straight off at the junction.

We had a map and took the road to Fontenay-sous-Bois, which was where they lived. There we were lost, and I stopped the car and asked a man in my best French if he could tell me where the 'Rue Charles Bassée' was. When I was in the last road before I actually reached the road I was looking for, I stopped the car, got out, went to the road and had a look. Sure enough the actual house was just around the corner.

So that was that, and we were welcomed by the French maid who happened to be at the entrance of the house when we arrived. I should have added that she had two of the children with her, whilst their mother was out teaching. During this and subsequent visits to Paris we saw all the sights, although we never went up the Eiffel Tower. We did go to the top of the Arc de Triomphe where one has a beautiful view of Paris. With our hosts in the evening we would go out for a meal at various restaurants they took us to. We got on very well as we both spoke French, and I will always remember one Alsace restaurant where I asked the waiter if I could have the empty bottles as I collected wine labels. He was compliant and offered to wash them out. At the end of the meal I asked him if they were ready, and he brought me all the labels, beautifully soaked off the bottles, dried, and placed between the leaves of a book on their wines which he presented to me. I was very moved! We spent several days looking around Paris and visited the Arc de Triumph, the Champs Elysées and similar places.

On one occasion, when we were staying with Pauline and Camille at St Molf we went to spend a few days with Madame Mitchell who had a bungalow at St Hilda de Rousse. Whilst there we would visit various friends of hers, for a meal in the evening probably, and it was quite a relaxed and social place to be. One person who lived a hundred yards or so from her was Madame Gilberte Messmer, the wife of the French Prime Minister, Pierre Messmer. She often came in for a cup of coffee and a chat in the mornings, so we met her quite a few times and got to know her well.

When we were in Paris, once there was a sale of work in aid of the Free French Forces, so we went along to visit it. When we went in we found Madame Messmer dressed in the full costume of Brittany manning one of the stalls, so we had a chat with her, and came away with a few things of interest. She was a very friendly person and we got on well with her. She would telephone me at home in the evening and ask me if I could do something for her in England. Some of these things she did not wish to go through the French Ambassador. The first one concerned a young French girl of about eighteen years of age who had failed English in her Baccalaureate and was associating with a somewhat undesirable person. They would like to get her away to England to study English as she had failed it in her exam and could I help? As it happened, a former senior advisor in the Education Office was now running a college in the house which was originally occupied by the founder of the Scout movement. It was now an international school for students studying English. I went to see him, told him all about it and he said he would be very pleased to interview her with a view to taking her on, if I could get her over to England.

This was arranged and I met her at the port of Southampton and brought her home. Unfortunately, we could not accommodate her at the time because we were full up already, so I arranged for her to have a room for a few nights at a house in Christchurch Road.

She came to us in the daytime and on the Monday I took her to see the head of this college and he accepted her without any hesitation. It was a residential establishment and she moved in there and we used to go to all the functions which took place, on behalf of her parents. Quite a pleasant social experience. At Christmas her parents came over and I booked a room for them and for her in a local hotel and they had Christmas dinner with us. In the afternoon, I took them out because he wanted to see the house where Montgomery lived. I would have knocked on the door but being Christmas day I didn't think it was quite the right occasion. I then wanted to give them afternoon tea in a hotel and tried two which were not serving anything at that hour. Eventually, I went to one at Alton and saw the receptionist and told her that I wanted to give these French people tea. She said the restaurant was closed, but that she would make us some tea and bring it to us in the reception area. So we managed to have our Christmas tea in style after all.

On a later occasion, I was asked by Madame Messmer whether I could fix up somewhere for a girl who wished to come over as an au pair. I succeeded in arranging for her to stay with a family from Littleton, although I cannot remember anything else about it now.

Later, she rang me somewhat agitated to say that another young French girl had come over to the London area to act as an au pair but was apparently dissatisfied with her job, and had suddenly left without saying a word. Nobody knew where she was. Could I possibly trace her without involving the police? This, I think, was one of the most difficult assignments I had received. But a youth adviser in the County Education Office had recently come from the London area, so I rang him and asked him if he had any ideas as to what I might do. He said that there was a particular Roman Catholic priest in that district of London who helped visitors from abroad to get settled in. As the young lady was a Catholic this was a good start.

He also said there was a youth club which flourished very well, and had a lot of French girls in it. He had a word with the priest and within twenty-four hours, to my amazement and relief, she had been located. It appeared that the house to which she came was a Jewish household and she arrived on a Friday. This, of course, is the Jewish Sabbath – there was no food, nothing to do, and she was virtually kept in silence for the first day. This was too much for her, and so the next day she walked out without saying anything, taking her belongings. It appeared that she had got a job in the French Embassy and was working there, I think, as a typist. She had only been there three days, however.

I telephoned Madame Messmer and told her and she asked me if I could arrange for her to be sent back to France. I said I wasn't very sure about this because, if she worked at the French Embassy and she suddenly disappeared, I thought the French Ambassador would get worried and would report it to Scotland Yard. On reflection, she said she agreed with me, and said she would ask the French Ambassador to arrange for her to come back to France. I think that my links with France as a result of the war might well have helped in a very delicate situation.

The outstanding event was, however, to come. Once when we were in France, Madame Mitchell had received an invitation to attend a garden party in the grounds of the French War Office in honour of Admiral De la Hay, the Commander in Chief of the French Navy. She would like us to take her to the French War Office at the height of the rush hour, and to join her in the garden party. Needless to say, I was very worried because I didn't know how I'd get there through the rush hour. Anyway, off we set, with her sitting beside me in the front of the car and giving me directions as to whether to turn right, turn left or carry straight on. Eventually, we got into the centre of Paris in the rush hour, and this really was a nightmare.

I was well aware of the French highway rule that you give priority to anything on the right. I had been advised that in this situation, it was wise not to look to the left, otherwise if the drivers knew you had seen them, they would dash ahead and beat you to it. I followed this guidance with considerable trepidation, and somehow got through and eventually we were in the area of the government offices and heading for the grounds of the French War Office. We arrived at a sign saying 'road closed', and there was a policeman standing in the middle of the road. He held his hand up because we hadn't got a permit to enter the area showing on the front of the car. As I was sitting on the right and he was in the middle of the road, he came to the passenger side and Madame Mitchell opened the window. The minute he saw her he said, 'Ah, bonjour, Madame Mitchell, how nice to see you. Are you heading for the War Office? Good, carry on.' This happened three times, I think, and on each occasion we were waved through, and then we went to park in the grounds of the Ministry next to the War Office building. The sentry at the War Office saluted and we were admitted without question.

This was a quite incredible event. We were welcomed by Admiral De la Hay and his wife having been introduced to them by Madame Mitchell. Subsequently, we saw Madame Gilberte Messmer who gave us an equally warm welcome. Her husband was not present because he was on an official engagement elsewhere. We were also introduced to a wealthy business man and his wife who, we were told quietly, was one of the wealthiest manufacturers in France. It may come as no surprise, I suppose, to discover that he produced accessories for the fashion trade! And, no doubt, he had a very busy business. We were walking round on our own and talking to various people, and everybody was very pleasant and happy. There was a form of bran tub in which presents wrapped up were buried and one paid a figure, I cannot remember what, probably somewhere around one or two pounds, to pick something out. We acquired a bineau which is a very small version of the French bagpipes and still hangs in the kitchen. Another treasured possession is a small bucket based on a bucket lowered into a well, but with a lid. On the side is painted the head, in full regalia, of a French lady.

We joined in the singing when we could, including the 'Marseillaise' and altogether it was a really marvellous day. There were wine and snacks and so on, and also a refreshment tent where one could have a cup of coffee if one wished. Marjorie was wearing a silk scarf round her neck in red, white and blue and she was congratulated frequently for wearing the colours of the French flag. She did not tell them that it was the scarf which Madame Mitchell wore when General de Gaulle marched in triumph down the Champs Elysées at the end of the occupation by the Germans.

Some time later, I commented to Admiral De la Hay that nobody was taking any photographs and asked if it was permitted. Unfortunately, by then it was getting a little dark, so I increased the aperture slightly and increased the exposure. I discovered later that I had moved the two levers in the wrong directions and all the results were rather dim. But our local photographer knew of one firm in the country who could produce a lighter version of a dark slide, and this was done. I now have a photograph, on display in the lounge, of Marjorie chatting to Madame Messmer: and also in the group is Madame Mitchell. Another one is of Admiral De la Hay and his wife, and Marjorie is there again. This really was the highlight of all of our visits to France.

It was a constant reminder to us that although the war involved considerable hardships it also brought very great benefits at the same time. If I had not been in French North Africa and in Corsica none of this would have happened. Also, if I had not volunteered for Coastal Forces, I would not have had the opportunity to go ashore to any extent in these countries either. Similarly, Madame Mitchell would not have come to Wellingborough and set up a convalescent home for Free French soldiers so that Marjorie could meet her daughter and visit the home as often as she could. It is an example of how war can widen one's horizons. Unfortunately, there is also the old adage that one man's gain is another man's loss.

Another interesting experience was the visit to Avignon in the south of France. We obtained a room in a hotel where we were on the third floor, which seemed a bit disappointing in a way, but when we got up there we realised that we had a good view over the town and particularly along the main road. For example, we saw a coach load of English visitors arrive. We thought how lucky we were that we were not with a party of English people who were speaking English all the time, and that we could get absorbed into the French countryside and the French way of life.

In the other direction we could see a building which we had never heard of before and which turned out to be the 'Palais des Papes'. This being the French equivalent of the Vatican City. We visited this with a group of about fifteen or twenty people and a guide. Again we did not speak English so that we had no risk of being interrupted or missing any part of it. We discovered that the popes were in France for about a hundred years. I believe they were exiled from Italy for this period of time. The building must have been three stories high and we must have gone just about everywhere in it.

Another interesting experience in France was a visit to the bridge on the Avignon River. I imagine most people will know the song *Sur le pont d'Avignon, l'on y danse, l'on y danse*. We were surprised to discover that to gain access to the bridge we had to go in a gift shop and upstairs then, for which there was a charge. When we got up there we could walk on to the bridge.

There was no road leading to it and to our surprise the bridge went into the river for about three arches and then ended abruptly. Whether it was never completed, or whether it was completed and washed away, or demolished to allow the passage of ships up river, I don't know. In any case, I took a photograph of Marjorie dancing on her own on the bridge, although this seemed rather an unusual place to dance. Afterwards, we went down again into the shop and had a look around. I will now let you into a closely guarded French secret, which is that when we looked at all the souvenirs in the shop, we realised that the dancers were not on the bridge but under the bridge, on the grassy bank. This seemed much more appropriate and likely, so we concluded that the song really should be *sous le pont d'Avignon*. So if you ever happen to be singing the song, remember where the dancers really were, even though if you're in France stick to the traditional wording!

We decided to visit the 'Gouffre de Padirac'. First of all, we travelled along the valley and it was surprising to see a valley where, to all appearances, there should have been a river flowing down the middle – but there wasn't a sign of anything. This is because the river was flowing underground, and when it arrived at the Gouffre it was flowing through caves. We could gain admission and walk through beside the underground river.

We paid a modest sum for entry and went downwards until we reached the river level, where we could walk along the rocks at the side of the river towards its source. It was quite fast flowing higher upstream and really was most impressive. We could not normally see further than thirty or forty feet ahead, owing to the bends in the river, and rocks hiding the view. I imagine we must have gone some distance, approaching a quarter of a mile, when we arrived at the point where we could not really go any further. Here, visitors embarked in a small narrow boat about twenty feet long, I suppose, with a man standing at the stern with a long pole, presumably to ensure its safe passage back down the stream. There were several French visitors about to embark, and when we arrived they recognised us as English, presumably by our clothes, and told us to get in the front two seats. We protested that we were quite happy to follow them, but they were absolutely insistent that we must get in the first two seats. We did so with some concern because we wondered whether at a bend, if the boat had missed its course or something and crashed into the rocks, we would be the ones to bear the brunt of the collision. Of course, there was the possibility that we all might get washed away.

However, we all got embarked and the boat pushed off and headed down river, erratically going from one side to the other with the current, sometimes pointing dead ahead, sometimes not quite, and so on. It all became clear when there was a sudden flash ahead of us from somewhere up the side of the rocks and we realised that a man was taking a photograph of the party passing through. The same thing happened again a little further on from the other side of the stream, and eventually we reached our destination and drew alongside a little quay which had been formed. The boat was secured and we all disembarked. It then transpired that this was the normal procedure, which they were well aware of, and they wanted us to be at the front and in the best position for the photograph. We thanked them profusely when we realised that it was out of consideration for us that they had done it. When we were going out we had the offer of a copy of the photograph on payment of a small sum which I cannot remember now. I think we paid for one of each of the photographs, and they arrived through the post at the address of the friends we were heading for later on our tour. It is still a vivid reminder of what happened.

We then went on to Rocamadour, on the River Aizou. The town was on the north side of the valley and the side was extremely steep and rocky but we decided to climb up to the top to admire the view and also to see the attractive buildings en route. It was quite impressive and the views also were magnificent, looking south across the countryside. I expect after our climb we stopped for a cup of coffee and then we went back down again where, equally, the views close to the river were magnificent. We travelled westwards along the valley in the car because we knew that the scenery was very attractive, and periodically we would stop to admire it from a particular vantage point. The river ultimately fed into the Dordogne, but we spent the night at Payrac.

On another occasion, after we had visited Limoges, the centre of the china industry in France, we headed eastwards towards the coast because we wished to visit the distilleries of Cognac. On the way we passed through Jarnac which is on the River Charente as is Cognac. We booked in for the night at a hotel in Cognac which did not serve meals. As we liked the look of Jarnac we drove back along the road and up through the small town and were surprised to see people lining the sides of the road. We realised that something must be about to happen. So we pulled into a side road and parked the car, and walked back to join the crowd.

We were just in time to see a procession of decorated vehicles, bands and everything coming through the town and past us, so we joined in the cheering. I cannot remember what it was in aid of but it was probably a saint's day. When the crowd had cleared, we turned back down the road and went alongside the river and parked the car. We chatted to a couple tending their allotment and walked down the river a way, then back up, across the bridge and went to the other side. This being a Saturday evening, many of the villagers were having a walk beside the river. We went a certain way, turned back again, crossed the road to the other side and walked along the side of the river towards the sea for a while. We had moved the car to that side of the river by then.

The river bank was quite wide. On our way back Marjorie said, 'I wonder what that building is across the road? It looks very interesting.' We asked an old lady and she said, '*Ah, c'est chez Bisquit.*' We immediately recognised this as the Cognac distillery, well known in England for its product. She went on to tell us that her son was a head of department in the distillery. When we said we would very much like to visit the distillery, she said, 'Oh well, I'll have a word with my son and he will no doubt arrange it for you if you go in on Monday and ask for him.' All the conversation was, of course, in French!

She obviously wanted someone to chat to so we walked up and down with her for quite a time, and she then began to tell us her life story. She, her husband and two sons had fled from Paris on the arrival of the Germans and kept going southwards until they found somewhere they thought they could settle in which was Jarnac. Her husband secured an appointment in the Bisquit distillery and eventually became the cellar master – the person who controlled the fermentation of the spirit. Her sons grew up and one of them was a senior manager in one of the distilleries in Cognac and the other was now in the Bisquit distillery.

There was a speedboat on the river with a man in it and a young lady aged about twenty to twenty-five, I suppose. She told us that he was a relative of hers, as was the young lady, and asked us if we would like to have a trip on the river. I said, 'I think it's getting a little too late for that now,' as by then it was about nine o'clock. Just after that the boat tied up a little way downstream on our side, and the young lady came and joined us. The lady we had been talking to asked whether we would like to come to her flat, which was over the timber yard across the road, for a cup of coffee and a biscuit. We accepted, and we all went along, up some wooden stairs over the place where all the wood was stored. At the top was a flat still in the wooden structure, very luxurious and well appointed. The window looked out over the river, and we sat there drinking our cup of coffee and chatting. She then asked us if we would like a glass of Cognac, and of course, being polite, we said, 'Yes.' Out she came with a bottle which she said was thirty-year-old Cognac. It really was quite an experience to drink a Cognac of that age, as I did not even know that it existed.

When we were ready to leave she came out and presented me with a half litre bottle of the thirty-year-old Cognac which I treasured for a long time. An example of the hospitality of the French people when visitors speak to them in their own language! We then hurried back to our hotel in Cognac, wondering whether we would be locked out by that time, but fortunately the door was open, so we went in, went to our room, and had a good night's sleep.

We spent the Sunday looking around Cognac which had quite a pleasant park in the centre, and one distillery was open to visitors. We went in and had an official visit and, of course, ended up with a glass of brandy each afterwards.

On the Monday morning we visited the Bisquit distillery and said that we had been told by the mother of this person that he would arrange for us to have a look around. Unfortunately, they couldn't recognise the name and this caused some confusion. They said in the end, that they would fetch somebody who spoke English, as there happened to be somebody in the building at the present time. The man who came was an Englishman who represented Bisquit in this country. He realised that I had got the pronunciation slightly wrong and that was what was causing the confusion.

The French man we were looking for came then, and said regretfully that he could not show us around then because he was busy that day, but he would arrange for a member of his staff to do so. We went back at about two thirty as arranged, and a man came to meet us. He of course spoke virtually no English, but we got on very well. He said he hadn't got his car with him that day and asked if I would mind taking mine, and he would show me where to go. This was somewhat of a surprise but we drove some five or six miles away from Jarnac where we were taken to see the vineyard and this really was a huge expanse of vines. We went into the building where the Cognac was distilled and chilled, and this was a colossal place and quite impressive.

We then went back to Jarnac and went into the building, not the one we had seen across the river, but one slightly to the back of it where the main headquarters of the company were. We went through the side of a dining room where there were some forty or so people finishing their lunch, through to the main reception room next to it where we sat down in luxury seats to await the tasting at about half past four. This would take place when the party next door came through from the end of their meal. At this point they started singing and I said to the guide who had taken us around, 'That is a song of Algeria, is it not?' He said, 'Yes, how did you know?' and I replied that I had spent quite a lot of time in Algiers and in North Africa. When they were settled I was introduced to the singers as a great friend of Algiers. They were told that I had taken part in the landing and had travelled along the Algerian coast also. This produced a cheer from the crowd, and so then I stood up and said a few words to them, wishing them well, and saying how much I liked Algiers.

The tasting then began, and we started off with a taster of the normal Cognac. We then moved up to one that I think was about twelve years old, and this was even better. We then moved on to the Bisquit VSOP in a black bottle which was quite superb. I asked the guide if I could have the cork as a souvenir, and he said to the person who had been taking us around, 'I think we can do rather better than that, can't we.' I had the cork anyway. Afterwards our guide, with Marjorie and me, went into the administrative building which we had seen from across the river. We went up to the Directors' suite where we all sat down for a rest, and he asked us if we would like a drink, and suggested that a nice glass of cool beer might be the best thing. We all agreed and sat there drinking our beer. We were then presented with a litre bottle of Bisquit black label together with a brochure on the whole organisation. Our visit had taken four hours and we had been treated like royalty, and all this was because we had been talking to a lonely old lady the night before!

Although it seems ironic, none of this existence and enjoyment we had later could possibly have happened unless there had been the war, I had served in the Royal Navy and Marjorie had met a French family in England. It led to many visits by French people to our house and many visits by us to their houses in France and to us touring the whole country. Also, if I had not volunteered for Coastal Forces I would never have been so close to the people of the countries in the Mediterranean. If I had spent my whole Naval career on destroyers and fighting ships, life would have been quite different and I would only have visited Naval ports, or ports regularly used by the Navy.

An example of the friendship of the French people was when we were on the coast of Brittany somewhere and we were going to have a picnic lunch but hadn't bought anything to have with our dessert. I think we had some fruit, but we saw a shop which had sets of four pots of yoghurt in the window. We went in and I said to the man, 'Is it possible to buy two of the pots of yoghurt separately, please?' He said, 'No, only the fours I'm afraid.' I said, 'Well, we were just hoping to have a couple of pots to follow our lunch and we would like either peach or strawberry, I think.' He picked up one of the packs of four, broke it in two and set two down on the counter in front of us. I thanked him very much. Later in the same village we were walking along the road when we saw a mother with her daughter aged about twelve, beautifully dressed in some special costume – it really was a very special sight, such as I have never seen in England. I imagine she was either going to be confirmed in the church or that it was for some ceremony connected with the saint's day.

Another experience we had in France which I have never seen in this country ever, was that Camille was to have a birthday party and we, of course, had to go along. It was in a village some ten miles from St Molf. We went there and entered the restaurant where we occupied a long table with about ten or twelve people seated on either side, with him sitting at the end of the table. It was a special anniversary, but I cannot recall how many years it was celebrating. All the visitors, who were people we knew already and members of the family and so on, were seated at the table and I was sitting on the opposite side to Marjorie. Needless to say, the lunch went very slowly, as is the custom in France. Towards the end, there was the sound of a small band playing outside and somebody suddenly called out, '*Un mariage.*' Everybody immediately left the table, leaving their food just as it was, and went outside. The entire staff of the restaurant came out as well, including the cooks who presumably switched off all their cookers. We were in time to see approaching a small orchestra followed by the bride and bridegroom and all the wedding guests walking along the road. They were heading for the reception which was to be held a little further along the road and everybody who could came out to cheer them. This was when we found out that this was quite a normal procedure in France. It seemed so remarkable – so different from the English method, and so much more attractive.

Our fondness for the French then began to extend to other nationalities as well. Education officers would have frequent visitors from abroad to study our educational system. We would invite them home to visit us, and take them to see various places of interest around Winchester – this led to further relationships. One person who used to visit us became a senior political figure in Kenya, another was the Poet Laureate of Trinidad, who visited us also later on with his wife and family. Although thousands of people are killed in war, and this causes much sadness, there are ultimately some benefits for those who survive.

I think I have one last thought. I like Great Britain to be Great Britain, France to be France, Italy to be Italy, and every country to have its independence as much as possible. Although I accept that we are part of Europe I have no great desire for this to develop into a Euro currency. I say, 'Long live Great Britain and the British traditions and also the traditions and independence of all other countries.' I think that a great part of the attraction of foreign travel is the difference which one experiences, not only in currency, but in habits and outlook and everything. I would much prefer to be left alone. After all, the war we fought was for the United Kingdom and basically was for Europe. I see no point in abandoning the United Kingdom and its own traditions, customs and money after all we went through! There is one country in Europe, not on our side, who appears to want to dominate Europe, this time by decree, rather than war.

Appendix I

Ports and Harbours Visited by the Author in the British Isles between 1940 and 1946

Portsmouth	Gosport
Littlehampton	Bursledon
Hamble	Portland
Weymouth	Lulworth
Lundy	Falmouth
Milford Haven	Douglas (Isle of Mann)
Fisguard	Tobermory
Fort William	Holyhead
Sandbanks	Greenock
Cardiff	Swansea
Avonmouth	Bristol
Ilfracombe	Tenby
Pembroke Dock	Larne
Porthcawle	Clovely
Padstowe	Fowey
Ardrossan	Lamlash
Oban	Loch Foyle
Loch Tuath	Loch Ewe

Scapa Flow North Shields
South Shields Liverpool
Thurso

Appendix II

Ports and Harbours Visited by the Author in the Mediterranean between 1942 and 1945

Gibralta
Bordalise Rock
(D-Day landing)
La Perouse
Dellys
Tigzert
Bone
Bizerta
Tripoli
Filfia

Augusta
St Paul's Bay
Milazzo
Messina
Salerno
(D-Day landing)
Naples

Torre Annunziata

Algiers

Bougie
Port Gueydon
Collo
Cherchell
Malta
Sousse
Avola Beach
(D-Day landing)
Noto
Palermo
Termini
Acireale

Castellamare di Stabia
Sorrento

Marina di Equa
Ischia

Procida
Pozzuoli
Bastia
Ile Russe
Calvi

Port de Centuri
Pianosa
Bonifaccio
Piambino
Marsa Scirroco
Erbalunga
Capri

San Tropez
St Raphael

Leghorn
Catania
Riposta

Syracuse –
Pisa, Florence and Rome

Volturno River
Anzio
(D-Day landing)
Posillipo
Maddalena
San Florent
Porto Vecchio
Elba – Golfo di Campo
(D-Day landing)
Ile de la Giraglia
Porto Longone
Rio Marina
Macinaggio
Tamarone Bay
Reggio
Gulf of Frejus
(D-Day landing)
Rade d'Agay
Baie de Pampalonne
Civita Vecchio
Lagugna
Via Reggio –
Arno River

and
Rejkavik, Iceland